DISTRIBUTED
PROCESSING SYSTEMS

ROBERT J. THIERAUF, Ph.D., C.P.A.

Professor of Management
and Information Systems

Chairman, Department of Management
and Information Systems

D. J. O'Conor Memorial Professor
in Business Administration

Xavier University
Cincinnati, Ohio

DISTRIBUTED PROCESSING SYSTEMS

PRENTICE-HALL, INC., Englewood Cliffs, New Jersey 07632

Library of Congress Cataloging in Publication Data

Thierauf, Robert J.
   Distributed processing systems.

   Includes bibliographies and index.
   1. Management information systems.
2. Electronic data processing—Distributed
processing. I. Title.
HF5548.2.T442   658'.05'4   78-8100
ISBN 0-13-216507-4

Printed in the United States of America

10 9 8 7 6 5 4 3 2 1

Prentice-Hall International, Inc., *London*
Prentice-Hall of Australia Pty. Limited. *Sydney*
Prentice-Hall of Canada, Ltd., *Toronto*
Prentice-Hall of India Private Limited, *New Delhi*
Prentice-Hall of Japan, Inc., *Tokyo*
Prentice-Hall of Southeast Asia Pte. Ltd., *Singapore*
Whitehall Books Limited, *Wellington, New Zealand*

CONTENTS

PREFACE

In the past few years, the trend has been toward the "small computer" for business and away from the large, centralized computer. This new thrust in DP operations was predicted years ago by many computer experts. As an example, Captain Grace Murray Hopper forecasted the trend in 1973. At the time, she said, "There was never any rule which said that accounts receivable and payroll had to be on the same computer. Once we go to the minicomputers and dispersed computing, we will be able to devote those computers functionally to a particular job . . . put them where they are needed and give them to the people who need them and must use them."

Distributed processing has opened up a whole new train of thought. Although the technology has been around for some time, it needed a push. The impetus for distributed processing came from utilizing large computers for most DP activities which caused large data input bottlenecks and also created situations where the feedback of the business data necessary to run the business occurred, after long delays. In effect, dispersed data processing arose out of the need to get data processing power where it is needed, that is, to handle DP chores that can be done more efficiently in the field than at the home office. The concept still allows the use of the large computer at central headquarters while off-loading it with dispersed processing.

The real payoff from distributed processing is the increased responsiveness of the EDP function to the user's needs by providing data entry/inquiry capabilities, coupled with processing power, at the appropriate level—in particular, the lower levels. Not only does this give local and regional managers more control over and involvement with data and the information system, but also a burden is taken off the central facility. And because more processing is done locally and regionally, the overall system now can be utilized to do what it does best, i.e., repetitive processing with responsiveness improved in the process of fulfilling management's informational needs. Thus, distributed processing is the ability to place computing power where it is needed within an organization from the lowest level to the highest level. Although the current direction is satisfying user needs at the lower levels, future distributed processing systems will focus on satisfying user requirements from the lower to the higher levels within an organization.

The structure of the book follows a logical sequence for presenting a comprehensive treatment of distributed processing, namely, past, present, and future developments. The major topics covered are:

Part One, Prior Developments to Distributed Processing Systems. Initially, the various types of business information systems that have been developed and implemented over the years are reviewed, with particular emphasis on real-time management information systems (Chapter 1).

Part Two, Current Developments in Distributed Processing Systems. The essential characteristics of distributed processing systems are discussed (Chapter 2), followed by a methodical approach for studying the feasibility of going to distributed computing (Chapter 3). Once the best distributed system has been determined by the feasibility study group and approved by top management, the next important phase is implementation (Chapter 4). In many cases, distributed networks and data bases are the focal point of such a system (Chapter 5). No matter the level of sophistication for the distributed processing environment, typical applications currently found in business organizations are presented (Chapters 4 and 5).

Part Three, Case Study of Current Distributed Processing Systems. After presenting a brief background on the American Products Corporation (Chapter 6), the essential components of its marketing subsystem in a distributed processing environment are set forth (Chapter 7). In a similar manner, the manufacturing, physical distribution, and accounting subsystems are illustrated as an integral part of a distributed processing system (Chapters 8, 9, and 10).

Part Four, Future Developments in Distributed Processing Systems. Based upon current directions in distributed computing (including concurrent developments in hardware and software), the new and emerging characteristics of future distributed processing systems are explored (Chapter 11).

Finally, the various types of distributed processing systems to be found within the organization and extending beyond the organization of the future are presented (Chapter 12).

The text is designed for use by management information systems specialists, systems analysts, information systems managers, and programmers who wish to broaden their knowledge of present situations and current directions in distributed processing systems. Similarly, the text is suitable for an undergraduate or graduate course examining the fundamentals of distributed computing. The material is suitable for one quarter or one semester. No matter the orientation, the book's structure is designed to stimulate the reader's interest in this innovative approach to business information systems.

For a project of this magnitude, I wish to thank the following professionals who read the manuscript and contributed their helpful suggestions. I am deeply indebted to Richard D. Coverdale of Four-Phase Systems, David P. Enoch of Honeywell Information Systems, Robert C. Hale of American Telephone & Telegraph, and John F. Niehaus of Xavier University.

ROBERT J. THIERAUF

DISTRIBUTED PROCESSING SYSTEMS

part one

PRIOR DEVELOPMENTS TO DISTRIBUTED PROCESSING SYSTEMS

SYSTEMS PRIOR TO DISTRIBUTED PROCESSING

1

The current vogue in business information systems, namely *distributed processing systems,* is an attempt to answer the difficulties experienced with earlier computer systems. The utilization of large centralized computers in the 1960's and 1970's created large data input bottlenecks as well as situations where the feedback of business data necessary to run the business occurred after long delays. Distributed processing arose out of the need to get computer power where it is needed and to handle data processing operations that can be done more efficiently in the field, i.e., local and regional levels rather than at the home office. Thus, a distributed processing approach to business functions not only gives local managers more control over and involvement with their computerized information systems but also takes a burden off the central computing facility.

Another way of viewing distributed processing is that it represents the next logical step after the teleprocessing wave of the late 1960's and early 1970's when, as communications became practical, users "wired" many locations with terminals for talking to and for feeding data to large, powerful central computer complexes. Since that time, several things have happened. Terminals have become "intelligent" as small processors have been built into them. And since the cost of communications has not dropped as fast as the cost of computation and memory, one solution is to let small computers, located near the data, do much of the processing and send only summary data to headquarters. From this view, distributed processing represents a new form of technology for designing and implementing business information systems.

Before enumerating the essentials of distributed processing systems (refer to Chapter 2), in this chapter we shall provide background on prior information systems. Initially, the relationship of a system to information is followed by examining the significance of information and the need for information systems. After the information needs for lower, middle, and top management are explored, information systems prior to and including real-time management information systems are set forth. Not only are their essential characteristics detailed, but also their respective deficiencies are enumerated. This orderly study places continuing developments of information systems, namely, distributed processing, in their proper perspective.

RELATIONSHIP OF SYSTEM TO INFORMATION

Prior to discussing the significance of information and the need for information systems, it would be helpful to review the meanings of some basic terms—*data, information,* and *system.* The term *data* (plural of datum) is defined as unstructured facts, forming the necessary inputs to an information system. On the other hand, *information* is defined as selected data that represent output from a system and are meaningful to the user of that output. In simple terms, then, the function of the system is the transformation of data to information. As noted in Figure 1-1, a *system* is defined as an ordered set of methods, procedures, and resources designed to facilitate the achievement of an objective or objectives. This very general and simplistic definition also applies to all types of information systems, i.e., business information systems, with accent today on distributed processing systems.

SIGNIFICANCE OF INFORMATION

Information, the logical output of an information system (Figure 1-1), is of vital importance to the managers of a firm to achieve short-, intermediate-, and long-range goals. Management needs a fairly accurate measurement of its sales and cost factors for various time periods. It must maximize its income through higher selling prices and/or larger inventory turnover and minimize costs of products and services. In short, management wants a combination of selling prices, turnover, costs and profit per unit that will provide the highest return on invested capital. Given adequate information on these essential facts, management can rely more on deduc-

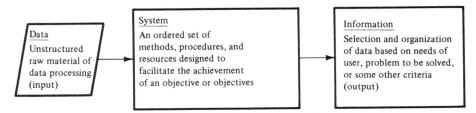

FIGURE 1-1. An effective system (i.e., a business information system) stores, organizes, and retrieves
the required data to produce meaningful
information.

tive and analytical methods than on guesses and intuitive judgment, which it must
employ when many of the relevant facts are missing. Many wrong decisions have
been the result of insufficient or inadequately processed information.

*There is a growing awareness that accurate and timely information is a vital
resource of the firm and that an effective information system is a means of providing the needed information.* Many top managers are finding that information is a
source of competitive power. It gives them the ability to out-maneuver their rivals
at critical times, especially when introducing new products. If the data processing
system does not produce the information necessary for management to handle its
operations effectively, an "out-of-control" condition may result and the firm may
never recover. An examination of firms that have experienced difficult times over
the years will verify this point.

THE NEED FOR INFORMATION SYSTEMS

The need for an effective information system is of paramount concern to the firm
now as well as in the future. Because the firm does not operate in a vacuum, it
must coordinate its operations with the business universe. Of prime importance is
information about markets in which it operates, current knowledge of its customers
and competitors, availability of capital, capabilities of available personnel, and
knowledge concerning sources of supply. Increasing prices of purchased materials,
rising labor costs, and foreign competition signal the need for an information system that describes the firm's economic environment and coordinates the external
environment with the internal factors to provide meaningful management information (Figure 1-2).

The information system, in addition to recognizing trends external to the
firm, must treat changes that have occurred and will yet occur in the internal
business environment. Advancements in the behavioral sciences, continuing developments in management science, and increasing utilization of paperless computer
output terminals must be reflected in the design of the information system. Inter-
departmental approaches have transcended the traditional, functional lines of business in complex systems. Still other system technology developments have occurred

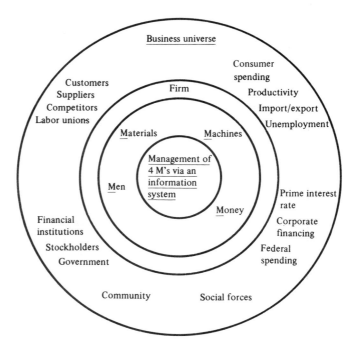

FIGURE 1-2. The relationship of the internal and external factors to the firm's information system.

regarding methods, procedures, computer equipment, and data communications equipment. By no means is this listing of internal factors complete, but it does serve to exemplify what is causing the firm's information system to change.

The changes taking place within and outside the firm generally do not stand alone; each advancement tends to affect and overlap another development. As a result, there is a need for an information system capable of integrating these advances with the needs and capabilities of the firm. It is a generally accepted fact that more frequent and more accurate information leads to better decisions, thereby enhancing operational efficiency.

INFORMATION NEEDS OF MANAGEMENT

Because the output of a business information system is directed toward management, it is beneficial to relate the managerial levels to the following types of information:

- operational
- tactical
- strategic

Generally, lower management is concerned with operational information, while tactical and strategic information is applicable to middle and top management, respectively. The type of information supplied has to do with the relative position of the manager in the company's hierarchy and the activities with which the information is concerned—the internal environment of the organization and the external environment in which it operates. It is a generally recognized fact that internal information should be increasingly summarized as the level of management for which it is prepared rises in the hierarchical structure, with top management receiving the most comprehensive reports. The rationale for this is that internal data are control-oriented, and the lower echelons of management are the most control-oriented; top management, however, is more planning-oriented.

Information concerning the external environment of the firm should be summarized exactly opposite to that of the internal environment. That is, because the upper levels of management are more planning-oriented and because planning necessitates more information concerning the organization's external environment, information concerning the external environment should be increasingly summarized and selective as the position of the receiver decreases in the managerial hierarchy. Thus, the amounts of time spent in planning and controlling for lower, middle, and top management complement one another in a management information system (MIS) environment, as indicated in Figure 1-3. As will be indicated in the forthcoming chapters, present distributed processing systems focus on satisfying the operational needs of lower management and, to a degree, those of middle management. However, future distributed processing systems will center on satisfying most information needs at the various managerial levels in an organization.

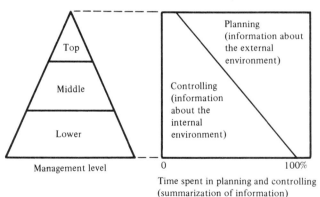

FIGURE 1-3. The relationship of the managerial levels to time spent on planning and controlling and to the summarization of information.

OPERATIONAL INFORMATION FOR LOWER MANAGEMENT

Operational information, being at the lowest level, is concerned with structured and repetitive activities that are measurable in achieving specific results. It allows line managers, such as plant foremen and department heads, to measure

FIGURE 1-4. Operational information needed to control the major subsystems of a typical manufacturing firm.

performance against predetermined results, including standards and budgeted figures. Similarly, operational information allows lower management to comment on how operating standards and policies can be improved to assist day-by-day operations. The feedback of essential information from this low level keeps higher levels of management aware of unfavorable as well as favorable results. Illustrated in Figure 1-4 is operational information employed to control the major subsystems of a typical manufacturing firm.

TACTICAL INFORMATION FOR MIDDLE MANAGEMENT

Tactical information that covers relatively short time periods (not greater than 12 months) is used by middle management to implement strategic plans at functional levels. As with operational information, tactical operational data are used by a large number of people. Examples are a functional budget report comparing actual to estimated amounts, a production report that evaluates assembly opera-

FIGURE 1-5. Tactical information needed to implement strategic plans for the major subsystems of a typical manufacturing firm.

tions, and a vendor performance evaluation report that rates overall vendor performance. Typical tactical information generated in a manufacturing firm is shown in Figure 1-5.

STRATEGIC INFORMATION FOR TOP MANAGEMENT

Strategic information is used primarily by top management and their staff to cover a long time span—generally one to five years. This type of information is used for planning purposes and for analysis of problem areas to discover the underlying reasons for specific problems or situations. In many cases, the objective of strategic information is to find answers to the question *why* rather than *what* or *where*. Examples are found in Figure 1-6.

FIGURE 1-6. Strategic information needed to plan, organize, direct, and control the major subsystems of a typical manufacturing firm.

Before strategic information can be forthcoming, planning must be undertaken. Strategic planning concerns itself with the establishment of objectives and policies that will govern the acquisition, use, and disposition of the resources needed to achieve those objectives. It is normally conducted at the highest level of management and at a very broad level of detail. Primarily, it requires large amounts of information derived from or relating to areas of knowledge outside the organization. Finally, strategic planning is original and covers the entire spectrum of the organization's activities.

INFORMATION SYSTEMS PRIOR TO
REAL-TIME MIS

Information systems prior to real-time MIS (management information systems) have been backward-looking; that is, they have concentrated on producing various types of historical reports. For the most part, they were not designed to produce relevant information for controlling current operations or future operating conditions. These systems centered around the following:

- custodial accounting systems
- responsibility reporting systems
- integrated data processing systems
- integrated management information systems

Briefly, each of these systems will be explored along with their respective deficiencies.

CUSTODIAL ACCOUNTING SYSTEMS

Information systems, prior to the introduction of computers, were concerned generally with historical facts, in particular, the balance sheet and the income statement of a company. There was very little concern for control of operations day by day or hour by hour. The accent was centered on what had occurred and not on what might be done to control current operations. This orientation led to what is now termed *custodial accounting*.

The designers of custodial accounting systems were not concerned about the basic needs of management, that is, obtaining feedback of critical information to compare actual performance with a predetermined plan or standard. However, the blame for this "backward-looking" approach should not be placed entirely on the systems designers. In most cases, managers were not trained to utilize such information. Consequently, they did not ask that timely management reports be provided.

Deficiencies of Custodial Accounting

For custodial accounting systems, manual methods, bookkeeping equipment, and punched card equipment were used to process the batched data. The major subsystems were treated as separate entities where record keeping was concerned. There was no attempt to integrate records that might serve several functions at the same time. Not only was there a proliferation of excess records in the firm, but it also generally took a long time to produce historical reports. By the time data were assimilated, it was much too late for meaningful analysis. In total, the custodial accounting system approach had more bad points than good points.

The important characteristics of custodial accounting systems, as well as other approaches to business information systems prior to real-time MIS, are summarized in Figure 1-7.

RESPONSIBILITY REPORTING SYSTEMS

An outgrowth of custodial accounting was the preparation of reports on the basis of responsibility assignments. A responsibility reporting system accumulates historical data for specific time intervals according to the various activities and levels of responsibility. The basis for determining responsibility is the firm's organization structure. Responsibility reporting is concerned with those activities that are directly controllable and accountable by the individual. A typical set of reports in a responsibility reporting system (manufacturing firm) is found in Figure 1-8.

Under responsibility reporting, each manager, regardless of level, has the right to participate in the preparation of the budget by which he or she is evaluated monthly. Although noncontrollable costs are included in the reports distributed, the manager is held accountable only for unfavorable deviations of controllable costs from the predetermined plans or the budget. The budget is constructed from the top level of management to the lowest level, that of a foreman, department head, or supervisor. Only in this manner can the individual be held responsible and accountable for costs that he or she controls directly.

More Timely Historical Reports

The adoption of this type of reporting system required too much time when manual methods and bookkeeping machines were used. Even with punched card equipment, the problem of preparing detailed cards, handling the cards manually, and running off the reports was a time-consuming task. The utilization of a batch processing computer system to perform the required manipulation of data and storage of prior data expedited the preparation of historical reports (Figure 1-8). Instead of waiting weeks under an older accounting system, management had reports in hand within a week after the close of a period. With the operations relatively fresh in their minds, they were able to review results sooner—unfavorable as well as favorable deviations from the established plans.

Deficiencies of Responsibility Reporting Systems

Overall, the responsibility reporting system was an improvement over the custodial accounting system. Although output was oriented toward historical reporting of accounting activities, it failed to take into account the integration of a company's subsystems, i.e., marketing, manufacturing, etc., with accounting. Thus, the responsibility reporting system was extremely narrow in its perspective.

Important Characteristics of Data Processing Systems	Custodial Accounting System	Responsibility Reporting System	Integrated Data Processing System	Integrated Management Information System
Type of System	Backward-looking control system and subsystems	→	→	→
Reports Prepared	Historical output reports for the firm	Historical output reports on a responsibility reporting basis	Historical output reports to various operating levels	Output reports directed to all levels of management for past operations
Exception Reporting	Very few accounting exception reports	Accounting exception reports	Accounting and other exception reports	Management exception reports
Information Orientation	Output-oriented	→	→	→
Processing Mode	Batch processing	→	→	→
Data Elements	Primarily accounting data	→	Common files	Common data bank
Type of Files	Sequential access file storage	→	→	Sequential and random access file storage
Mathematical Models	—	—	—	Limited use of standard operations research models

⟶ *Denotes continued use and improvement.*

FIGURE 1-7. Important characteristics of business information systems prior to real-time management information systems.

Organization Structure—
Individual responsible and accountable

Responsibility reports

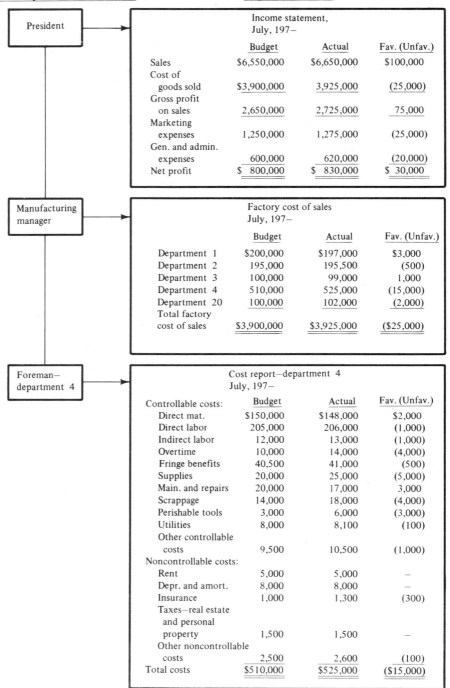

President

Income statement,
July, 197—

	Budget	Actual	Fav. (Unfav.)
Sales	$6,550,000	$6,650,000	$100,000
Cost of goods sold	$3,900,000	3,925,000	(25,000)
Gross profit on sales	2,650,000	2,725,000	75,000
Marketing expenses	1,250,000	1,275,000	(25,000)
Gen. and admin. expenses	600,000	620,000	(20,000)
Net profit	$ 800,000	$ 830,000	$ 30,000

Manufacturing manager

Factory cost of sales
July, 197—

	Budget	Actual	Fav. (Unfav.)
Department 1	$200,000	$197,000	$3,000
Department 2	195,000	195,500	(500)
Department 3	100,000	99,000	1,000
Department 4	510,000	525,000	(15,000)
Department 20	100,000	102,000	(2,000)
Total factory cost of sales	$3,900,000	$3,925,000	($25,000)

Foreman—
department 4

Cost report—department 4
July, 197—

	Budget	Actual	Fav. (Unfav.)
Controllable costs:			
Direct mat.	$150,000	$148,000	$2,000
Direct labor	205,000	206,000	(1,000)
Indirect labor	12,000	13,000	(1,000)
Overtime	10,000	14,000	(4,000)
Fringe benefits	40,500	41,000	(500)
Supplies	20,000	25,000	(5,000)
Main. and repairs	20,000	17,000	3,000
Scrappage	14,000	18,000	(4,000)
Perishable tools	3,000	6,000	(3,000)
Utilities	8,000	8,100	(100)
Other controllable costs	9,500	10,500	(1,000)
Noncontrollable costs:			
Rent	5,000	5,000	—
Depr. and amort.	8,000	8,000	—
Insurance	1,000	1,300	(300)
Taxes—real estate and personal property	1,500	1,500	—
Other noncontrollable costs	2,500	2,600	(100)
Total costs	$510,000	$525,000	($15,000)

FIGURE 1–8. A responsibility reporting system for a
typical manufacturing firm.

INTEGRATED DATA PROCESSING SYSTEMS

An examination of the responsibility reporting approach indicates that its initial accounting applications were discrete and were processed individually. There were several reasons for this approach. First, computers were regarded as large accounting machines that represented only a further mechanization of the accounting section. For example, first payroll was designed and programmed, followed by accounts receivable, then inventory, and so forth. Second, this piecemeal approach was the result of following the organizational boundaries that have traditionally existed. Third, these early installations were justified not on the basis of giving management more information and control over their entire operations but on the basis of the computer's ability to perform accounting jobs faster and more economically. Because of the stress on accounting applications, the computer system generally became a part of the accounting department within its existing framework.

As time passed, systems designers recognized that operations go considerably beyond the accounting aspects. They saw the great need for a system that integrates all subsystems that can be logically interrelated. The system must integrate men, machines, money, materials, and management (refer to Figure 1-2) in conformity with the firm's objectives, policies, methods, and procedures. The net result is a unified system, commonly known as an *integrated data processing system.*

Single Data Entry for Multiple Uses

In addition to a network of related subsystems developed according to an integrated scheme for carrying out an organization's major functions, integrated data processing systems have other distinguishing characteristics, like single data entry for multiple uses. Data entered into the system are based on the *single record concept,* i.e., data are entered once for multiple uses. To state it another way, single data entry for multiple uses transcends organizational boundaries whereby data are stored in a machine-processible form that can be used by many functional areas of the firm. Records that are kept for one purpose may actually have several other uses. Related elements in different processing activities are combined into common coordinated procedures and work flows. This is made possible by having the whole business system interrelated. For example, bills of materials which are prepared by the engineering department can be utilized as is or manipulated by manufacturing, purchasing, accounting, and other appropriate departments. The manufacturing section can determine material requirements from the bills of materials, which, in turn, can be the basis for ordering from vendors, initiating production orders, and pricing the final products.

Responsiveness to Changes—Flexibility

Another distinguishing characteristic of an integrated information system is its responsiveness to change, namely, its flexibility. Since activities, methods, procedures, responsibilities, and similar items are continually changing, many times it is easier to effect changes with computer systems than manual systems because many of these can be programmed without the need for retraining personnel with new equipment and procedures. Hence, flexibility is generally an important part of an integrated data processing system.

Deficiencies of Integrated Data Processing Systems

The integration of many data processing activities reduced the duplication of data and files as well as improving the coordination of the firm's major functions with one another. However, the integration of major functional activities does not, in itself, guarantee optimum results. Although historical output reports were prepared for various operating levels, output for controlling current operations was needed. In essence, reports that could better facilitate the managerial functions were lacking in integrated data processing systems.

INTEGRATED MANAGEMENT INFORMATION SYSTEMS

Several of the deficiencies of integrated data processing systems were remedied by improving upon its basic concepts. Among the improvements was the preparation of output reports for all management levels of past operations so that the system could take over routine decision making. The net result of this system upgrading was an *integrated management information system*—a system designed to provide selected decision-oriented information needed by management to plan, control, and evaluate the activities of the organization. It is designed within a framework that emphasizes profit planning, performance planning, and control at all levels. It contemplates the ultimate integration of required business information subsystems, both financial and nonfinancial, within the organization.

Reports to Assist Management

Formerly, the primary interest of business information systems was developing financial statements. When an integrated MIS is installed, its major purpose is the production of reports that will assist management. The periodic financial reports are secondary, representing a by-product of the information processed to assist in controlling current operations. From this standpoint, data processing records can serve several uses, thereby reducing costs of obtaining essential managerial reports.

Performance of Routine Decision Making

A true integrated management information system involves more than a mechanical linking together of various organizational functions. Going one step further, it aids management by taking over routine decision making. If a manager can define his or her decision criteria, they can be computerized. Thus, management can concentrate its efforts on those areas that are not routine.

Integrated MIS Illustrated

The introduction of a customer order creates an open order file that forms the basis for preparing invoices and for updating the accounts-receivable file at a later time. The customer order also affects the raw material orders, manpower scheduling, production scheduling, finished goods inventory, shipping orders, sales commissions, and marketing forecasts. Incoming orders, through their effect on inventory levels, may trigger an automatic computer reordering subroutine through the issuance of a purchase order. (The reorder quantity is based on reorder levels and quantities determined by mathematical formulas designed as part of the system.) The purchase orders, in turn, create a liability, requiring payment to vendors. In such a system, the operations aspects of order entry, billing, accounts receivable, inventory control, purchasing, and accounts payable are interwoven. This approach is illustrated in Figure 1-9.

In addition to illustrating the foregoing parts of this integrated management information system, Figure 1-9 shows data input (from major business functions) being sent to a computer system on some predetermined periodic basis. Inputs in previous periods have resulted in master magnetic tape files of data relating to customers, employees, inventories, and all other business phases accumulated from previous processing cycles. As current data are processed by the computer system, the appropriate master magnetic tape files are updated. From these, documents, forms, and reports are prepared automatically. The kinds and number of control and information reports generated from the basic data are dictated by the needs of management and the capabilities of the equipment.

Although the preceding discussion has centered around sequential access files, integrated MIS can also employ random access files. The reader is reminded that random access files were not illustrated in Figure 1-9.

Major Characteristics of Integrated MIS

An integrated management information system, then, is a network of related subsystems, integrated to perform the functional activities of an organization. Its essentials include producing meaningful output for management and taking over routine decision making. Activities that are common to all departments are stored in a data file or data bank. Transactions that affect more than one functional area are captured but once and processed in a manner appropriate for all users of the information. It is, thereby, a considerable improvement over prior systems.

Deficiencies of Integrated MIS and Prior Systems

Even though the integrated management information system rectified the problem of being accounting-oriented and is a business information system that provides feedback in the form of reports through its various subsystems, it is still deficient in one important respect. Data must be accumulated for a period of time before processing is feasible. Whether sequential (i.e., magnetic tape) or random

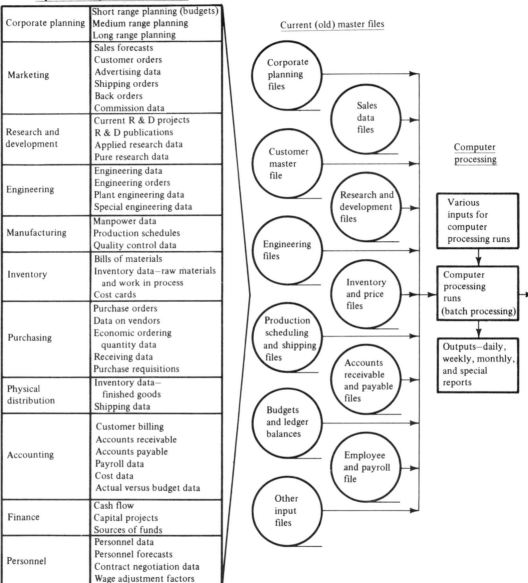

Inputs from major business functions

Corporate planning	Short range planning (budgets)
	Medium range planning
	Long range planning
Marketing	Sales forecasts
	Customer orders
	Advertising data
	Shipping orders
	Back orders
	Commission data
Research and development	Current R & D projects
	R & D publications
	Applied research data
	Pure research data
Engineering	Engineering data
	Engineering orders
	Plant engineering data
	Special engineering data
Manufacturing	Manpower data
	Production schedules
	Quality control data
Inventory	Bills of materials
	Inventory data—raw materials and work in process
	Cost cards
Purchasing	Purchase orders
	Data on vendors
	Economic ordering quantity data
	Receiving data
	Purchase requisitions
Physical distribution	Inventory data— finished goods
	Shipping data
Accounting	Customer billing
	Accounts receivable
	Accounts payable
	Payroll data
	Cost data
	Actual versus budget data
Finance	Cash flow
	Capital projects
	Sources of funds
Personnel	Personnel data
	Personnel forecasts
	Contract negotiation data
	Wage adjustment factors

Current (old) master files

Corporate planning files

Sales data files

Customer master file

Research and development files

Engineering files

Inventory and price files

Production scheduling and shipping files

Accounts receivable and payable files

Budgets and ledger balances

Employee and payroll file

Other input files

Computer processing

Various inputs for computer processing runs

Computer processing runs (batch processing)

Outputs—daily, weekly, monthly, and special reports

FIGURE 1-9. Integrated management information system for a typical manufacturing firm—data stored on magnetic tapes can be used for more than one report.

18

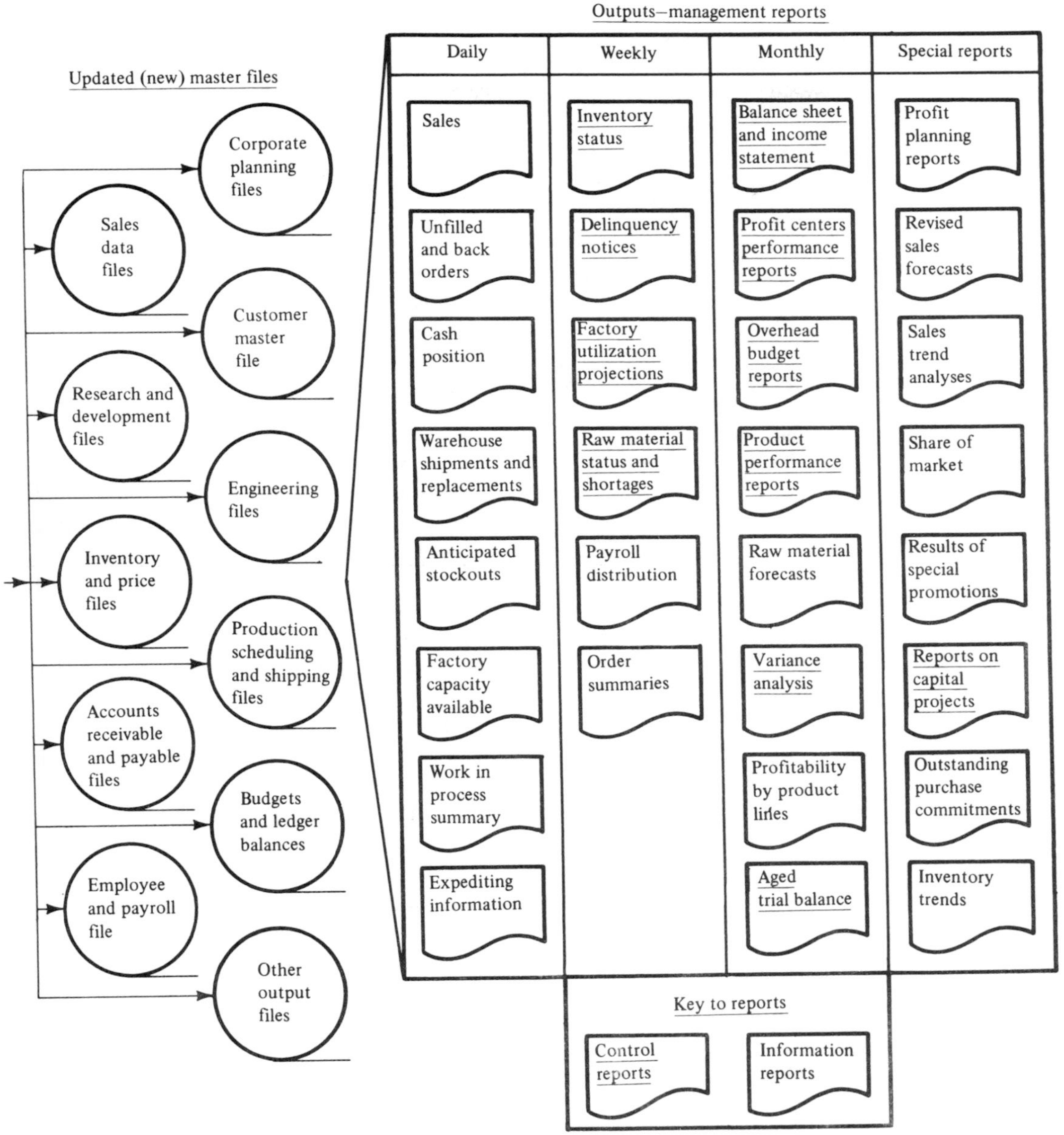

Outputs—management reports

Updated (new) master files

Daily	Weekly	Monthly	Special reports
Sales	Inventory status	Balance sheet and income statement	Profit planning reports
Unfilled and back orders	Delinquency notices	Profit centers performance reports	Revised sales forecasts
Cash position	Factory utilization projections	Overhead budget reports	Sales trend analyses
Warehouse shipments and replacements	Raw material status and shortages	Product performance reports	Share of market
Anticipated stockouts	Payroll distribution	Raw material forecasts	Results of special promotions
Factory capacity available	Order summaries	Variance analysis	Reports on capital projects
Work in process summary		Profitability by product lines	Outstanding purchase commitments
Expediting information		Aged trial balance	Inventory trends

Corporate planning files

Sales data files

Customer master file

Research and development files

Engineering files

Inventory and price files

Production scheduling and shipping files

Accounts receivable and payable files

Budgets and ledger balances

Employee and payroll file

Other output files

Key to reports

Control reports	Information reports

19

access (i.e., magnetic disk or drum) files are utilized, there is still the problem of time lag. For this reason all prior systems, whether they are custodial accounting, responsibility reporting, integrated data processing, or integrated management information systems, are called *backward-looking control systems.* The methods, procedures, and equipment look to past history before reports are produced for feedback. What is needed is a "forward-looking control system"—one that looks to the present and future. Such an approach is found in a *real-time management information system.*

The foregoing data processing systems prior to real-time management information systems were summarized previously in Figure 1–7. Their important characteristics are set forth for comparative purposes.

REAL-TIME MANAGEMENT INFORMATION SYSTEMS

Although the foregoing systems are still operating in organizations of various sizes (despite their deficiencies), one current trend in newer business information systems is the implementation of real-time management information systems, sometimes referred to as *on-line real-time* systems. Typical applications within such an environment include accounts receivable, airline reservation systems, bank desposit and withdrawal accounting, hotel accounting and reservations systems, law enforcement intelligence systems, patient hospital records, savings and loan deposit accounting, and stock market information.

An essential characteristic of this type of system is the on-line real-time concept. All information is *on-line,* that is, *all data are sent directly into a computer system as soon as they come into being.* The whole operation is in *real-time,* which means *data are processed and fed back to the appropriate source in sufficient time to change or control the operating environment.* Basically, then, any system that processes and stores data or reports them as they are happening is considered to be an on-line real-time system. Company personnel will receive a response from the system in time to satisfy their own real-time environmental requirements. The response time may range from a fraction of a second to minutes, hours, and days, depending on the attendant circumstances.

To illustrate the concept of real-time in a business information system, the production planning department has developed a computerized on-line daily scheduler. Since all variable manufacturing data are entered as they occur in the local on-site computer system, the on-line data base for this function as well as others is always up-to-date. Before the start of each day, the computerized scheduler simulates the activities of the factory for that day. Knowing what has occurred during the previous day, that is, where jobs are backed up or behind schedule and where production bottlenecks are currently occurring, this manufacturing simulation model can determine what will happen as the day begins and, thereby, alerts the foremen and plant supervisor about critical areas that need immediate attention. A response, then, has been fed back in sufficient time to control the upcoming manufacturing activities.

Integration of All Subsystems

A real-time system must be integrated in order to be effective. Data acquired from one source are often used in many subsystems. If this approach is not used, there is much wasted motion and extra cost since each subsystem must treat the same data without taking advantage of processing accomplished by other subsystems.

Common Data Base Elements

The integrated data accumulated from the many detailed on-line transactions are commonly referred to as the data base elements or the organization's data base. In addition to having all data collected in one place (basically secondary on-line storage), a firm's data base must be data-oriented. The same inventory data base may be used by a number of departments, such as manufacturing, production control, inventory control, purchasing, and finance. In another example, a data base element is an employee skill number that can assist in preparing weekly payroll, referencing personnel records, filling new job openings, preparing contract negotiations, and the like. Thus, a data base refers to elements or data bits in a common storage medium that form the foundation for operational information, although the data base may be physically dispersed.

Structure of Common Data Base

Before the organization's data base can be structured in a meaningful manner, it is first necessary to identify the information requirements of management. Second, the data base elements must be fully identified, that is, where they are located, how they are obtained, how large they are, and what their specific contents are. The last requirement dictates that relationships among the data base elements be clearly known so that they can serve many information requests with a minimum amount of programming. The data elements should be capable of being related to as many different outputs as possible, in particular, those needed for timely managerial reports (Figure 1–10).

Reports to Lower and Middle Management

Designing a structured data base for accommodating the various levels of management (lower, middle, and top) is a formidable task. Currently, systems designers are concentrating on satisfying the needs of lower and middle management for organizing, directing, and controlling activities around the established plans, being in conformity with the firm's objectives. Hence, real-time management information systems are focused on such areas as improved forecasting for all phases of the firm, optimum marketing budget, improved shipping schedules and service to customers, better utilization of production facilities, improved vendor performance, higher return on short-term assets, and improved negotiations with

On-line input (I/0 devices)

Corporate planning

Marketing

Research and development

Engineering

Manufacturing

Common data base

Data base elements and programs

Corporate planning	Marketing	Res. and dev.	Engineering	Manufacturing	Inventory	Purchasing
Short range planning (budgets) Medium range planning Long range planning	Sales forecasts Customer orders Advertising data Shipping orders Back orders Commission data	Current R and D projects R and D publications Applied research data Pure research data	Engineering data Engineering orders Plant engineering data Special engineering data	Manpower data Production schedules Quality control data Bills of materials	Inventory data—raw mat. and work in process Cost cards	Purchase orders Data on vendors Economic ordering quantity data Receiving data Purchase requisitions

On-line I/0 devices

Machine tools

Microcomputers and minicomputers

Industrial processes

Analog computers

Central processor (on-line real-time processing and remote batch processing)

Various outputs as required

On-line I/0 devices

Inventory
On-line I/0 devices

Purchasing
On-line I/0 devices

Physical distribution
On-line I/0 devices

Accounting
On-line I/0 devices

Finance
On-line I/0 devices

Personnel
On-line I/0 devices

Inputs from major business functions

FIGURE 1-10. Real-time management information system for a typical manufacturing firm—data base elements stored on line can be used for more than one report.

Physical distribution	Accounting	Finance	Personnel
Inventory data—finished goods / Shipping data	Customer billing / Accounts receivable / Accounts payable / Payroll data / Cost data / Actual versus budget data	Cash flow / Capital projects / Source of funds	Personnel data / Personnel forecasts / Contract negotiation data / Wage adjustment factors

Input/output

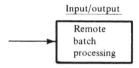

Remote
batch
processing

Input/output

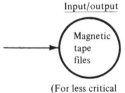

Magnetic
tape
files

(For less critical
and voluminous files)

Outputs—management
reports, refer to
Figure 1—9

On-line output—typed or visual (I/O devices)

Corporate planning
Budget data
Short range planning data
Medium range planning data
Long range planning data

Marketing
Customer order status
Back order status
Finished products available
 for sale

Research and development
Research references for
 review
Graphic displays
Pure and applied reasearch
 results

Engineering
Plotted engineering data
Results of mathematical
 calculations
New engineering designs

Manufacturing
Production order status
Inventory levels on
 specific items
Production control data

Purchasing
Purchase order status
Results of vendor
 comparison

Finance
Cash flow status
Capital projects data
Cost of capital data

Personnel
New personnel needs
Payroll forecasts
Available personnel
 within to fill new
 job openings

Inventory
Shipments received
 over quantities
 ordered
Location of stock items
Items available
 in stock

Physical distribution
Routing information
Data on location of
 goods to be shipped
Shipping schedule
 data

Accounting
Net profit to date
Expense accounts
 exceeding budget
Accounts receivable
 status on individual
 accounts
Credit check
Accounts payable
 by vendors
Overdue invoices

labor. Other outputs found in a real-time MIS for a typical manufacturing firm are given in Figure 1–10.

On-Line Input/Out Devices

Within a real-time MIS environment, there are a number of on-line input/ output devices that are located throughout the firm's operations. Teletypewriters and visual display devices are capable of sending as well as receiving information. They may be many miles away from one another but are linked through a data communication network from the local computer and/or regional computer to the central computing facility.

A real-time system at the home office, for example, may be so designed that input data from an I/O device will trigger a production order when inventory reaches a predetermined level. The number of units to be produced will be based on an economic order quantity (mathematical model). The computer program will scan the present production schedules of the many plants scattered throughout the country and determine which plant will produce the order, based on its capacities and previous production commitments. Likewise, the computer program will indicate to which warehouse the products will be shipped, based on proximity to the factory and level of present inventory. During this on-line process, the computer files are updated simultaneously to reflect these changing conditions.

Remote Batch Processing

An examination of Figure 1–10 reveals other devices, such as minicomputers, analog computers, and magnetic tape that provide input for the system. A real-time system is capable of handling remote batch processing for applications that are not ideal candidates for real-time processing. In effect, a real-time MIS computer is capable of handling remote input/output devices as well as remote batch processing, the question being which is best suited for the activity.

Major Characteristics of Real-Time MIS

There are many essential characteristics of a real-time management information system. A real-time MIS, being a forward-looking control system, maintains data base elements on-line which are available to the computer system when needed. The firm's data base (locally, regionally, or centrally located) is always updated as events occur and can be interrogated from many I/O terminals. With source data being entered as they happen, the real-time approach reduces repetitious recording, makes data available to all subsystems needing them, and reduces the error in conflicting reports that arise from varying coding or interpretations and unsynchronized timing. As a result, all departments work with the same information, thereby making it possible to tie in their decisions with those of other functions. Also, information stored on-line can be obtained upon request from a number of locations at a distance from the main computer system. It is possible to process data in real-time so that output may be fed back almost instantaneously to control current operations. The on-line computer's ability to interact with people on a timely basis with important information is its greatest asset. Management can be made aware of trends, exceptions, and results of recent decisions in order to initiate corrective action that meets predetermined business plans. Environmental feedback alerts the manager as to how the total business is operating, favorably or unfavorably, in relation to internal and external conditions.

Deficiency of Real-Time MIS

Even though lower and middle managers can obtain updated information about the firm's basic business operations through some kind of input/output device, the same cannot be said for top management with a real-time management information system. Although the system does respond to the managerial needs of the first two levels, it falls short of the information desired by top-level executives. Those in top management are responsible and accountable for the full range of business activities. Their principal task revolves around long-range planning or strategic planning. No matter what name is used for future planning, a real-time system does not provide long-range information per se. However, it does respond with immediate feedback on present operations, which is essential in order to modify future plans.

A comparison of the important characteristics for integrated MIS and real-time MIS is given in Figure 1-11. For further information on these management information systems, consult the author's book on real-time management information systems[1] as well as the selected references at the end of the chapter. In addition, integrated MIS will be illustrated in Part III of this text.

CHAPTER SUMMARY

Prior to distributed processing systems, several different approaches to business information systems have been designed by systems analysts for managerial use. Before the dawn of the computer age, management was fact-minded rather than information-oriented—accounting-oriented in terms of reports rather than toward information for controlling all of the firm's basic business functions. It dealt with today's problems in the light of yesterday's results. This approach, represented by the custodial accounting system, was appropriate for the times. The structure of the firm and its markets was static, and changes came gradually. As a result, today's problems were not too different from yesterday's. With the arrival of the computer, management found it could produce many accounting reports for a more comprehensive approach. This led to the development of a responsibility reporting system that was capable of producing accounting-oriented reports for all levels of management.

These accounting-oriented approaches satisfied management during the first

[1] Robert J. Thierauf, *Systems Analysis and Design of Real-Time Management Information Systems,* Englewood Cliffs, N.J.: Prentice-Hall, Inc., 1975.

Important Characteristics of Management Information Systems	Integrated Management Information System	Real-Time Management Information System
Type of System	Backward-looking control system and integrated subsystems	Forward- and backward-looking control system and integrated subsystems
Reports Prepared	Output reports directed to all levels of management for past operations	Output reports directed mainly to lower and middle management for past, current, and future operations
Exception Reporting	Past activities contained in management exception reports	Current plans and objectives used for management exception reports
Information Orientation	Output-oriented	Input/output-oriented with I/O terminals
Processing Mode	Batch processing	On-line real-time processing and remote batch processing
Data Elements	Common data bank	Common data base
Modularity	Very little modularity of systems design	Use of modular design approach
Type of Files	Sequential and random access file storage	Accent on random access on-line file storage
Mathematical Models	Limited use of standard operations research models	Great use of standard and some complex operations research models

FIGURE 1-11. Comparison of important characteristics for integrated and real-time management information systems.

generation of computers. The dynamics of the ever-changing business world, the volume and complexity of producing needed managerial information, and the recognition of the computer's potential by personnel in the data processing field provided the initial thrust for better systems. Simultaneously, management began to realize that the information potential of the computer had not been fully exploited. Based on these initial developments, integrated data processing systems were developed and were further refined into integrated management information systems. These systems and prior ones were backward-looking and generally batch-processing-oriented.

The state of the art has progressed in terms of both computer hardware and software for the implementation of real-time MIS. A real-time MIS has been shown to be a forward-looking control system that maintains data base elements on line and is available to the central processing unit when needed. The organization's base is always updated as events occur and can be interrogated from remote I/O terminals. With source data being entered as they happen, the real-time approach reduces repetitious recording, makes data available to all integrated subsystems needing them, and reduces conflicting reports that arise from varying coding or interpretations and unsynchronized timing. As a result, all departments work with the same information, thereby making it possible to tie their decisions with those of other functions. Also, information stored on line can be obtained upon request from a number of locations at a distance from the main computer system. *The computer's ability to interact on-line with people on a timely basis is its greatest asset.* Management can be made aware of trends, exceptions, and results of recent decisions in order to initiate corrective action that meets predetermined business plans. Feedback alerts the manager as to how the total business is operating— favorably or unfavorably—in relation to internal and external conditions. Thus, a real-time MIS has great potential for certain business applications. However, a more practical easy-to-use and less costly approach for many business applications is *distributed processing,* the subject matter for the remainder of the text.

QUESTIONS

1. Define the following terms:
   a. information
   b. system
   c. subsystem
   d. data bank

2. a. Distinguish between a custodial accounting system and a responsibility reporting system.
   b. How does a responsibility reporting system effect better control over a custodial accounting system for a typical firm?

3. a. What are the essential differences between an integrated data processing system and an integrated management information system?
   b. In what ways is an integrated MIS better than integrated data processing (DP) from a management point of view?

4. a. What is meant by a backward-looking control system?
   b. What systems are of this type?

5. What caused the development of management information systems? Explain.

6. a. Distinguish between a backward-looking control system and a forward-looking control system.
   b. What type is a real-time management information system?

7. Why is output from a real-time MIS directed basically toward lower and middle management?

8. What part does the management by exception principle play in a real-time management information system?

9. What are the advantages of an on-line data base in real-time versus off-line files in batch processing?

10. What are the essential differences between an integrated management information system and a real-time management information system?

SELECTED REFERENCES

Anderson, D. R., "Viewing MIS from the Top," *Journal of Systems Management,* July 1973.

Argyris, C., "Management Information Systems: The Challenge to Rationality And Emotionality," *Management Science,* Feb. 1971.

Bentley, T. J., "Defining Management's Information Needs," *AFIPS Conference Proceedings* (National Computer Conference), Vol. 45, 1976.

Blackman, M., *The Design of Real-Time Applications,* New York: John Wiley & Sons, Inc., 1975.

Borovits, I., and Segev, E., "Real-time Management—An Analogy," *Academy of Management Review,* April 1977.

Boulden, J. B., and Buffa, E. S., "Computer Models: On-Line Real-Time Systems," *Harvard Business Review,* July–Aug. 1970.

Boutell, W. S., *Computer-Oriented Business Systems,* Englewood Cliffs, N.J.: Prentice-Hall, Inc., 1973.

Brown, W. F., and Hawkins, D. H., "Remote Access Computing: The Executive's Responsibility," *Journal of Systems Management,* June 1972.

Burch, J. G., and Strater, F. R., "Tailoring the Information System," *Journal of Systems Management,* Feb. 1973.

Burdeau, H. B., "Environmental Approach to MIS," *Journal of Systems Management,* April 1974.

Davis, G. D., *Management Information Systems: Conceptual Foundations, Structure, and Development,* New York: McGraw-Hill Book Company, 1974.

Dearden, J., "Myth of Real-Time Management Information," *Harvard Business Review,* May–June 1966.

——, "MIS Is a Mirage," *Harvard Business Review,* Jan.–Feb. 1972.

Dearden, J., McFarlan, F. W., and Zani, W. M., *Managing Computer-Based Information Systems,* Homewood, Ill.: Richard D. Irwin, Inc., 1971.

Field, R., "MIS Comes Percolating up the Organization," *Computer Decisions,* May 1972.

Hanold, T., "An Executive View of MIS," *Datamation,* Nov. 1972.

Head, R. V., *Manager's Guide to Management Information Systems,* Englewood Cliffs, N.J.: Prentice-Hall, Inc., 1973.

Kanter, J. *Management-Oriented Management Information Systems,* Englewood Cliffs, N.J.: Prentice-Hall, Inc. 1977.

Kneitel, A. M., "Operating Management—The 'Real Users' of MIS," *Infosystems,* Oct. 1975.

Llwellyn, R., *Information Systems,* Englewood Cliffs, N.J.: Prentice-Hall, Inc., 1976.

Lohara, C. S., "A New Approach to Management Information Systems," *Journal of Systems Management,* Part I, July 1971, and Part II, Aug. 1971.

Mancinelli, T. B., "Management Information Systems, The Trouble with Them," *Computers and Automation,* July 1972.

Martin, J., *Design of Real-Time Computer Systems,* Englewood Cliffs, N.J.: Prentice-Hall, Inc., 1967.

Murdick, R. G., and Ross, J. E., *Information Systems for Modern Management,* Englewood Cliffs, N.J.: Prentice-Hall, Inc., 1975.

____, *Introduction to Management Information Systems,* Englewood Cliffs, N.J.: Prentice-Hall, inc., 1977.

Paretta, R. L., "Designing Management Information Systems: An Overview," *The Journal of Accountancy,* April 1975.

Prince, T. R., *Information for Management Planning and Control,* Homewood, Ill.: Richard D. Irwin, Inc., 1975.

Rothstein, M. F., *Guide to the Design of Real-Time Systems,* New York: John Wiley & Sons, Inc., 1970.

Seese, D. A., "Initiating a Total Information System," *Journal of Systems Management,* April 1970.

Shults, E. C., and Bruun, R. J., "The Hard Road to MIS Success," *Infosystems,* May 1974.

Spiro, B. E., "What's a Management Information System," *Datamation,* July 1972.

Sprague, R. H., Jr., and Watson, Hugh J., "MIS Concepts, Part I and Part II," *Journal of Systems Management,* Jan.–Feb. 1975.

Strassman, P. A., "Managing the Costs of Information," *Harvard Business Review,* Sept.–Oct. 1976.

Swanson, E. B., "Management Information Systems: Appreciation and Involvement," *Management Science,* Oct. 1974.

Taplin, J. M., "AAIMS: American Airlines Answers the What Ifs," *Infosystems,* Feb. 1973.

Thierauf, R. J., *Systems Analysis and Design of Real-Time Management Information Systems,* Englewood Cliffs, N.J.: Prentice-Hall, Inc., 1975.

Urban, G. L., "Building Models for Decision Makers," *Interfaces,* May 1974.

Vandell, R. F., "Management Evolution in the Quantitative World," *Harvard Business Reivew,* Jan.–Feb. 1970.

Withington, F. G., "Five Generations of Computers," *Harvard Business Review,* July–Aug. 1974.

Yourdon, E., *Design of On-Line Computer Systems,* Englewood Cliffs, N.J.: Prentice-Hall, Inc., 1972.

part two

CURRENT DEVELOPMENTS IN DISTRIBUTED PROCESSING SYSTEMS

ESSENTIALS OF DISTRIBUTED PROCESSING SYSTEMS

2

Various approaches to information systems design, as set forth in the prior chapter, have evolved over the years where each new design is meant to try to correct deficiencies of the previous one. Currently, an important thrust in business information systems, i.e., comprehensive management information systems that provide managers throughout an organization with information they need to make decisions, is real-time MIS. On-line real-time capabilities of such information systems require extensive use of costly random access devices and remote terminals, which involves large financial commitments at the initial stage of implementation. Many organizations may neither have nor be willing to risk such enormous amounts of capital and time on such sophisticated information systems. In view of these realities, many organizations are moving in the direction of simpler and easier-to-use systems, such as *distributed processing systems*. Not only are the costs lower, but also the time to implement such systems is substantially less.

Although the declining costs of microcomputers, minicomputers, and small general-purpose computers as well as "smart" and "intelligent" terminals have provided the economic justification for distributed computing, there are other reasons for moving in this direction. These are described in the opening section of this chapter. After discussing the need for distributed processing systems, their specific characteristics are delineated. These features of a distributed processing environment are the main part of the chapter. Finally, distributed processing systems are defined. The orientation of such systems is toward answering the reporting needs of lower and middle management as set forth in the prior chapter.

THE NEED FOR DISTRIBUTED PROCESSING

In the history of computers, as pointed out in the prior chapter, most computing capabilities were dependent on one or more large central processing units that were programmed to perform various data processing (DP) functions. The use of centralized systems created input bottlenecks. Likewise, they created situations where the feedback of business data necessary to run an organization occurred after substantial delays. Due to these difficulties, distributed processing arose out of the need to get computing power where it is needed, namely, at the lower levels in an organization. This approach to data processing is actually a spin-off of the "small business computer" concept. In many cases, the computer equipment used is the same; however, the accent is on who is using it and how it is programmed.

Another way of viewing the need for distributed processing is applying the 80:20 rule, i.e., putting computer processing power where 80 percent of the work is done or where results are needed. In general, distributed data processing makes economic sense if 80 percent of the data generated at a downline site is used primarily for that site. Otherwise, other DP approaches, such as those enumerated in the prior chapter, may be more suitable for meeting an organization's data processing needs.

Fundamentally, distributed processing can be characterized as an approach for making computer systems more amenable and responsive for use by humans. Instead of having one or two large central processing units perform most of the data processing work, often inefficiently, distributed processing means adding to the system a series of linked mini- or microcomputers where terminals can be programmed to react more quickly to the user's needs. With smaller "building blocks" or "modules," users can put together systems to meet highly specific needs. For example, point-of-sale terminals and bank cash machines can be configured to meet the operating needs of personnel at the local level for source data entry. In a similar manner, various types of "intelligent" terminals can be programmed to do much of the processing of data before they communicate and interact with divisional or central computers. Thus, DP needs at the local and regional levels in an organization can be performed more efficiently as well as be integrated with DP operations at central headquarters. Likewise, DP operations can be undertaken at less cost in the field (local and regional levels) than at the central office level.

ESSENTIAL CHARACTERISTICS OF DISTRIBUTED PROCESSING SYSTEMS

Having established a need for distributed processing systems, there are several essential characteristics that focus on placing computing processing power where it is needed within an organization. These are discussed below as well as set forth in Figure 2-1. Although some of these characteristics will be found in systems detailed in Chapter 1, specifically integrated MIS and real-time MIS, nevertheless, they are the distinguishing ones found in a distributed processing environment. Additionally, these characteristics will be highlighted in Chapters 4 and 5—current applications for distributed processing systems—as well as in Part III of this text for the case study of the American Products Corporation.

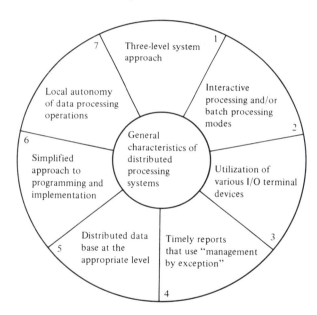

FIGURE 2-1. General characteristics of distributed processing systems.

THREE-LEVEL SYSTEM APPROACH

Because a distributed processing environment can be structured many ways, it is helpful to think in terms of various level system approaches for implementing such an information system. Basically, three different levels which make them attractive for a wide range of applications include

first-level system—local processing of source data entry

- *second-level system*—local processing of source data entry, transactions, and management reports
- *third-level system*—network of distributed processing systems

Not only will the essentials of each level system be explored, but also its operating characteristics will be delineated. Such a presentation serves to highlight the essential differences among the three-level systems in a distributed processing environment.

First-Level System—Local Processing of Source
Data Entry

The main thrust of this first-level system is distributing the power of the computer to the operating level. In other words, a major part of distributed processing at this level is the increased responsiveness of the DP function to the user's needs by providing data entry/inquiry capabilities of the computer at the local or regional level. Such an approach not only gives local managers more control over and involvement with the data and the information system, but also a burden is taken off the central computing facility. And because more is done locally or regionally, the overall system can be utilized to do what it does best, i.e., repetitive processing with responsiveness to the user's needs improved in the process.

Since distributed processing gets computing power where it is needed at the lower levels, management is concerned with operating ease for its personnel. In particular, the DP manager is concerned with the ease with which a system can be implemented and supported for data entry applications. Currently, extensive remote file checking, source validation, and correction are made possible by small processors and "intelligent" terminals to reduce errors and eliminate reentry. Easy-to-run preprocessing and postprocessing routines at the department level allow many standardized tasks to be off-loaded from the main computer. Proven and reliable communication ensures fast and accurate transmission to a centralized computer system if necessary.

For a local processing orientation of a distributed processing system, a first-level system that is easy to use should encompass the following operating characteristics. It should

- aid the user by prompting and checking all entries on a display which looks like the source document itself.
- be conveniently adaptable to any number of data entry forms for various applications.
- perform editing and all logical and arithmetic operations.
- allow for keyed files to be automatically stored on cassette or diskette in a proper format for transmission to the DP center.
- permit the daily input file to be retrieved for review or editing and for push-button printing of part or all of the records.

- allow for communications to the main computer which are accurate, fast, and easy to operate, employing automatic error detection and retransmission.

- prevent fragamation of the professional data processing staff since programming languages are easy to use and systems support from the main DP center is at a minimum.

Examples of the first-level system will be found in Chapter 4. Basically, these local processing systems are oriented toward assisting lower management in controlling day-to-day operations.

Second-Level System—Local Processing of
Source Data Entry, Transactions, and
Management Reports

Going beyond the first-level system where the focus is on source data entry, distributed processing at the local or regional level also includes transaction processing. An integral part of processing all transactional data is the ability to generate some type of managerial reports for local or regional managers. In effect, this second-level system for distributed processing gives both the manager and operating personnel more control over ongoing operations, i.e., the manager gets reports about current operations, and operating personnel process the entire transaction versus just capturing source data.

The second-level system has several operational characteristics. Such a system should

- follow the same entry procedures that existing users are familiar with but, in addition, process complete transactions as they are entered.

- permit expansion to transaction processing inasmuch as local master files are compatible with existing data entry.

- interface with completed and verified transactions as well as their files which are stored for fast access on local disks or diskettes so they can be sorted and listed for display or be printed.

- provide for generating reports that give operational management an up-to-date picture of their operations while communication of summary data to the central DP center ensures timely information for overall control.

Based on these operational characteristics, this second-level system of distributed processing is capable of handling both local and regional operations and of producing management information. If operating management can define their operations and their needs, these requirements can be implemented and summary reports can be integrated into the system at the lower levels. Also, information is forwarded to the central computer system so that appropriate reports can be produced for the various management levels.

For this second-level system, distributed processing examples are set forth in Chapter 4. Accent is not only on data entry and transaction processing but also on producing managerial reports at the local and regional levels.

Third-Level System—Network of Distributed Processing Systems

As noted for the second-level system, management information at the lower levels is an important part of the distributed processing system. However, with this third level, namely, a network of distributed processing systems, management information is a necessary element in the success of not only corporate management but also of operating management. Today, an organization can structure its DP functions to fit the operating structure and generate important management information as a natural by-product of regular day-by-day operations. Distributed processing at the third-system level permits accessibility of information to management, in particular, at the operating levels.

It should be noted that specialized corporate DP resources cannot be fragmented to perform every possible remote request within a network. Thus, the answer is a group of well-managed remote processing centers that are an integral part of the distributed processing network. The total system must operate, for the most part at the local and regional levels, without professional EDP staffing—like the first and second levels—and yet it must accomplish major data processing tasks at the operating level and for operating management.

An essential part of a distributed processing system network is the use of data transmission equipment from the remote processors to the central computer facility. Within such an environment for this third-level system, certain operational characteristics are found. The system should

- allow a number of small computers, i.e., microcomputers, minicomputers, and small business computers, to be combined to form an operational DP center at more than one location. A network of these centers sharing computerized files provides a powerful data processing capability at local and regional levels.

- provide on-line data entry to the local and regional data bases for concurrent processing of multiple independent jobs. An operational DP center performs the required DP requirements of the remote site while it maintains concurrent high-speed communication with the central computer and other DP centers in the network.

- permit the development of network applications that can be solved by the existing DP staff where the accent is on simplicity of operations.

- provide for generating reports within the network that give operational management control over their operations as well as allow for generating summary information for higher levels of management.

Because several different network arrangements can be configured by connecting network elements through communications lines, these basic network types, described below, provide insight into the organization and operation of any network.

Point-to-Point Network. This simplest of computer networks employs a communications line to link two processors, minicomputers, or computers together. In this configuration, one machine is used primarily to process the data into an acceptable format that can be used to make a forecast or a decision. On the other hand, the other machine, which may be a special-purpose device, performs communications control, message switching, and data concentration. In essence, each one performs a complementary function, as illustrated in Figure 2-2.

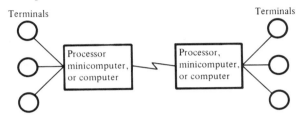

FIGURE 2–2. **Point-to-point network of distributed processing systems.**

Hierarchical or Tree Network. In this arrangement, processors, minicomputers, or computers that perform a dedicated function are linked to another, usually larger, computer that monitors their activities and serves as a backup should one fail or encounter a problem that it cannot handle. The larger computer itself may, in turn, also be monitored by yet another larger computer that may also carry out higher-order processing. In any case, communications in a hierarchy configuration take place between processors, minicomputers, and computers at different levels and not among the machines at the same level. Most distributed processing networks currently in use are of this type. An example of a hierarchical or tree network is given in Figure 2–3 and in Part III for the American Products Corporation.

Star Network. The remote processors, minicomputers, or computers in this network configuration all report to a central computer. Organizationally, a star is similar to a two-level hierarchy but differs in that it entails a heavy flow of communications back and forth between the machines and the central unit, as in an airline reservation and ticketing system. In such a network application, a small processor keeps a local file, formats the tickets, and causes them to be issued. A large computer connected to the smaller ones via dedicated lines draws on a master file to determine seat availability on any one of numerous flights; also it updates the file to reflect new reservations or cancellations.

The star configuration is effective in mini-micro networks. A typical example of a star network is given in Figure 2–4.

Loop or Ring Network. The organization of this network is relatively

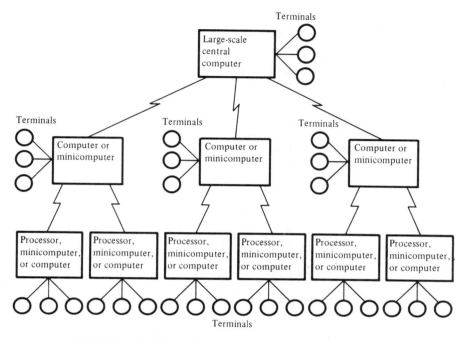

FIGURE 2-3. Hierarchical or tree network of distributed processing systems. Note: Most distributed networks now in use are of this type.

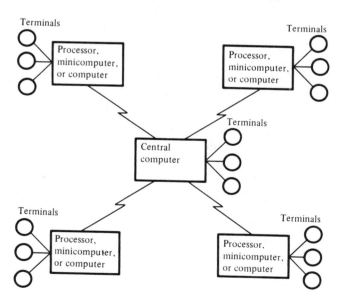

FIGURE 2-4. Star network of distributed processing systems.

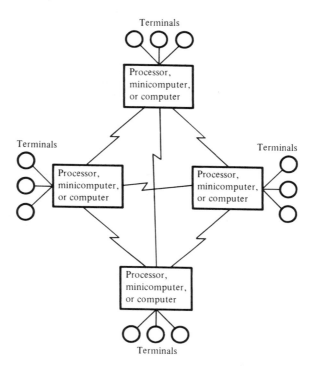

FIGURE 2-5. Loop or ring network of distributed processing systems.

simple; that is, several processors, minicomputers, or computers are linked together to form the equivalent of a ring. Data lines connect each unit only to adjacent ones; any communication between more distant units must be routed through the intermediate units. For this reason, the computers in a ring network must be physically close together. Otherwise, the extensive communications lines cause the configuration to be uneconomical. This network configuration is illustrated in Figure 2-5.

Fully Connected Ring Network. Because of the limitations within a loop or ring network, it is seldom used in its pure form. Rather, it is generally structured as a fully connected ring network, as shown in Figure 2-6. Composed of processors, minicomputers, and computers that have powerful local or regional processing capabilities, each unit can communicate directly with the others—usually in an interactive processing mode. As an example, the fully connected ring network is found in a banking environment.

Hybrid-Type Networks. The preceding five basic network types can be combined to create hybrid-type networks. Several central computers, for example, whereby each is surrounded by a separate star network of satellite processors, can also be connected together in a star network of their own. Such a multistar config-

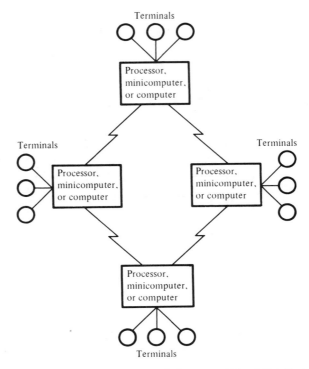

FIGURE 2–6. Fully connected ring network of distributed processing systems.

uration is an alternative to the high-cost ring network where the main processors are remote from one another.

To illustrate the foregoing, a network is intended to serve a city-wide department store chain where each store has a computer that is linked to point-of-sale cash registers in a star configuration. The computers of all the stores, in turn, are also tied together in a star via communications lines. Additionally, one of these is the host to the other computers as well as to its own satellite processors. Such an arrangement allows department store management to obtain inventory information, sales data, special order inquiries, and other management information quickly, separated by individual store or applied to the chain collectively.

As with the prior two-level systems, examples for the third level will be found in Chapter 5. Within these illustrations, summary information that is needed for higher levels of management is forwarded from the local or regional levels to the centralized computer facility for appropriate processing. Thus, detailed information needed for local and regional operations remains at that level; summary information needed to plan, organize, direct, and control overall operations is forwarded from the lower levels and is handled by the central computer.

INTERACTIVE PROCESSING AND/OR BATCH PROCESSING MODES

The processing mode(s) in a distributed processing environment is contingent upon the type of equipment employed. Within the three-level systems discussed previously, one of the following would be appropriate:

• interactive processing mode
• batch processing mode
• combined interactive and batch processing mode

Generally, the first- and second-level systems are interactive at the local or regional levels, while data are transmitted to the home office in a batch mode. Also, for the third-level system, both types of processing modes are employed. As indicated previously, current distributed processing applications for these three levels will be illustrated in Chapters 4 and 5. In addition, the case study of the American Products Corporation in Part III of the text will highlight both processing modes.

Interactive Processing Mode

Within a distributed processing environment, one type of interactive processing mode is the ability of the data entry units to interact with the processor. There must be the ability to change input data that have been entered incorrectly before being stored on magnetic tape or disk. In turn, these data are used for communicating data to the central office. As illustrated in Figure 2–7, data entry units are attached to a processor for entering and verifying data input in an interactive mode; i.e., data are corrected in an interactive mode before becoming a source of input for data transmission.

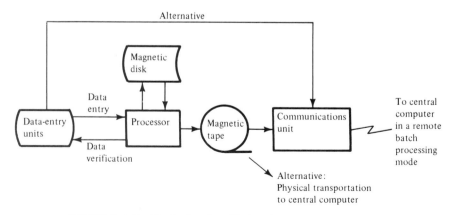

FIGURE 2–7. Method of utilizing interactive processing (local or regional) in a distributed processing environment.

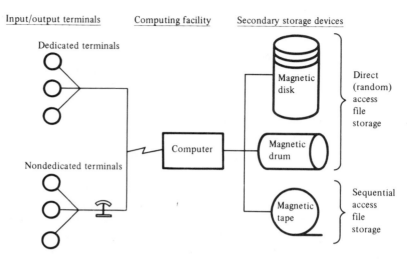

FIGURE 2–8. Interactive processing, i.e., real-time processing, from and to input/output terminals with a computer that utilizes direct (random) access and sequential access file storage.

Another type of interactive processing mode is real-time processing, which is capable of processing information within short time intervals. There is a fast conversion (or turnaround) of input to output that has the ability to affect the operation(s) of the current environment.

Distributed processing systems operating in real-time vary in their capabilities. Some maintain a continuous connection between the many dispersed terminals (commonly called dedicated terminals) and the computer facility, as depicted in Figure 2–8. Also, as illustrated, if a continuous connection is not required between geographically dispersed terminals (commonly called nondedicated terminals) and the computer, the telephone can be used to forward and receive information. Generally, an input transaction from an on-site or an outlying location triggers immediate processing of the data, with the answer being returned immediately if deemed necessary. Not only is the computer capable of updating data files (on secondary devices, such as magnetic disks) from input transactions, but it can also route output to another terminal location either immediately or at a future time.

Batch Processing Mode

The outstanding feature of *local batch processing* in a distributed processing environment is that data at the local or regional level are grouped in batches for better control of input processing. As illustrated in Figure 2–7, data entry units produce tape output which can be physically transported to the central computer facility for further processing.

To overcome the problem of time lag experienced with a local processing approach, *remote batch processing* combines data transmission with batch processing and is used to process data created at points distant from the central computer.

Based on a predetermined schedule, data are transferred over the data communications channel to the central computer in one of two ways: (1) onto a machine-processible medium, such as magnetic tape or disk, for future processing (off-line) or (2) into the computer itself for processing (on-line). The transfer of output information involves basically the same steps but in the opposite direction—that is, from the main computer to the outlying data processing locations. The remote batch processing mode is illustrated in Figure 2-7.

When remote batch is used in an *off-line mode,* there are neither enough transactions to warrant a permanent communication with the main computer nor a continuing need for an immediate response. All data are first captured on some machine-processible medium before computer processing at a central facility is initiated. The chief advantage of this off-line approach is the comparatively low data communications cost.

The other approach to remote batch is an *on-line mode* whereby accumulated data are transferred to and from the computer with little manual intervention. It is also possible to maintain a permanent communication link with the central computer to eliminate the need for establishing a manual connection (via telephone) when a group of data is to be transferred. This type of remote batch is used when there is a large number of transactions to be transferred and/or a large number of locations for transferring data.

Combined Interactive and Batch Processing Mode

The foregoing two approaches may be combined for a more sophisticated approach to distributed processing. While interactive processing is utilized at the local and regional levels for entering and verifying source input data, real-time processing might be used at these same levels for critical areas, such as production scheduling and inventory control. Similarly, critical applications at the home office level might rely on the on-line real-time mode of processing. However, the general procedure at the local and regional levels is to batch data before sending them to the home office. The rationale is that these outlying processing points do not have sufficient volume to warrant a permanent connection with the home office. Thus, a mixture of interactive and batch processing modes might be a more pragmatic and less costly approach than utilizing one of the two approaches by itself.

UTILIZATION OF VARIOUS I/O TERMINAL DEVICES

Based on the approach to distributed processing, various types of input/output terminal devices are required. Currently, there are three types available:

- "dumb" terminals
- "smart" terminals
- "intelligent" terminals (and systems)

Due to the power of microprocessor circuits, some of these terminal devices are virtually indistinguishable in performance from a microcomputer or a minicomputer. Hence, a wide range of I/O terminal devices is available to the user; the attendant circumstances will dictate which is the best hardware configuration for the distributed processing system.

"Dumb" and "Smart" Terminals

To understand the difference between the three basic types of I/O devices, they are defined as follows. A "dumb" terminal is a simple device that is either a standard typewriter unit or video display (CRT) unit which is connected to some type of computing power. Fundamentally, such a unit is a method of providing direct access to and from some type of computer. An example is the standard Teletype unit. The second type of terminal is the preprogrammed "smart" terminal, which can edit and check for errors. These terminals are widely used in data entry and inquiry applications.

"Intelligent" Terminals (and Systems)

The third type of terminal device is the "intelligent" terminal, which is programmable by the user. An intelligent terminal generally consists of a desktop keyboard and video display, and it does not look unlike some remote terminals that have been around for years. But internally it is equipped with powerful microcircuits, and it is often linked with such devices as a printer, plotter, tape drive, and disk storage. Such a system, commonly known as an "intelligent system," is capable of calculating a payroll, updating an inventory, printing an invoice—almost every task a computer is capable of performing.

Currently, users are reaping the benefits of the increasing intelligence of terminal systems by programming them to perform many of the routine tasks that utilize valuable central processor time. For example, these terminal systems are finding their way into sophisticated computer networks for controlling warehouses, managing production lines, and providing accounting services at remote locations.

Clustered Terminals

Going beyond the three basic types of terminals, an important approach for distributed processing has proven to be the clustered display (an approach pioneered in 1970 by Four-Phase-Systems). At each site, whether local or regional or on some other basis, a cluster of keyboard/video terminals share a single processor whereby terminals can easily be added or removed to suit the site's functional requirements and transaction volume.

The flexibility offered by the clustered display concept is an important part of an organization's orderly growth plan for the implementation of distributed processing. When a network evolves along an orderly growth path, each increment of growth is triggered by economic benefits proven in the previous increment. This approach, then, is a cost-efficient way to implement a distributed processing system.

TIMELY REPORTS THAT USE "MANGEMENT BY EXCEPTION"

Within a distributed processing environment that ranges from simple to complex, timely management information is an essential part of it. In straightforward systems, managerial reports may be prepared at periodic intervals during data processing operations. However, in more sophisticated systems, data files are maintained on-line that are available to the central processor when needed for controlling present and future operations. The company's data elements are updated as events occur and can be interrogated from remote I/O terminals. Company personnel receive responses from the system in time to satisfy their own real-time environmental requirements. In some cases, the response time may be a fraction of a second; however, in other cases, it may range from minutes to hours or days, depending on the circumstances.

Regardless of the approach used in a distributed processing system, the *management by exception* principle is an integral part such that only extraordinary events—favorable or unfavorable—are brought to the attention of those responsible and accountable. Often, exceptions to established plans, procedures, or standards are referred to the next higher level of command. Viewing the principle from this perspective, a manager give his or her attention only to those matters which deviate from an established level and thereby require some type of action. The management by exception principle also ensures that normal events are processed without necessitating management's attention. Company personnel at lower- and middle-management levels work within established ranges of authority and responsibility. The exception principle, then, is designed to serve several purposes (especially at the lower- and middle-management levels):

- It specifies areas of direction and supervision, the contents of which can be processed according to normal routine.
- It identifies the unique problem or the unusual event requiring higher decision.
- It establishes a system for handling problems on a higher level when those problems cannot be solved on the level at which they occurred.

To make the exception principle function properly, there are problems of relative balance in job assignment and in the managerial direction at each specific level of organization. First, there is the matter of balance with respect to the functions that constitute a job—the selection of those functions which fit and those which do not fit. Collectively, the functions should be structured so that authority actually fits responsibility and accountability. Second, balance is dependent on the priority of functions which comprise the job. A ranking of order is required to determine which of the functions has to be discharged first, which comes second, and so forth. Without this priority of functions, the manager would be flooded with information, some of which is not necessary. Relativity of job balance that makes the management by exception principle feasible then, revolves around authority, responsibility, and accountability.

DISTRIBUTED DATA BASE AT THE APPROPRIATE LEVEL

Referring to the prior chapter, several problems were uncovered with a common data base (centralized data files in a real-time MIS environment). For one, the data base became enormous. In a heavily loaded multiprogramming and/or teleprocessing environment, the data were not always available. Line failures and other teleprocessing problems separated the remote users from the data and users were concerned about data security. In addition, many central processors became overloaded handling too many jobs. Although several solutions to these problems were offered, such as upgrading to more powerful and more expensive computers or juggling job schedules and job mixes to take the load off the machine, these solutions were largely ineffective.

To overcome objections to a large, centralized common data base, DP strategists came up with the idea of distributed data bases where the user's files are placed at or near the point that transactions occur. This way, the user's data are always available; the concern about data communications failures is no longer necessary. In addition, distributed data bases caught on for other reasons. Low-cost minicomputers have peripherals and processing power almost equal to general-purpose computers. If the local processing load is taken off the main computer, large-scale systems at the central headquarters level became more manageable since the data base becomes smaller, as does the size of the application programs. Distributed processing systems can then operate more autonomously at the local and regional levels and, at the same time, be an important part of a processing cooperative. The distribution of data bases at local, regional, divisional, and home office levels not only makes for more manageable data files but also allows the data to be located where they are needed in an organization.

A distributed data base is a logical integration of related data bases at individual installations. Integration permits users to produce reports summarizing information from different locations, as it also provides a means of using data stored in another data base. Purists would like to see distributed data bases with no redundant data. However, while this is technically feasible, it is operationally undesirable for reasons of backup, security, and integrity. Hence, a distributed data base is a logical integration of related but potentially redundant transactions at individual installations distant from one another.

Before an organization's data base can be distributed and structured in a logical manner, it is first necessary to identify the information requirements of management, that is, which data base elements are required for management reports. Second, the data base elements must be fully identified: specifically, where they are to be located, how they are to be obtained, how large they are to be, and what their specific contents are to be. The last requirement dictates that relationships among the data base elements be known as clearly as possible so that many different information requests can be served with a minimum of programming. The data elements should be related to as many different outputs as possible, in particular to those needed for timely managerial reports.

Data Base Management Systems

Today, numerous generalized data base management systems are available to the user. For instance, a data base management system may be designed to allow selective retrieval of information and to produce managerial reports with a minimum of time and effort. Generally, the system establishes, for a given data base, a dictionary containing all the information necessary to define not only the file or files comprising the data base but also each field within the data base. When the dictionary is written, a search name which can be referenced is assigned to each field whereby the system gains flexibility and can be used for a different data base by simply creating a new dictionary. Numerous data base management systems, then, are currently available to handle the distribution of an organization's data base efficiently and economically.

SIMPLIFIED APPROACH TO PROGRAMMING AND IMPLEMENTATION

Programming and implementing a distributed processing system at the local and regional levels must be different from that employed at the home office level. The DP manager at headquarters recognizes that he (or she) cannot afford to fragment the professional staff of systems analysts and programmers with each installation at the lower level. He cannot justify an on-site programmer, for example, for a hardware installation of less than $1000 per month. Thus, he must select distributed processing equipment at the operating level which can be programmed and maintained by non-EDP personnel. Such an approach results in a simplified approach to data processing activities at the local and regional levels.

Currently, most distributed processing systems being installed are capable of being programmed and utilized by operating personnel. Operating managers at the local level, as an example, are employing easy-to-operate data entry equipment that existing personnel can use without extensive training. Such a source data input system provides computer power during processing of input data. Likewise, operating managers employ easy-to-use distributed processing equipment to sort data into meaningful operating categories and produce timely management information for themselves before the data are transmitted to the DP center. In effect, management information is produced as a normal by-product of a distributed processing system, operated by non-EDP personnel. Such an approach minimizes the impact on the home office data processing staff and, thereby, prevents this staff from being spread too thin. Distributing computer capabilities are available to the user without the necessity to distribute expensive computer experts at the lower levels for long periods.

LOCAL AUTONOMY OF DATA PROCESSING OPERATIONS

A distributed processing system provides autonomy at the local and regional levels both in terms of hardware operation and processing requirements. From an equipment standpoint, the remote system keeps working, performing complete transaction processing even during temporary lapses or unavailability of the centralized computer system. In addition, unique or critical processing requirements can be handled at the operating level because of the ease of program development on a small independent system. Overall, control over local and regional data processing operations is assured.

Not only is there better control over hardware and processing requirements at the operating levels, but also there is more autonomy in terms of DP applications. Operational activities and extraordinary items, peculiar to one operational system, can be accommodated more easily in a distributed processing environment, resulting in more flexibility. This added dimension of flexibility makes the system more accommodating to the user. Overall, development of distributed processing applications for unique, operating-level requirements not only ensures responsive service to lower-level management but also minimizes the impact on the central system resources, thereby preventing fragmentation of the organization's data processing staff.

RECAP OF ESSENTIAL CHARACTERISTICS OF DISTRIBUTED PROCESSING

Within the framework of the foregoing characteristics, distributed processing, broadly speaking, involves the movement of processing capability to new and ever expanding locations within organizations. It ultimately results in an integrated information network which extends throughout an organization and is generally customized to meet the particular needs of the user. This entails arranging computing power according to the levels of complexity, creating local and regional data bases, and developing communications capabilities. Distributed processing takes many forms because it parallels the structure of the using organization. From this view, distributed processing is an integral part of the organization structure.

The essential characteristics of distributed processing are summarized in Figure 2-9 for the reader's convenience. These serve as a basis for a better understanding of distributed computing and provide a means for defining such systems. Likewise, many of these distinguishing characteristics will be an integral part of the emerging ones for future distributed processing systems, the subject matter for Chapter 11.

DISTRIBUTED PROCESSING SYSTEMS DEFINED

Before stating what distributed processing is and is not, it is helpful to define the word *distribute*. It is defined as "to divide and give out in shares, to scatter or spread out, to arrange according to classsifications, or to put in various distinct

1. *Three-level system approach:*
   First-level system—focuses basically on the local processing of source data entry.
   Second-level system—combines local processing of source data entry and transaction processing with preparation of management reports.
   Third-level system—provides a network of distributed processing systems for meeting the needs of users at the local, regional, and home office levels.

2. *Interactive processing and/or batch processing modes:*
   Gives the user the option of an interactive processing mode, a batch processing mode, or a combination of the two for meeting an organization's DP needs.

3. *Utilization of various I/O terminal devices:*
   Consists of using preprogrammed ("smart") terminals for editing and checking errors and programmable ("intelligent") terminals and systems for undertaking many of the routine tasks that a computer can perform.

4. *Timely reports that use management by exception:*
   Employs the appropriate processing mode (interactive, batch, or a combination) for providing timely management reports that set forth exception items.

5. *Distributed data base at the appropriate level:*
   Provides for locating the data bases where they are needed as well as allowing for accessability to and from other locations if required.

6. *Simplified approach to programming and implementation:*
   Incorporates an easy-to-program approach and a simplified installation method for use by operating personnel.

7. *Local autonomy of data processing operations:*
   Allows personnel at the local and regional levels to develop more of their data processing applications without the necessity for continued support from the central systems group.

FIGURE 2–9. Essential characteristics found in distributed processing systems.

locations." Within these various meanings, distributed processing, as it is being implemented today, reflects the full range of these definitions.

Distributed processing does not mean using a front-end processor to handle data communications from the central site, using several minicomputers or general-purpose computers located at the central facility to replace one large computer, or using "intelligent" terminals at remote locations to enter data which are then transmitted to the central site. On the other hand, distributed processing does mean locating individual processors, microcomputers, minicomputers, and small business computers in locations remote from central headquarters and letting these machines do the major processing of given applications that were originally processed on the central system. Control of the distributed applications is distributed to operational management at the local and regional levels who are responsible for processing and maintaining the applications. Summary information, in turn, is communicated from the remote processors to the central site for management review and, many times, is stored on the centralized data base.

Based on this overview, i.e., what distributed processing is and is not, and the essential characteristics set forth in the chapter, distributed processing can be defined as "an approach to placing low-cost computing power, starting at the various points of data entry, and linking these points, where deemed necessary, with a centralized computer via a distributed communications network." In effect, it is an approach to placing computing power where it is needed in an organization for efficient and economical DP operations. Similarly, it is a viable alternative to centralized data processing due to the declining costs of programmable terminals, microprocessors, microcomputers, minicomputers, and small business computers. Because the focus of current distributed processing systems is placing computer power at the lower levels in an organization, generally their output centers on assisting operational (lower) and functional (middle) management.

CHAPTER SUMMARY

The changing technology of today has been a most important stimulus in the movement toward distributed processing systems. To prove this point, consider the early days of the industrial revolution where technical and economic factors dictated that all factory equipment be driven from the same power source—either water wheels or steam engines—through a system of shafts, pulleys, and belts. This highly centralized approach presented a number of problems. The load capacity of the prime mover was limited so the number of users had to be restricted or performance of individual machines would be degraded. The breakthrough came when fractional horsepower electric motors went into mass production. It then became feasible for prime movers to be distributed throughout a factory.

The analogy between motion and computation should be apparent. Microprocessors, microcomputers, minicomputers, and small business computers have become sufficiently powerful and economical that they can be distributed throughout an organization and assigned useful local data processing functions. However, in most broad-based organizations, there is also a need for a network structure to regulate and coordinate local operations. The various types of network structures were enumerated in this chapter. Thus, the type of distributed processing network is contingent upon the user's DP needs.

Underlying the essential characteristics of distributed processing, as presented in this chapter, is the goal of improving productivity through the better management of information. The basic resources of men, machines, materials, money, and management can be made more productive through implementation of a distributed processing network. Specifically, distributed processing brings usable computer power directly to the front-line manager, speeds communications throughout an organization, reduces the information error rate, and adds flexibility so that all organizational levels can adjust rapidly to changing business and processing needs. These advantages are achieved by improving and simplifying the data input function, handling data at the point of most familiarity, accomplishing much of the actual data processing at the source of data, and constructing the flow and configuration of information to meet the needs of a wide range of users.

QUESTIONS

1. Relate the 80:20 rule to the need for distributed processing.

2. How does the "building block" or "modular" approach apply to distributed processing systems? Explain.

3. Of what importance is the three-level approach to an understanding of distributed processing systems? Explain.

4. Of the various types of distributed networks presented in this chapter, which one(s) is (are) the most widely used? Why?

5. Why do current distributed processing systems tend toward an interactive processing mode? Explain.

6. a. How important is the clustered terminal concept in distributed processing? Explain.
   b. How important is the management by exception principle in distributed processing? Explain.

7. What is the chief benefit of distributing an organization's data base?

8. In what ways is distributed processing a simplified approach to programming and implementation? Is this simplified approach related to autonomy of operation at the lower DP levels?

9. What is (are) the principal reason(s) for an organization to install a broad-based distributed processing system? Explain.

10. Criticize the following definition of distributed processing: "A distributed processing environment is one in which the focus is on the pre- and postprocessing of data where the data originate while maintaining central control of the overall DP functions."

SELECTED REFERENCES

Alter, S. "Why Is Man-Computer Interaction Important for Decision Support Systems?," *Interfaces,* Feb. 1977.

Barna, B., "Can the IRS Go Distributed?," *Computer Decisions,* June 1977.

Booth, G. M., "Distributed Information Systems," *AFIPS Conference Proceedings* (National Computer Conference), Vol. 45, 1976.

Burnett, G. J., and Nolan, R. L., "At Last, Major Roles for Minicomputers," *Harvard Business Review,* May–June 1975.

Business Week Special Report, "Glowing Prospects for Brainy Computer Terminals," *Business Week,* Oct. 25, 1976.

Computerworld Special Report, "Distributed Processing: A Concept in Search of a Definition," *Computerworld,* March 28, 1977.

Down, P. J., and Taylor, F. E., *Why Distributed Computing?*, Rochelle Park, N.J.: Hayden Book Company, 1977.

Feidelman, L., "Distributed Computing: It's a Small World," *Infosystems,* April 1977.

Gilder, J. H., "Distributed Processing: Keyword for Tommorrow's Super-computers," *Computer Decisions,* April 1976.

Horn, B. K. P., and Winston, P. H., "Personal Computers," *Datamation,* May 1975.

Hunter, J. J., "Distributing A Database," *Computer Decisions,* June 1976.

Kallis, S. A., Jr., "Networks and Distributed Processing," *Mini-Micro Systems,* March 1977.

Kaufman, F., "Distributed Processing—A Discussion for Executives Traveling over Difficult EDP Terrain," New York: Coopers & Lybrand, 1977.

Kelley, N., "Bank of America Goes Distributive," *Infosystems,* March 1977.

Levin, K. D., and Morgan, H. L., "Optimizing Distributed Data Bases— A Framework for Research," *AFIPS Conference Proceedings* (National Computer Conference), Vol. 44, 1975.

Luke, J. W., "Unraveling the Confusion of Distributed DP," *Infosystems,* Dec. 1976.

Lusa, J. M., "Infosystems Report: Distributed Computing," *Infosystems,* Nov. 1976.

Masi, C., and MacDonald, A., "Wang on Distributed Data Processing," Lowell, Mass.: Wang Laboratories, Inc., 1976.

Myers, E., "AMA Conference: Distributed Processing," *Datamation,* Nov. 1976.

Paretta, R. L., "Designing Management Information Systems: An Overview," *The Journal of Accountancy,* April 1975.

Ritchie, R. D., "Intelligent Terminals and Distributed Processing," *Computer Decisions,* Feb. 1975.

Simonette, I., "Ring in Distributed Computing," *Computer Decisions,* Jan. 1976.

Stein, P. "Distributed Processing and Reality," *Computer Decisions,* Aug. 1976.

Tersine, R. J., "Systems Theory in Modern Organization," *Managerial Planning,* Nov.–Dec. 1973.

Vickers, W. H., "What To Look for in Distributed (Source) Data Processing," *AFIPS Conference Proceedings* (National Computer Conference), Vol. 46, 1977.

FEASIBILITY STUDY OF DISTRIBUTED PROCESSING SYSTEMS

3

An elaboration of distributed processing essentials in the prior chapter brings to the forefront the issue of decentralization versus centralization. Initially, in this chapter we shall examine this important aspect, with emphasis on decentralization of data processing tasks, i.e., distributed processing at the local and regional levels and centralization of those functions which cannot be handled efficiently and economically at the lower operating levels.

Next, we shall discuss important design criteria for distributed processing which are very important for determining the feasibility or nonfeasibility of going distributed. If distributed processing appears to be a viable alternative for current DP operations, a feasibility study is initiated in which feasible system alternatives are developed along with their specific savings, costs, and intangible benefits. An analysis of this information forms the basis for selecting the best distributed processing system. An integral part of the feasibility study is the evaluation of the equipment to be utilized in the new DP environment. The equipment selection process concludes the feasibility study—the final part of the chapter.

DECENTRALIZATION VERSUS CENTRALIZATION
IN A DISTRIBUTED PROCESSING ENVIRONMENT

Before discussing the pros and cons of decentralization versus centralization in a distributed processing environment, it would be helpful to define each. Fundamentally, *centralization* creates one functional unit within an organization which has prime responsibility for providing information processing services for all of the operating units in the organization. On the other hand, *decentralization* creates a functional unit within each operating unit which has the primary responsibility for servicing the information processing needs of the operating unit. The basic difference between centralization and decentralization, then, is the degree to which information processing decision making, authority, and responsibility are disseminated throughout an organization.

Many organizations in the past have centralized their computer operations for the purpose of reducing DP costs. The most frequent argument advanced in support of centralization is that it results in economies of scale—the first item in Figure 3-1. The reduced costs are the result of several factors: (1) decentralized small computers may have unused capacity; (2) individual small computers may be overloaded, generating pressure for upgrading equipment or purchasing service bureau time; (3) the costs in a single large installation for items such as floor space, electricity, air conditioning, and other facilities are less than in multiple small installations; (4) large installations need fewer support personnel than small installations; (5) large installations require fewer management and staff personnel; and (6) a large computer is more cost effective than a group of small computers. Likewise, large computers, with their higher internal speeds, greater primary storage, and higher channel capacity, may make certain applications practical that are not feasible on smaller equipment. Examples of this include scientific computation, sophisticated data base management systems, and the maintenance of and access to hierarchically structured files for manufacturing systems.

Another reason for centralizing is improved efficiency in systems development—the second item in Figure 3-1. Centralization permits the design and use of common data bases as well as common standards for data entry and input validation. It can also facilitate the use of development and project techniques that result in specific benefits to the organization.

Larger installations seem to attract and retain highly qualified technical people. These individuals can provide management with a wide range of alternative solutions to problems. This fact reduces the cost of development, operation, and future maintenance of the systems. Additionally, other reasons can be given for centralizing data operations. These are noted in Figure 3-1. Likewise, the disadvantages of centralization are set forth in this illustration.

The reasons advanced for centralization are generally based on *efficiency*. In contrast, the arguments for decentralization deal with *effectiveness*. As illustrated in Figure 3-1, until recently, no one could argue that decentralization offered anything but added cost. However, in the last few years, the minicomputer

Centralized Processing	Decentralized Processing
Advantages:	*Advantages:*
• Economies of scale in terms of hardware and software	• Capture of data input at the local level and placement of error correction where it belongs
• Improved efficiency in systems development and programming	• Tailoring output to place information in the hands of the user, particularly at the lower levels
• Better control of operations and standards	• Lower total system communication costs
• Greater growth and expansion of CPU, I/O devices, and peripheral devices	• Higher reliability for dispersed computer systems
• More efficient usage of magnetic tape storage, data bases, and data management software	• Less computer time allocated to overhead, i.e., operating system, for the computer
• Improved total compatibility, thereby allowing for tighter control and security	• Smaller incremental costs for expansion and off-loading from the main computer
• Capacity to process large, complex applications	• Easier and faster accessibility to local files
• Reduction in duplication of effort	• Lower cost and more effective backup capability
Disadvantages:	*Disadvantages:*
• Less flexibility for tailoring programs to meet end user's needs	• Higher costs due to duplication in terms of hardware, software, data, space, and people
• Higher total system costs for communication and transmission of data	• Duplication of input, operating procedures, and processing
• Lower reliability of total system	• More difficult control of system development, programming, standards, and data bases
• More computing power and time allocated to overhead, i.e., operating system, for the computer	• Restricted growth, i.e., CPU power, storage capacity, and I/O device selection
• Larger incremental expansion steps and costs	• Possible incompatibilities among distributed equipment
• Restricted and slower access to centralized files	• Application size and complexity restrictions
• Higher cost of backup or redundancy	

FIGURE 3-1. Advantages and disadvantages of centralized processing and decentralized processing.

has held out the promise of substantial savings. A single-purpose mini, programmed for a specific application, is relatively inexpensive. If it is used as an office machine, it does not require a trained operator or the programming and technical support that a general-purpose computer does. Some minis can provide on-line inquiry, saving the cost of telecommunications. The high cost of communications, the overhead associated with large general-purpose computers, and the possibility that a large installation's capacity will not be fully utilized combine to weaken the case against decentralization.

In the area of applications, there are problems when an organization attempts to meet local needs from a central site. Often, applications developed for a centralized operation are far more complex and costly than those developed for local needs. Also, maintaining the system for one operating unit could potentially affect all units. If the central computer becomes inoperative for any reason, all units are adversely affected. Not only are the risks increased, but centralization forces operating units into a common mold that may be inappropriate for their needs. These different needs could be satisfied by smaller installations at reduced cost and complexity.

Advocates of decentralization state that local analysts are more attuned to local needs and have a deeper understanding of local operations, managerial preferences, and organization structures. This enables them to establish requirement specifications and to design systems that are best suited for the local user. The local analyst can also respond more quickly to emergencies and changes in priorities of local management. In contrast, a manager at the local level in a centralized environment has to battle with other users for the central system's development resources. In addition, the close association between the analyst and the user means that the user will be better informed about the benefits and limitations of data processing. The user can assume tighter control over DP personnel and the quality of their work.

Even though most centralized installations allocate their costs to users according to the resources used, the local manager has little responsibility for total data processing costs. Salaries paid to central personnel, overhead rates, choice of equipment, time spent on projects, and share of resources used all seem to be beyond the manager's control at the local level. As a consequence, the allocations are viewed as arbitrary. The manager's only objective is to obtain as much service as he or she can from the centralized installation. In the long run, this drives up costs. However, if the data processing resource is local, the manager has direct knowledge of all the elements of cost and an incentive to control them. Thus, the manager at the local level knows that there is better control over operations in a decentralized environment.

Having stated briefly the important benefits for both centralization and decentralization (refer to Figure 3-1), we can now raise the question, Which is the best approach for distributed processing? Although the definition offered in the prior chapter leans heavily toward decentralization, typical business organizations would be well advised to combine the best features of centralization and decentralization for a distributed processing environment. To do this effectively, the feasibility study must evaluate what elements of both are best suited for the organization.

If the organization's data processing problems are in the area of service, cost, or effectiveness, it will be necessary for the feasibility study group to balance the requirements of the decentralized units against those of the organization as a whole. In this evaluation process, the DP manager should pay close attention to developing alternative organizational designs and comparative costs. In some cases, cost information may be all that top management needs to resolve the problem. However, if management is primarily concerned with service rather than cost, a different approach may be necessary. Thus, the feasibility study's objectives will determine what elements of centralization and decentralization will be found in the distributed processing system.

In the case study of the American Products Corporation found in Part III, certain functional activities for marketing, manufacturing, physical distribution, and accounting that can best be handled at the corporate level are left at that level. However, many data processing functions are off-loaded from the corporate level to the local level. In this manner, the benefits of centralization and decentralization are obtained by this combined approach to distributed processing. Overall, the accent for the American Products Corporation is toward off-loading the central site for distributed computing at the plant level.

CONSIDERATIONS FOR DESIGNING DISTRIBUTED PROCESSING SYSTEMS

Prior to discussing general and specific design criteria for a distributed processing environment, it is helpful to examine a typical data processing system, such as that illustrated in Figure 3–2. In such a system, there are many procedural steps involved in the processing of data. Fundamentally, eight steps are involved in the *data preparation* phase and the same number of steps are needed for *data conversion.* In turn, a number of steps is required in the computer room for validity checking and control whether *computer processing* is performed at the local, regional, or headquarters level. In effect, a long and drawn-out structure of personnel, equipment, procedures, and programs has been built to convert organizational data to meaningful information. Or looking at the structure another way, many of the data preparation and data conversion procedures are not equipment-oriented but rather entail manual handling, procedures, and data control. In fact, studies have indicated that more than half of all information processing efforts concern just these functions.

In view of these realities of a typical DP installation, a distributed processing system should demonstrate improved productivity where it is needed most—in the labor-intensive areas. Likewise, it should fit into the existing scheme of operations. If a distributed processing system fails on these two important points, there is generally little or no incentive to make the move.

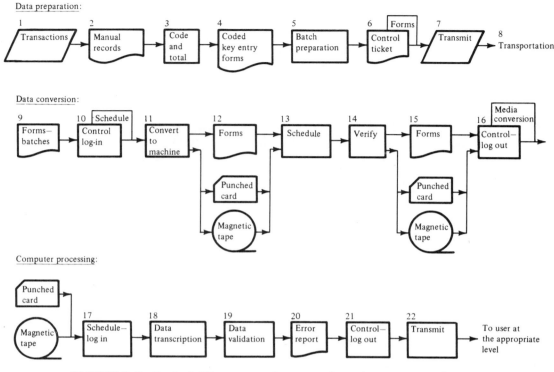

FIGURE 3-2. Typical DP system of personnel, equipment, procedures, and computer programs found in many organizations.

When evaluating the move to a distributed processing environment, many design criteria from a general standpoint must be kept in mind. Similarly, specific design criteria peculiar to these systems should be reviewed. General and specific design criteria, as set forth below, provide the systems designer with adequate guidelines for devising an effective distributed processing system.

GENERAL DESIGN CRITERIA FOR DISTRIBUTED PROCESSING

Within a distributed processing system, or, for that matter, within any type of information system, there are many important design criteria. Implied from a management viewpoint in the development of systems design, the distributed processing system must be designed to meet *management goals and objectives,* especially the degree of decentralization contemplated. The goals and objectives must be satisfied at all levels of the organization's management. Likewise, it must provide various levels of management within the organization with the necessary elements of information for planning, organizing, directing, and controlling present and

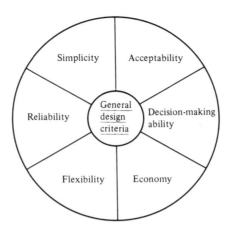

FIGURE 3-3. General design criteria for distributed processing systems.

future operations. This implies summary for top levels of management and more detailed information concerning quantitative and qualitative data for management directly responsible for operations.

From a general design viewpoint, there are several important criteria, which are set forth in Figure 3-3. Although these are discussed below, any distributed processing system that is not acceptable to organizational personnel will generally fail even though it encompasses all of the other general design criteria that are found in a well-designed system.

Acceptability

Success of a new distributed processing system pivots on its acceptance or nonacceptance by company personnel. If operating personnel are convinced that it will not benefit them, that it is a poor system, or that it does not follow established company policies or have some other legitimate reason, the new system is in serious trouble. To overcome this resistance, their participation is essential, particularly during the design and implementation phases, for in reality they constitute the organization that must use and live with the newly designed system. In effect, the human element can "make or break" any distributed processing system.

Decision-Making Ability

An effective distributed processing system allows decisions to be made on a timely basis. Similarly, it must be able to utilize techniques that can allocate available resources most effectively. Hence, a distributed system is designed to make decisions as efficiently and automatically as possible. Decisions that cannot be made automatically as a result of the nature of the system must be relegated to the appropriate level of management or nonmanagement personnel, thereby making the firm's objectives obtainable.

Economy

For economic operations, data should be captured or created in machine language as near to the source as possible and allowed to flow through the distributed processing system automatically from that point on. Activities that must be performed in sequence should be located as closely together as possible, both organizationally and physically. Eliminating duplicate information files, reducing the provision for every possible contingency, and eliminating small empires in the firm's functional areas are other examples of economically improving DP operations.

The question of system cost versus the potential savings must be considered. Generally, no information or service should be produced that is not justified by its cost to the firm. It is often expensive to develop one functional area of the overall system that has greater capacity than its integrated and related parts. In essence, there is need for a proper balancing of the distributed systems and their related parts to effect economy of operation. For example, it makes no sense to develop fast-order processing methods and procedures for improving customer service if the company's plants are not geared on a comparable basis for providing prompt service.

In deciding whether to centralize or decentralize the performance of the firm's functions, the economy of specialized operations and the elimination of duplicate functions must be compared with the reduction of communications and paperwork costs under decentralized conditions. Also, the reduction in time cycles, the increased flexibility, and the greater unity of control and responsibility possible under decentralized operation must be considered (as set forth in a prior section).

Flexibility

To be effective, the distributed processing system must be flexible—capable of adapting to changing environmental conditions. There will always be variations of products, manufacturing processes, and accounting procedures, to name a few. Managers must be prepared to adjust their DP operations to changing conditions. Without this ability, the firm may lose customer goodwill as well as encounter problems with its own personnel. Thus, a well-designed distributed processing system should be able to withstand change by providing for ease of expansion and for added output of production capacity.

Reliability

Reliability of the distributed processing system refers to consistency of operations. In other words, are data input, processing methods and procedures, and output information consistent over an extended period of operation? The degree of reliability can range from a constant and predictable mode of operation to a complete breakdown of the system. Although most distributed processing systems do not operate at these extremes continuously, they do operate somewhere between them. A high degree of reliability can be designed into the system by providing for good *internal control*—that is, numerous control points where variances from established norms and practices can be detected and corrected before processing continues. Control functions should be allocated to organizational units that are independent of the functions to be controlled. In all cases, controls should be an integral part of a distributed processing system.

Simplicity

The trademark of any effective distributed processing system is simplicity. Simplicity can be affected by providing a straight-line flow from one step to the next, avoiding needless backtracking. Input data should be recorded at their source, or as close to it as possible, to reduce or eliminate the need for recopying. Functions should be assigned to organizational units in a way that will reduce the need for coordination, communication, and paperwork. To state it another way, the distributed system should be easy to use. In addition, each organization group should have the authority and responsibility for its area and be held accountable for its performance to one superior only. Thus, the simpler the distributed processing system is, the fewer chances there are of having major problems and foul-ups.

SPECIFIC DESIGN CRITERIA FOR DISTRIBUTED PROCESSING

Going beyond the general design criteria explored above, there are several specific design criteria that must be considered in a distributed processing environment.[1] First, *procedures are as important as technologies,* perhaps even more important. The integrity of data depends more on the way they enter, move, and are screened in a system than on any other factor; much of this processing, in turn, depends on the labor content. The conclusion to be drawn is that a distributed processing system should either displace or support labor content. In this manner, the system will be cost effective.

Second, for *data handling to be accurate and efficient at the local or higher levels, it requires measurement.* The more precisely the measurements can be made, the more accurate and efficient they will be. This means that any systems designer planning to convert to distributed processing equipment must insist that a vendor provide a clear methodology on how to measure performance, at every level—from the operator interaction to central-site computation. In turn, such measurements are critical for determining cost allocations at the local and higher levels.

Third, from the viewpoint of *network effectiveness, it must be a function of the system and not depend on any individual operator, group of operators, or departments.* By definition, a distributed system is used by all kinds of persons in all types of environments—local, regional, and central; skilled and unskilled; rigidly controlled and noncontrolled. Thus, the control of quality, accuracy, and completeness of the entire system is paramount. Such an approach leads to overall

[1] Refer to William G. Moore, "Going Distributed," *Mini-Micro Systems,* March 1977, p. 44.

optimization of the entire distributed processing environment versus letting one area exercise control over the new system requirements.

Last, *systems productivity must be planned for, insisted upon, and expected from the system.* It is not a natural by-product of the prior criteria. The goal should be to improve performance on the part of each local operator, local site, and central component in the system. Otherwise, there can be no real economic justification for going to a distributed system.

DISTRIBUTED PROCESSING SYSTEM— FEASIBILITY STUDY

Having established the important design criteria for distributed processing, the DP manager and his (her) staff will find the process of evaluating alternative systems much easier. Fundamentally, evaluation of such systems is a process of matching the desired functions to be performed against the capabilities of available equipment. For best results, an in-depth feasibility study is necessary to determine what functions can be distributed and what equipment can be acquired to perform these functions. To do otherwise generally leads to less than optimum results.

To determine the feasibility of going distributed, the study team should accent the following items. First, the feasibility study should determine whether the present system will benefit from distributing tasks for both present requirements and future needs. If the organization is diversified and the current system must allocate a large percentage of processing time to communications, it is likely that distributed processing could prove a valuable alternative.

Second, it is important to consider the corporate structure, the size and location of the organization, and its operating units. In a very large corporation, the concept of one totally centralized computer operation, serving everyone, is a difficult if not an impossible task. Hence, the need for distributed computing would be apparent. However, an organization which has many similar operating units, all requiring the same basic data, is generally not a prime candidate for distributed processing.

Last, it is advisable to monitor current system activity through software monitors provided by the computer manufacturer, or software and hardware monitors offered by independent manufacturers, to determine the percentage of mainframe processing time being spent on communications housekeeping tasks that could be distributed.

Upon completion of these aspects of the feasibility study, a clear picture of the current data processing environment should emerge. If the overhead for the computer system is not too great and the projected increase in work load can be handled, the current computer system is probably adequate and the low work load will make distributed processing unnecessary. In these cases, however, the desire to distribute processing may not be related to the computer's work load. Rather, it may be desirable because it offers better control over input/output functions of divisions or subsidiaries with specialized processing needs. In addition, the central processing center is too large to be economically or functionally responsive to user needs. An in-depth feasibility study of these factors, then, should provide sufficient information to determine the economic trade-offs involved in a distributed processing system versus a centralized processing system.

FEASIBLE DISTRIBUTED PROCESSING SYSTEM ALTERNATIVES

Before feasible distributed processing system alternatives can be developed by the study team, proposed system requirements must be clearly defined. They are determined from the desired objectives initially determined in the study. Likewise, consideration is given to the strengths and the shortcomings of the existing system. Required distributed processing requirements, which must be clearly defined and conform to the study's objectives, are

1. outputs to be produced, with emphasis on managerial reports that utilize the exception principle
2. data files (data bases) to be maintained with on-line and off-line processing capabilities
3. types of input/output terminals to be utilized in the appropriate processing mode
4. input data from original source documents for processing by the system
5. methods and procedures that show the relationship of inputs and outputs to the data files (data bases)
6. work volumes and timing considerations for present and future periods, including peak periods

One starting point for compiling the above requirements is the outputs. After they have been determined, it is then possible to infer what inputs and on-line and off-line files are required and what methods and procedures must be employed. Although it is possible to start with the inputs, the output-to-input procedure is recommended because the outputs are related directly to the firm's objectives, the study's most important consideration. The future work loads must be defined for the inputs, the data files (data bases), and the outputs in terms of average and peak loads, cycles, and trends.

Flexible System Requirements

The requirements of the new system may appear at first to be fixed. A closer examination, however, often reveals that these specifications have flexibility. For example, the objectives set forth in the study state that certain file data must be updated once a day. Perhaps the best solution is to incorporate the data into a data base that is updated as actual transactions occur. This approach is within the constraints as initially set forth and introduces a new way of maintaining files. The important point is that alternative methods are available in data processing areas which may have the outward appearances of being fixed. With this approach in mind, it is possible to design a number of different systems with varying features, costs, and benefits. In many cases, more alternatives will be investigated and analyzed when flexible system requirements are considered.

Consultant's Role in Feasible System Alternatives

A clear understanding of the new system requirements is the starting point for developing feasible system alternatives. This phase is by far the most important and difficult undertaking of the study to date. An outside consultant's experience is of great value to the study group. His (her) knowledge of many installations can help immeasurably to reduce the number of possible solutions for the firm. Too often, a study group goes off on a tangent about a specific systems approach which should have been discarded as unfeasible. The outside consultant can make certain that time is not wasted on trivial matters. Also, he can point out the shortcomings of a certain approach which may have been strongly advocated by certain DP personnel. The consultant's objectivity in judging the merits and weaknesses of a new distributed processing system can enhance the firm's chances of selecting an optimum one. The key to developing promising system alternatives and selecting the optimum one is to employ fully the talents and experience of the DP feasibility study group.

SAVINGS, COST FACTORS, AND INTANGIBLE BENEFITS FOR EACH ALTERNATIVE

After developing feasible distributed processing alternatives, the next step is to determine the estimated savings and incremental costs for each alternative. Estimated savings (sometimes referred to as cost displacement) are enumerated in Figure 3–4. Incremental costs are segregated into two categories: one-time costs and additional operating costs. These are listed in Figure 3–5. The difference between

- Reduction in the number of personnel, lower salaries and wages
- Lower payroll taxes and fringe benefits with fewer people
- Sale or elimination of some equipment—depreciation and/or rental—no longer applicable
- Reduction in repairs, maintenance, insurance, and personal property taxes
- Lower space rental and utilities
- Elimination or reduction in outside processing costs

FIGURE 3–4. Feasibility study—estimated savings.

Estimated one-time costs:

- Feasibility study
- Training of programming and operating personnel
- Documentation of all feasibility study applications
- Programming of these applications
- Program assembly and testing of programs for new system
- Data file (data base) conversion
- Site preparation (includes construction costs, remodeling, air conditioning, and power requirements)
- Parallel operations (the old and the new system operate concurrently—duplication of personnel and equipment for a given time period)
- Conversion activities (from existing system to new system)
- Other equipment and supplies (includes forms-handling equipment, files, magnetic disks, and magnetic tapes)

Estimated additional operating costs:

- Data processing equipment (processors, computers, and related equipment)—monthly rental and/or depreciation
- Maintenance of equipment (if not included above)
- Program maintenance (programmers)
- Wages and salaries of data processing personnel (direct supervision, equipment operation, and other data processing jobs), payroll taxes, and fringe benefits
- Forms and supplies (for new data processing equipment)
- Miscellaneous additional costs (includes insurance, repairs, maintenance, and personal property taxes on equipment purchased; power costs; etc.)

FIGURE 3-5. Feasibility study—estimated one-time costs and estimated additional operating costs.

the estimated savings and estimated one-time costs and additional operating costs represents the estimated net savings (losses) to the company before federal income taxes.

Accurate figures for a five-year period are of great importance, which indicates a need for accounting department assistance. Often the best way to increase the accuracy of the figures compiled by the study group is to have the outside consultant assist the group and review the data. His (her) knowledge of current data processing equipment will save time in this phase of the study. His exposure to other similar cost studies will add creditability to the final figures, including the selection of a distributed processing system.

	Years from Start of Systems Implementation					Five Years Total
	1	2	3	4	5	
Estimated Savings:						
Reduction in personnel (including payroll taxes and fringe benefits)	$120,200	$400,500	$440,300	$490,500	$540,500	$1,992,000
Sale of equipment	120,000					120,000
Rental (space) savings	25,000	51,000	54,500	58,000	61,800	250,300
Elimination of rental equipment	2,050	4,380	4,690	5,000	5,300	21,420
Other savings	3,000	3,060	3,210	3,370	3,540	16,180
Total Estimated Savings	$270,250	$458,940	$502,700	$556,870	$611,140	$2,399,900
Estimated One-Time Costs:						
Feasibility study (for this year and prior year)	$ 95,000					$ 95,000
Training	50,000					50,000
Systems and programming	255,500					255,500
Data base conversion	272,500					272,500
Other conversion activities	75,500					75,500
Site preparation	55,400					55,400
Other one-time costs	22,300					22,300
Total Estimated One-Time Costs	$826,200					$ 826,200
Estimated Additional Operating Costs:						
Data processing equipment rental (include maintenance)	$110,000	$120,800	$127,400	$134,100	$141,000	$ 633,300
Additional personnel for new system (includes payroll taxes and fringe benefits)						
Program maintenance	34,000	60,700	62,300	63,400	64,600	285,000
Forms and supplies	20,000	30,700	32,200	33,800	36,000	152,700
Other additional operating costs	10,000	21,500	23,000	24,500	26,000	105,000
	4,400	12,400	12,800	13,200	17,600	60,400
Total Estimated Additional Operating Costs	$178,400	$246,100	$257,700	$269,000	$285,200	$1,236,400
Net Savings (losses) before Federal Income Taxes	($734,350)	$212,840	$245,000	$287,870	$325,940	$ 337,300

FIGURE 3-6. Feasibility study—distributed processing system alternative 3 of net savings (losses) for a five-year period (rental basis).

Projected Savings and Cost Factors

It is not desirable to base the estimates of savings and incremental costs on the present data processing work load. Rather, the trend of growth or cutback in the firm's work load should be analyzed and projected for the next five years. These data can then be utilized to project savings and costs, as shown per the analysis in Figure 3-6. In this feasibility study for alternative 3, consideration has been given to higher future costs. Salaries and wages are generally increased by 5 percent. Cost reduction through work simplification in the present system has been incorporated in the analysis.

Because the projected savings and costs factors in a feasibility study are for five years (starting with systems implementation), the difference between the two sums, after taking into account federal income taxes, should be discounted back to the present time. The purpose of the discounted cash flow is to bring the time value of money into the presentation. This is shown in Figure 3-7 for system alternative 3. Notice that the net savings after federal income taxes of $175,396 over the five-year period (anticipated life of the system), when discounted, shows a negative present value for this alternative of $27,229. With a discounted 20 percent estimated return on investment for this alternative, this one should not be chosen (the firm's cutoff point for capital investments is 20 percent). Even though the revised discounted rate of return is approximately 16 percent (based on present value factors), additional benefits should be considered.

Year	Net Savings (Losses) Before Federal Income Taxes (Per Figure 3-6)	Federal Income Tax @ 48% Rate	Net Savings (Losses) After Federal Income Taxes	At 20%	
				Present Value of $1	Present Value of Net Savings (Losses)
1	($734,350)	($352,488)	($381,862)	.833	($318,091)
2	212,840	102,163	110,677	.694	76,810
3	245,000	117,600	127,400	.579	73,765
4	287,870	138,178	149,692	.482	72,152
5	325,940	156,451	169,489	.402	68,135
Totals	$337,300	$161,904	$175,396		($ 27,229)

FIGURE 3-7. Feasibility study—distributed processing system alternative 3 discounted cash flow based on 20 percent return after federal income taxes (rental basis).

Intangible Benefits

While the foregoing calculations have taken into account the projected savings and costs or quantitative factors, a number of intangible factors or qualitative factors will be uncovered by studying the potential contributions of the new distributed processing system. A list of these factors is found in Figure 3-8. Even though qualitative factors are nonquantifiable initially, their ultimate impact is in quantitative terms, reflected in the financial statements.

- Improved customer service through faster order processing and inquiry capabilities.
- Ability to handle more customers faster with custom-designed equipment.
- Needed information is more readily available in formats which are oriented toward the operating levels.
- Processed information is more accurate because data input error rates are reduced.
- Efficiency of the central processing facility rises as it is relieved of many time-consuming tasks.
- Better decision-making ability through more timely and informative reports.
- Closer control over capital investments and expenses through comparisons with budgets or forecasts.
- Improved scheduling and production control, resulting in more efficient employment of men and machines.
- Greater accuracy, speed, and reliability in information handling and data processing operations.
- Better control of credit through more frequent aging of accounts receivable and analysis of credit data.
- Greater ability to handle increased work loads at small additional costs.

FIGURE 3–8. Feasibility study—intangible benefits from a distributed processing system.

An analysis of Figure 3–8 indicates that the intangible benefits of the system ultimately offer two major benefits: increased revenues and decreased costs. Better customer service and relations should enable the organization to increase sales to its present customers and to many potential ones who are looking for these characteristics in its vendors. A distributed processing environment affects the organization not only externally but also internally in terms of faster and more frequent reporting of results. In addition to accuracy, speed, and flexibility, distributed processing equipment allows operating management at the local and regional levels to plan and organize activities and, in turn, direct and control according to the original plans.

SELECTION OF THE BEST DISTRIBUTED PROCESSING SYSTEM

Once a thorough analysis of the important factors has been completed, the DP manager and the study group will be in a position to compare the system alternatives. Although there are several approaches to evaluating alternatives that can be employed for a definitive conclusion to the feasibility study, the decision table approach, shown in Figure 3-9, is used. A *decision table* is helpful in resolving a complex management decision because it assembles all factors for every feasible system alternative. A complete summary of all factors pertinent to making the important decision should be a part of the decision table for it to be a fully effective management tool.

The conditions in the upper part of the figure represent benefits (tangible and intangible), while the lower part shows the possible courses of action. Each distributed system alternative represents a set of actions corresponding to a certain set of conditions. In this case, system alternative 3 indicates the highest return or 16 percent for distributed computing, although system alternative 4 has the same answers but has a slightly lower return of 15 percent. Their intangible benefits must be reevaluated for a final decision. Thus, an examination of Figure 3-9 indicates that alternatives 3 and 4 are best.

Now the question is which one of these alternatives should be implemented. On the surface, both have about the same benefits, except that alternative 3 gives a higher return on investment. A closer inspection, however, reveals that only alternative 4 utilizes many more "intelligent" terminals than alternative 3. Conversion today will mean no or minimal conversion costs in the future for this type of equipment. With this added advantage, the DP manager feels the future cost savings justify accepting a lower return. Therefore, his recommendation has been finally reached. As with all feasibility studies, all information gathered must be documented not only for future reference but also to serve as a framework for selecting the appropriate equipment.

BASIC TYPES OF DISTRIBUTED PROCESSING EQUIPMENT

Currently, a second industrial revolution, based on machines that can add decision making, arithmetic, and memory to their usual functions, is evident in distributed processing systems. The brains of this revolution is the *microprocessor*. Even though there is no general agreement on a precise definition, the microprocessor is a tiny chip of silicon, the size of a pencil eraser, that provides the arithmetic and logic capabilities of yesterday's large computers. The equivalent of a network of wires, switches, and transistors has been fabricated on the chip's surface.

Basic types of distributed processing equipment utilizing new technology are set forth below. They include

- remote batch terminals
- smart and intelligent terminals
- communications controllers
- microprocessors and microcomputers
- minicomputers and small business computers

	Table Name: Feasibility Study – Distributed Processing System												
Decision Table	Chart No: FS-ES-1			Prepared by: R. J. Thierauf						Page 1 of 1 Date: 7/25/7-			

	Rule Number											
Condition	*1*	*2*	*3*	*4*	*5*	*6*	*7*	*8*	*9*	*10*	*11*	*12*
Tangible benefits:												
Meets return on investment criteria—20% after taxes*	N	N	N	N	N							
Lower order processing costs	Y	Y	Y	Y	Y							
Lower investment in inventory	Y	Y	Y	Y	Y							
Less future cash requirements	N	Y	Y	Y	N							
Intangible benefits:												
Improved customer service	N	Y	Y	Y	Y							
Improved promotional efforts	Y	Y	Y	Y	Y							
Ability to handle more customers faster	N	N	Y	Y	Y							
Better decision-making ability	Y	Y	Y	Y	Y							
More effective utilization of management's time	Y	Y	Y	Y	Y							
Improved scheduling and production control	Y	Y	Y	Y	Y							
Closer control over capital investments and expenses	Y	Y	Y	Y	Y							
Better control of credit	N	N	Y	Y	Y							
Ability to handle more volume at lower costs	Y	Y	Y	Y	Y							

FIGURE 3-9. Feasibility study—decision table for appraising feasible distributed processing system alternatives.

Condition	Rule Number											
	1	2	3	4	5	6	7	8	9	10	11	12
More accuracy and reliability of data	Y	Y	Y	Y	Y							
Greater utilization of mathematical techniques	Y	Y	Y	Y	Y							

Action

Action												
Utilizes a distributed processing system	X	X	X	X	X							
Utilizes remote batch processing	—	—	X	X	X							
Minor changes of inputs and outputs	X	—	—	—	—							
Substantial changes of inputs and outputs	—	X	X	X	X							
Need for distributed data bases	X	X	X	X	X							
Moderate revision of methods and procedures	X	X	—	—	—							
Complete revision of methods and procedures	—	—	X	X	X							
Employ an additional consultant for study	—	—	X	X	X							
Recruit new data processing personnel	—	X	X	X	X							
Great use of intelligent terminals	—	—	—	X	X							

Other Information: 1-14%; 2-15%; 3-16%; 4-15%; 5-13%

FIGURE 3-9. Continued.

Within the discussion of each piece of hardware, the important component parts will be set forth as they pertain to distributed processing systems.

REMOTE BATCH TERMINALS

Most traditional remote batch terminals offer very little for the user interested in a true distributed processing system. However, the low cost of microprocessor technology has allowed manufacturers to add more capability to their batch terminals and incorporate local processors to create small business systems. The growing acceptance of distributed processing has encouraged these advances to the point where some systems even provide interactive processing and batch processing. Such terminals not only perform local job processing and interactive data entry but also support peripheral magnetic tape drives, disk storage devices, and local interactive terminals. A few of these new terminals can even support remote interactive terminals. In essence, current hardware advances allow remote batch terminals to perform a wide range of distributed processing functions.

SMART AND INTELLIGENT TERMINALS

The user should be careful to distinguish between "smart" or microprogrammable terminals and truly "intelligent," user-programmable terminals (refer to Chapter 2 for more information). *Smart terminals* do little to off-load the mainframe processing tasks. The only local data validation they can do is to restrict entry fields for alpha only or numerics only. And while some smart terminals have a buffer, they lack the necessary storage. Generally, microprogrammable terminals should not be considered vehicles for distributed processing. These terminals are not user-programmable. Changes to the logic must be done through the internal read-only memory, a task which must usually be performed by the manufacturer. Also, the architecture of most of these terminals limits the functions that can be changed to character generation and communications procedures, not data processing.

On the other hand, *intelligent terminals* are capable of performing more tasks than smart terminals, because they have some memory and control functions built in for programming. Within a programmed environment, they can stand alone or be configured in a cluster, sharing any or all of the computer power, storage, printers, and sometimes communications. CRT is the most common display technology for these types of terminals.

Generally, an intelligent terminal must have, as a minimum, the following characteristics:

- self-contained storage, random access memory
- user interaction with the terminal itself

- stored program capability
- processing capability at the terminal through a user-written program
- capability of on-line communications with another intelligent terminal
- human-oriented input, such as keyboard
- human-oriented output, such as a printer or a CRT

The trend today is for programmed intelligent terminals to perform multiple functions in data entry, data retrieval, inquiry/response, and monitoring and control. And this trend is expected to continue as the office becomes more automated. In response to this trend, terminal vendors are gearing up for the distributed processing era. For a current listing of the larger manufacturers of intelligent terminals, refer to Figure 3–10.

Beehive Medical Electronics, Inc.	Inforex Inc.
Bunker Ramo Corp.	International Teleproc. Systems, Inc.
Burroughs Corp.	Megadata Corp.
Computek Inc.	Mohawk Sciences Corp.
Conrac	Pertec Business Systems
Data 100 Corp.	Raytheon Data Systems
Datapoint Corp.	Sanders Associates
Delta Data Systems Corp.	Scope Electronics Inc.
Digital Equipment Corp.	Sycor Inc.
Four-Phase Systems	Tektronix, Inc.
Hewlett-Packard	Telex Terminal Comm. Inc.
Honeywell Information Systems	Texas Instruments
IBM Corp.	Wang Inc.
Incoterm Corp.	Zentec Corp.

FIGURE 3–10. Current listing of manufacturers of intelligent terminals.

COMMUNICATIONS CONTROLLERS

Functions that can be removed from the mainframe by communications controllers include error recovery, code conversion, polling, and network control. But like most intelligent remote batch terminals, intelligent communications controllers do no more than emulate their hardwired counterparts. When choosing a communications controller for a distributed system, the provision of adequate software support for these functions and implementation of these functions without major changes to the existing mainframe-resident communications software must be considered.

MICROPROCESSORS AND MICROCOMPUTERS

As indicated in the opening section, microprocessors provide the underlying technology for distributed processing equipment. Similar to the central processing unit (CPU) of a computer, a *microprocessor* manipulates data by interpreting and executing coded program instructions. This general-purpose, data processing device is contained on large-scale integrated (LSI) circuits which are produced by means of metal-oxide-semiconductor (MOS) technology. Fundamentally, a microprocessor consists of an accumulator, an arithmetic-logic unit, a scratch-pad, read/write memory, a register and decoder for instructions, a program counter and address register stack, a timing and control section, a parallel data and input/output bus, and a controller for input and output of data.

Potential applications for microprocessors are wide open for distributed computing. Present equipment includes data entry devices, intelligent peripherals, dedicated processors, point-of-sale units, CRT terminals, printers, and a variety of other input/output units. An important advantage of microprocessor technology is that low-cost computing power is made available for equipment at the local processing level.

Going beyond the capabilities of the microprocessor and below the processing capabilities of minicomputers and small business computers is the *microcomputer*. Although the microcomputer is a smaller version of a minicomputer, there is a tendency to blend these two types of computers into a virtually indistinguishable product line. However, there are certain distinguishing characteristics. Microcomputers tend to differ from minicomputers by having smaller word size, slower memory cycle time, and more limited instruction sets; being lower in cost; using less power; and having custom-fitted controls for specific applications.

Based on these important features, a microcomputer can be defined as a microprocessor affixed with memory and input/output logic or circuits so that it can perform a useful function. To state it another way, when the microprocessor (CPU) is incorporated as a CPU in a working system along with a data storage memory, a program memory, and input/output circuitry, it is called a microcomputer. Some firms produce complete microcomputers—CPU, data storage memory, program memory, and input/output circuitry—on one or two MOS-LSI circuits. The tendency in such cases is to call the unprogrammed circuits a microprocessor system.

Due to the steady advance in circuitry sophistication and miniaturization, the logic and memory circuits of a microcomputer can be held in the palm of one's hand. It is possible to have tens of thousands of components on a single chip requiring only milliwatt power. Based on their size and capabilities, it is expected that microcomputers will have a decided impact on distributed processing. Similarly, they will affect our lives in much the same way electric motors have. A listing of their present and future applications for distributed processing and other areas would include store sales information systems, information processing systems, measuring systems, control systems, and education systems.

MINICOMPUTERS AND SMALL BUSINESS COMPUTERS

For virtually all kinds of hierarchical distributed processing, minicomputers and small business computers are widely used. This will be apparent in the case study of the American Products Corporation found in Part III. Generally, they are located at multiple locations and are tied together via a data communications network. With this configuration, each small system functions as a combined data entry, computing, and printing system with the capability of performing simple processing tasks and transmitting the more complex processing to the larger system. This environment permits optimum use of the minicomputers and small business computers with the large computer in one integrated system.

Overall, the important distinguishing feature of minicomputers and small business computers is their level of communications support. Each machine should be able to support its own local and remote satellite terminals and perform high-speed communications with a host processor. Likewise, it should have a multi-tasking operating system—a system which is necessary for the machine to function simultaneously—and an extensive peripheral complement, especially a large disk storage to provide the necessary data base storage.

In price and performance, minicomputers and small business computers span a wide range between conventional accounting machines and minicomputers at one extreme and medium-scale computer systems at the other. Though the current systems differ widely in their architecture, data formats, peripheral equipment, and software, today's minicomputer and small business computer systems typically consist of a keyboard/CRT for data entry (cards, floppy disks, or cassettes may also be used), a processor that starts with about $8K$ bytes of memory, a disk for file storage, and a serial printer with a speed of about 30 characters per second. From there, the only way to go is upward, i.e., more memory, additional peripheral devices, faster printers, etc.

The small business computer market is served by distinct types of vendors. The first type is the "Fortune 500" companies, such as Burroughs, Honeywell, IBM, Litton, and NCR, all of which have vast product lines and resources. For these firms, the small business computer is just one of a broad line of products (although in the cases of NCR and Burroughs, business minicomputers now account for a sizable portion of total corporate revenues). A second group consists of minicomputer manufacturers, such as Digital Equipment Corporation, Data General, Computer Automation, Harris, Hewlett-Packard, Interdata, Microdata, and others. This group has watched the small business computer marketplace mushroom in size and now wants a piece of the action. Their answer to this segment of the marketplace is a packaged configuration consisting of a minicomputer and associated peripherals from their current product line, usually accompanied by some applications software. Most minicomputer vendors also offer assemblers and compilers for the user who wants to do its own programming or to solve business problems that cannot be handled by packaged software.

The major applications software packages usually offered are accounts payable, accounts receivable, billing, inventory, payroll, and sales analysis. Some vendors offer a full library of applications programs, while others modify their software to the customer's needs for a negotiated price. It is important for the buyer to determine beforehand the kind and degree of software support being offered in a distributed processing environment.

EQUIPMENT CRITERIA FOR DISTRIBUTED PROCESSING

To implement the recommended distributed processing system (as determined in a previous section), certain equipment criteria must be considered. This checklist is extremely important since a small distributed system in one local or regional area of an organization may eventually be enlarged to a nationwide basis. Similarly, the initial system may take on new applications. The following criteria, then, to achieve such flexibility and expandability include equipment that is capable of

- taking advantage of newer, lost-cost equipment as it can be economically justified
- improving throughput, i.e., the amount of data that can be processed within a specific time period.
- being used with current equipment and providing read/write media (magnetic disk, tape, etc.) that can be used by other devices in the system
- improving reliability for the user as well as greater accessibility for the user
- being configured as a single stand-alone piece of equipment or multi-terminal cluster or any combination
- performing local applications, working in a multipoint environment, or performing network control functions
- operating with no files, with small files, or with large disk configurations; offering a multiple of file access methods, from simple sequential to indexed to direct access
- facilitating the use of one industry-standard language or multiple languages
- being both fully programmable down to a single terminal level or not programmable at all
- supporting the intended applications via packaged software whether

these packages operate on a dedicated basis or under the control of a multitask operating system

- fitting a single large application in dedicated mode or readily converting to handle multiple applications

- being acquired on various bases, i.e., rental, outright purchase, option to buy, and third-party leasing (lease-back arrangement)

Of the foregoing, perhaps the most important criterion is that the entire hardware family should be *flexible* to meet most any distributed processing system and be *expandable* in place. As low-cost devices become even lower in cost in the future, an organization should be able to take advantage of lower-cost system developments. Also, it should be noted that the expense to replace, change, and maintain a system will become greater than the value of the system hardware itself. Thus, a distributed processing system should be flexible and expandable to take advantage of newer, low-cost equipment and, at the same time, be sensitive to the benefits and costs of converting to this new equipment.

An integral part of the foregoing equipment criteria centers on the type of CRT display terminal. In addition to selecting the business type of terminal, there are other important considerations, which include

- large-screen display features

- operator aids

- concurrent operations

- automatic logging

- security features

- record insert/delete capabilities

Each of these will be discussed briefly.

When *large-screen display features* exist, a terminal can accommodate at least a full-page source document on a single-screen image. This implies a 1920-character display, formable into lines and columns, with the most typical specifications being 80×24. A smaller screen, which may be appropriate in a specific application, slows down data entry, adds to its complexity, and may cause operator confusion.

Every equipment manufacturer utilizes *operator aids*. Such features make it easier for an operator to perform the assigned tasks with precision and accuracy. They include screen prompting; programmable keys that enable an operator to call a routine, or execute a command, with a single keystroke; error display messages; upper-/lowercase and video highlighting features; cursor control that speeds up data insertion, deletion, and correction in fields or records; and multiversion keyboards. These are all productivity aids that should be part of any large multiapplication system.

Concurrent operations enable operators to perform more than one task at the same time on an equipment configuration, such as a four-terminal local system that simultaneously executes data entry, file update, printing, and communications functions. The most often-stated advantage of concurrency is that equipment having the feature can perform either high- or low-volume work at the same time. A greater benefit, however, is that concurrency encourages and assures true distribution of equipment because it allows exceedingly cost-effective dispersal of linked equipment at a local, regional, or central site. Also, where a system has concurrency, it often causes serious degradation, with each task taking much longer to execute than it should. With a well-designed concurrent system, however, only extreme work-load queues should cause noticeable delays.

The next feature, namely, *automatic logging,* preserves data integrity at the point of initial entry, at the point of validation or audit, and at the point of re-creation when necessary. It also results in other benefits. Productivity, for example, is knowing how much work an operator turns out and its quality compared to all other operators. Automatic logging counts and compiles statistics on operators, jobs, specific sites, multiapplication usage, and almost every other transaction handled by the equipment. Hence, logging benefits productivity and systems control and is highly recommended.

Security features are one of the industry's most sought-after capabilities. Although total systems security is not attainable at this time, a fully secure or semisecure installation can achieve a very high degree of data and systems integrity. Features that provide a practical form of security include password sign-ons, physical terminal locks, and software lockouts. But regardless of the form, good protection demands that the system prevent entry into individual record fields, individual records, single or multiple files, and individual terminals. Also, there should be no access to specific commands.

In any data entry system where the two most common mistakes are failure to enter a record and to duplicate the entry, the *record insert/delete capability* is a must. If a terminal had no provision to correct an oversight, the result would be a major problem. All sorts of totals would be wrong, computer time would be wasted, and tracking down the missing or duplicated entry would consume a lot of time. Some early key-to-disk systems did not have insert/delete of a record capability. In a distributed system, the implications are the same or even worse; data could be lost.

EQUIPMENT SELECTION—CONCLUDING PHASE
OF FEASIBILITY STUDY

After the best distributed processing system has been selected from among the several feasible system alternatives, the appropriate equipment must be selected. Most organizations undertaking a distributed processing project have specific equipment under consideration. Because most of them have computer and related peripheral equipment salesmen calling on them at various times, they have had previous contact with most of the manufacturers. The representatives of the various equipment manufacturers should be contacted and invited to an orientation meeting on

Basic/Four Corp.	Honeywell Information Systems
Burrough Corp.	IBM, General Systems Div.
Cincinnati Milacron	Inforex
Computer Automation, Inc.	Interdata, Inc.
Consolidated Computer, Inc.	Lockheed Electronics Co.
Control Data Corp.	Logical Machinery Corp.
Cummins-Allison Corp.	Microdata Corp.
Data 100	Modular Computer Systems
Data General Corp.	Mohawk Data Sciences
Datapoint	NCR Corp.
Digital Computer Controls	Olivetti Corp. of America
Digital Equipment Corp.	Pertec Computer Corp.
Digital Scientific Corp.	Quantel Corp.
Entrex	Raytheon Data Systems
Four-Phase Systems	Seimens Corp.
Fujistu, Ltd.	Storage Technology Corp.
General Automation	Sycor, Inc.
General Computer Systems	Systems Engineering Labs, Inc.
Genesis One Computer Corp.	Texas Instruments Inc.
GRI Computer Corp.	Univac
GTE Information Systems	Varian Data Machines
Harris Corp.	Wang Laboratories, Inc.
Hewlett-Packard	

FIGURE 3-11. Current listing of manufacturers of distributed processing equipment.

the proposed system. During the course of the meeting, they should be instructed about the applications to be covered, general problems that will be encountered, approximate volumes (present and future), and other pertinent data. Each manufacturer should indicate in writing whether it wishes to receive a bid invitation. A listing of current distributed processing equipment manufacturers is set forth in Figure 3-11.

SUBMIT BID INVITATIONS TO MANUFACTURERS

Once letters of intent to bid are on file from equipment manufacturers, the company submits bid invitations to the interested equipment suppliers. The preferred approach when sending bid invitations is to mail the same set of data to all competing manufacturers. This permits bids to be placed on an unbiased basis and informs the manufacturers what requirements they must meet, keeps the number of questions to a minimum, and is a valid basis for comparison. Generally, the manufacturers will need additional information and assistance from the prospective customer as they progress with the preparation of their proposals.

Utilizing this approach, the respective manufacturers should have ample information to familiarize themselves with the company and its peculiar distributed processing problems. The recommendations made in their proposals should show clearly how the equipment will meet the customer's needs. Specifications lacking clear definition from the beginning will result in proposals with standard approaches that are applicable to any and all potential customers, making all the preliminary work a waste of time. It is of utmost importance that data submitted to manufacturers be as complete and self-explanatory as possible for the proposed distributed processing system.

Contents of Bid Invitation

Much of the material needed for the bid invitation can be taken directly from the data contained in the exploratory phase of selecting the best distributed processing system. The contents of the bid invitation include these areas:

1. general company information
2. future distributed processing plans
3. list of new system requirements
4. new system flowcharts and decision tables
5. list of equipment specifications (in general terms)
6. data to be forwarded by each manufacturer

In sections 1 and 2, the narrative should be brief so that attention can be focused on the remaining parts of the bid invitation. Data that are necessary for a thorough study are contained in sections 3, 4, and 5, forming the basis for the manufacturer's proposal. Section 3 is composed of five essential parts: planned inputs, methods and procedures for handling data, data files to be maintained (distributed data bases), output needs, and other requirements and considerations for the new system.

New system flowcharts and decision tables are contained in section 4. System flowcharts are needed for each functional area under study and to show the interrelationships among the areas. Decision tables should be an integral part of the bid invitation. This will enable the manufacturer to have a complete understanding of the programming effort envisioned and help determine the hardware that is needed under the existing conditions. Finally, this section of the bid invitation should contain a flowchart that depicts the overall aspects of the new system. This allows the equipment manufacturer to obtain an overview of the system and its subsystems.

Section 5 contains a listing of equipment specifications in general terms. Competing manufacturers must have a basic understanding of the data communications network, I/O terminal devices, auxiliary storage devices, the central processing unit, and other peripherals. The inclusion of this section not only details present owned equipment that is compatible with a distributed processing environment but also helps assure greater compatibility of bids from each competing equipment manufacturer.

In this final section, data to be included in each manufacturer's proposal are listed. Specifying in advance what the proposals should contain ensures that comparable information for a final evaluation will be forthcoming.

Conferences with Manufacturers

Even though bid invitations specify the numerous details of the new system, legitimate questions will be raised by the various equipment firms. Many of the questions center around those areas which may have need of modification, which may sometimes be necessary to take advantage of the equipment's special features. The result may be favorable benefits to the firm in terms of cost savings. Conferences between the manufacturer and the potential customer, then, can prove beneficial to both parties. However, caution is necessary on the part of the study group during this period because salesmen may use this time to sell the firm and the final proposal, making the final evaluation of the manufacturers' proposals not objective but subjective.

EVALUATE MANUFACTURERS' PROPOSALS

The distributed processing manufacturers should be given a reasonable amount of time to prepare their proposals. In most cases, approximately four to six weeks is adequate. When the proposals are completed, several copies are mailed to the customer for review and are then followed by an oral presentation by the manufacturer's representative(s). At this meeting, the salesman will stress the important points of the proposal and answer questions. After this procedure has been followed by all competing manufacturers, the DP manager and his staff should be prepared to evaluate the various proposals.

There are many criteria for evaluating a manufacturer's proposal. Among these are extent of automation proposed, evaluation of throughput performance—turnaround time, type of equipment, method of acquiring equipment, delivery of equipment, installation requirements, manufacturer's assistance, programming assistance, training schools, availability of reliable software, maintenance contracts, and other considerations. Finally, the proposals are evaluated in terms of how well they have complied with the bid invitation. Only after an intensive analysis of the facts can the DP group intelligently select the manufacturer(s) for distributed processing equipment.

SELECT EQUIPMENT MANUFACTURER(S)

Selection of the equipment manufacturer can be a difficult task since computer manufacturers have different ways of viewing distributed processing. Currently, the main difference between IBM's approach to distributive processing and that of other major competitors is that IBM apparently believes in *centralized host control over the network of distributed systems,* whereas Burroughs, Univac, CDC, and the minicomputer companies, such as Digital Equipment Corporation, believe in *distributed control within networked systems* or "netted" systems. On the other hand, Honeywell's current position appears close to IBM in this regard but may, in fact, provide an intelligent compromise between the two. Fundamentally, IBM clearly is against the "distribution of control" in that it would like to integrate the host computer, the front end, the network processors and multiplexers, concentrators, remote intelligent controllers, or satellite processors and terminals so each of these components and functions is ultimately dependent on the IBM central host(s) facility. This strategy frustrates the attempts of plug-compatible vendors to penetrate the IBM customer base and, at the same time, ensures greater total system or network control, improved data security and system integrity, and greater customer loyalty. In contrast, most other vendors cannot afford to be so restrictive due to their small market shares. Hence, this important factor should not be overlooked by the feasibility study committee.

The selection process is much easier if the equipment proposed is identical for all practical purposes. In such cases, the choice is normally based on the lowest-cost equipment. However, this approach is generally not followed because most manufacturers have certain unique equipment features, and this results in slightly different approaches to the customer's proposed system. To resolve this dilemma among the various competitors, several methods have been developed for evaluating and selecting equipment.

Method of Evaluation

One method of evaluation is utilization of a decision table, shown in Figure 3-12 on pages 86 and 87. A decision table for a final evaluation not only defines the important criteria in compact notation but also permits an objective evaluation because the values will have been determined before receipt of the manufacturer's proposals. In the illustration, the highest possible score is 100 points for each of the five distributed processing manufacturers. A value of 10 points is deducted for each *no* answer of a major criterion, while a value of 5 points if subtracted for each *no* answer of a minor criterion. The major criteria represent factors that have long-run effects on the firm in terms of profits and return on investment. Thus, the deduction of 10 points indicates greater importance attached to this particular criterion.

Values for another firm might be different from those found in Figure 3–12. For the study, this is a realistic approach in making the final decision for the selected manufacturer, vendor 2.

Signing of Equipment Contract(s)

The signing of the equipment contract by a top-level executive brings the study to a close. Generally, the feasibility study represents approximately one-third of the total time expended on a systems project. In the period just ahead—systems implementation—not only will more time be involved than in the feasibility study, but there will also be more involvement of organizational personnel. The problem of how to coordinate and control the activities during the coming period is a challenging task even for the most seasoned data processing manager and staff.

CHAPTER SUMMARY

The key to determining if distributed processing is feasible is to examine the DP operational aspects of an organization. Fundamentally, if the structure of the business is decentralized and a substantial amount of processing time is taken up with communications to headquarters, distributed processing can be a viable alternative. On the other hand, if the time spent for communication tasks is minimal now and in the future, distributed computing may be unnecessary. However, it may still be desirable to go distributed because of meeting specialized processing needs at the local and regional levels. Also, there may be better control over input/output functions at these levels.

The selection of the best distributed processing system is contingent upon performing a detailed feasibility study to determine the functions and tasks appropriate or desirable for distribution. Similarly, consideration must be given to the types of equipment and devices that are capable of performing these distributed functions and tasks. This information, in turn, forms the basis for forwarding bid invitations to equipment manufacturers. The receipt of the bids allows the DP manager and study group to select the appropriate equipment, thereby bringing the feasibility study of distributed processing to a formal close.

Building upon the material in this chapter, not only will systems implementation of distributed processing be discussed in Chapter 4, but also distributed processing applications at the first- and second-system levels will be presented. In addition, applications found in a distributed processing environment at the third-system level will be illustrated in Chapter 5. In a similar manner, selected subsystems for the American Products Corporation (case study) in a distributed processing environment will be the subject matter for Chapters 6 through 10.

Decision Table	Table Name: Criteria to Select Distributed Processing Equipment Manufacturer											
	Chart No: FS-SM-1				Prepared by: R. J. Thierauf				Page 1 of 1 Date: 8/30/7-			

	Rule Number											
Condition	*1*	*2*	*3*	*4*	*5*	*6*	*7*	*8*	*9*	*10*	*11*	*12*
Major criteria:												
Flexible to meet present and future user needs	Y	Y	Y	Y	N							
Expandability of equipment at all operating levels	Y	Y	Y	N	Y							
Low-cost data entry	N	Y	Y	Y	N							
Monthly rental within budgeted amount	Y	Y	Y	N	Y							
Dependable and efficient software	N	Y	N	Y	Y							
Full service backup with proven record	Y	Y	Y	Y	Y							
Minor criteria:												
High degree of automation proposed	Y	Y	Y	N	Y							
Availability of equipment when needed	Y	Y	N	Y	Y							
Capable of meeting installation requirements	Y	Y	Y	Y	Y							
Adequate programming assistance available	N	N	N	Y	N							

FIGURE 3–12. Criteria to select equipment manufacturer in a distributed processing feasibility study.

	Rule Number											
Condition	*1*	*2*	*3*	*4*	*5*	*6*	*7*	*8*	*9*	*10*	*11*	*12*
Good quality training offered	Y	Y	Y	Y	N							
Available equipment for compiling and testing program initially	N	Y	Y	Y	N							
Adequate personnel available	Y	N	Y	Y	Y							
Compliance with terms of bid invitation	Y	Y	Y	N	Y							
Action												
Subtract 10 points for each major criteria no (N) answer	X	—	X	X	X							
Subtract 5 points for each minor criteria no (N) answer	X	X	X	X	X							

Other Information:
Total points = 100 (6 major criteria $\times$ 10 pts + 8 minor criteria $\times$ 5 pts = 100)

Competitor's total points:
1, 70; 2, 90; 3, 80; 4, 70; 5, 65

FIGURE 3-12. Continued.

QUESTIONS

1. Why does a typical distributed processing system tend toward more decentralization rather than centralization? Explain.

2. Of the several general design criteria for distributed processing, which is the most important from a personnel point of view? Why?

3. Why have a distributed processing feasibility study? Why not save this expense and procure the lowest-cost equipment for the functional areas under study?

4. What is the recommended approach for determining the best of the many feasible distributed processing system alternatives?

5. What bearing does the introduction of intangible benefits have on a distributed processing feasibility study? Explain.

6. Why is equipment selection the final phase of the feasibility study?

7. Are there any problems associated with having various distributed processing equipment manufacturers draw up the appropriate specifications for an organization and having them submit bids on this basis?

8. What are the most important factors to consider when selecting distributed processing equipment?

SELECTED REFERENCES

Ainsworth, W., "The Primacy of the User," *Infosystems,* April 1977.

Bobick, S. A., Arman, E. J., and Yerkes, A. W., "Survey of Small Business Computers," *Datamation,* Oct. 1976.

Bowers, D. M., "Systems-On-A-Chip," *Mini-Micro Systems,* May 1976.

Brown, F., "Distributed Processing, There Ain't No Free Lunch," *Computer Decisions,* April 1977.

Burnett, G. J., and Nolan, R. L., "At Last, Major Roles for Minicomputers," *Harvard Business Review,* May–June 1975.

Business Week Special Report, "Minicomputers Challenge the Bit Machines," *Business Week,* April 26, 1976.

Business Week Special Report, "Glowing Prospects for Brainy Computer Terminals," *Business Week,* Oct. 25, 1976.

Colasanti, M., "Leasing and Distributed Processing," *Computer Decisions,* Nov. 1976.

Computerworld Special Report, "Distributed Processing," *Computerworld,* March 28, 1977.

Feidelman, L., "Distributed Computing: It's a Small World," *Infosystems,* April 1977.

Fortune Magazine, A Special Advertising Section on Distributed Processing/ Data Communications," *Fortune,* March 1977.

Foss, W. B., "Guidelines for Computer Selection," *Journal of Systems Management,* March 1976.

Gilder, J. H., "All About Microcomputers," *Computer Decisions,* Dec. 1975.

Hannon, J., and Fried, L., "Should You Decentralize?," *Computer Decisions,* Feb. 1977.

Hansen, J. R., "Terminals Get Smarter So Do Users," *Infosystems,* March 1977.

——, "Minis Move to the User," *Infosystems,* June 1977.

Hebert, B., "Multiprogramming on Minis," *Computer Decisions,* June 1977.

Igersheim, R. H., "Managerial Response to an Information System," *AFIPS Conference Proceedings* (National Computer Conference), Vol. 45, 1976.

Jaffe, M. T., "There's No Business Like Small Business," *Computer Decisions,* Aug. 1976.

Johnson, J. R., "Mini or Mainframe? An On-Line Question," *Infosystems,* April 1977.

Jones, J. H., "Distributed Processing—Age of the Application Analyst," *Infosystems,* June 1977.

Keider, S. P., "Once Again—Centralize or Decentralize," *Infosystems,* Dec. 1976.

Kelly, N. D., "Cutting DP Costs," *Infosystems,* June 1977.

Knottek, N. E., "Selecting a Distributed Processing System," *Computer Decisions,* June 1976.

LaVoie, P., "Distributed Computing Systematically," *Computer Decisions,* March 1977.

Lecht, C. P., "The Waves of Change," *Computerworld,* June 6, 1977.

Luke, J. W., "Unraveling the Confusion of Distributed DP," *Infosystems,* Dec. 1976.

Lusa, J. M., "Selecting Terminals Intelligently," *Infosystems,* Sept. 1976.

——, "Distributed Computing, Alive and Well," *Infosystems,* Nov. 1976.

Monrad-Krohn, J., "The Micro vs. the Minicomputer," *Mini-Micro Systems,* Feb. 1977.

Moore, W. G., "Going Distributed," *Mini-Micro Systems,* March 1977.

Reynolds, C. H., "Issues in Centralization," *Datamation,* March 1977.

Stiefel, M. L., "What Is an 'Intelligent' Terminal?," *Mini-Micro Systems,* March 1977.

Thierauf, R. J., *Systems Analysis and Design of Real-Time Management Information Systems,* Englewood Cliffs, N.J.: Prentice-Hall, Inc., 1975.

Wagner, F. V., "Is Decentralization Inevitable?," *Datamation,* Nov. 1976.

White, R., Guzeman, D., Pezzolo, D., and Berry, T., "Impact of Microcomputers 1980," National Computer Conference Handout, 1977.

Yasaki, E. K., "The Mini: A Growing Alternative," *Datamation,* May 1976.

IMPLEMENTATION AND APPLICATIONS OF DISTRIBUTED PROCESSING SYSTEMS (FIRST AND SECOND LEVELS)

4

Once the problem of what distributed processing equipment to acquire has been resolved, the feasibility study has been officially concluded. Even though a substantial amount of time and cost was expended on the study, considerably more of both will be spent on systems implementation. In reality, long hours for data processing and nondata processing personnel are just beginning, and extreme patience is required. Otherwise, the best-planned feasibility study can be upset by those personnel who fail to cooperate in executing the plans devised. In the first part of this chapter, the steps involved in systems implementation are discussed, thereby providing a logical framework for installing a distributed processing system.

The current trend, per Chapter 2, is to approach distributed processing from a three-level system viewpoint. By way of review, the first-level system focuses on local processing of source data entry, while the second-level system centers on local processing of source data entry, transactions, and management reports. The third-level system goes beyond local processing and is a network of distributed processing systems. Due to the complexity of the last system approach in a distributed processing environment, only applications for the first two levels will be explored in the last part of the chapter. The third-level system approach will be discussed in Chapter 5.

DISTRIBUTED PROCESSING SYSTEMS IMPLEMENTATION

The task of systems implementation for a comprehensive distributed processing system is a major undertaking because it generally cuts across the entire organization, i.e., the local, regional, and home office levels. This results in a great need for implementation planning. An understanding of specific tasks that need to be undertaken and the relationships among them is needed. Likewise, knowledge of the problems and the exceptions is necessary. This background permits the detailed planning of the various tasks that must be incorporated into a schedule having specific deadlines. The scheduling method should follow the natural flow of work to be undertaken. The usual questions of who, what, where, when, how, and why must be answered in developing the schedule. Implementation planning should include provisions for reviewing completed and uncompleted tasks so that the entire system project will be under control.

PREPARATORY WORK OF IMPLEMENTING DISTRIBUTED PROCESSING SYSTEMS

Certain preparatory work must be accomplished before a comprehensive distributed processing system, like those illustrated later in the chapter and, particularly, like those in the next chapter and in Part III, can operate on a day-to-day basis. Specifically, this includes preparing a detailed time and activity schedule, selecting and training qualified personnel, physical alterations to the premises, testing and accepting the new equipment, programming and testing programs, systems testing, and finally file conversion. Information gathered in the feasibility study provides a starting point for completing these phases. System flowcharts, decision tables, and the manufacturer's proposal constitute the major material necessary to get the work started. Even though the data have been compiled and documented properly, the time and manpower requirements for the systems project are just beginning. Thus, it is necessary that the DP manager be alert to keep costs within the confines of the feasibility study.

Scheduling the Installation

Installation work should be scheduled in sufficient detail so that each important milestone can be controlled. Even though uncertainty may exist for certain activities, accurate times should be developed as nearly as possible. Generally, the data set forth in the manufacturer's proposal can be used as a starting point in scheduling. (The user must consider lengthening the delivery time because it is possible for equipment manufacturers to experience difficulty.)

The scheduler must determine appropriate starting dates for each activity to find out whether or not personnel have ample time to complete all the necessary tasks before the equipment is delivered. It is possible that overtime and additional personnel may be required to meet the equipment delivery date. The ability today to foresee a future problem is a great help to the data processing group in controlling the project. One way of scheduling work is through the use of PERT, a refinement of the critical path method.[1]

Selecting and Training Qualified Personnel

The placement of the equipment order and scheduling its installation indicate the need for selecting and training qualified personnel for systems implementation as well as normal day-by-day operations. Not only are present personnel who are involved in existing DP operations an important source, but also non-DP personnel should be considered since distributed processing stresses simplicity and ease of operations for operating personnel.

There are many advantages to staffing from within an organization. Knowledge of present methods and procedures is helpful in understanding the specialized tasks that must be accomplished with the new system. This understanding of procedural exceptions and problem areas can be of great importance in complying with difficult system changes. The departmental managers know these people and what can be expected from them. For the most part, they are desirable employees who want training because it increases their professional status and pay. Thus, management's interest in them should increase their loyalty in return.

If the jobs in a distributed processing environment cannot be filled from within by qualified personnel, the DP manager has no alternative but to go outside the organization. This includes hiring trained personnel with no or some data processing experience, depending on the job requirements of the new system. Applicants need to be tested for their ability to handle positions for which they are being considered.

Considering the sources of qualified personnel to implement the new system, training of personnel will still be necessary. All equipment manufacturers provide training courses for their customers. These courses vary in length from several hours to several weeks, depending on the subject matter and its depth. By no means is training limited to those who will operate the new system. Management should have a good grasp of what the distributed processing system can do for them and how it can be applied effectively to the organization. Otherwise, there will be a gap between management and the new system.

---

[1]Refer to Robert J. Thierauf, *An Introductory Approach to Operations Research,* Santa Barbara, Calif.: Wiley/Hamilton, 1978, Chap. 5.

Physical Requirements and Alterations

The actual installation of the equipment may require more, less, or the same amount of space. However, requirements for conversion activities generally take more space because dual operations of the new and old systems must take place within the same general area. Alterations may be needed to handle new inputs, the distributed data bases, off-line files, and outputs as well as many I/O terminal devices. New methods and procedures may require physical modifications. In comprehensive distributed processing systems, new departments may replace old ones, while other departments will have need of extensive modifications. Others will no longer be needed, providing space for new departmental requirements.

The physical requirements and alterations necessary should be an integral part of the systems implementation schedule. Although the DP manager will not personally supervise the new equipment installation and its physical environment alterations, he is, nevertheless, accountable in the final analysis. It is best to determine as early as possible the layout of the new distributed processing system to permit the location of physical changes which may take a while to install. Too often in the past the physical aspects of a new system have been ignored because prior system changes have gone smoothly without any need for large modifications.

Testing and Acceptance of Equipment

No matter what type of new equipment is being installed, the manufacturer's field service engineers must test it thoroughly before its acceptance by the user. Only the manufacturer has the necessary diagnostic routines for this testing. A common method is to utilize field service programs which are capable of testing the various pieces of hardware in the system. This method can be supplemented with company programs that have proved to be thoroughly operational at another location.

Programming and Testing

A major task of a comprehensive distributed processing system is programming and testing computer programs. Although much time is allocated to other implementation areas, the task of programming and testing may be of such a magnitude that it must be supervised effectively in order to obtain the best results at all levels, i.e., local, regional, and central. Although the detailed steps involved in developing a computer routine will not be discussed, an overview of the important steps involved in developing an operational computer program in an interactive processing mode is set forth in Figure 4–1. Similarly, a listing of the steps involved in a batch processing mode are set forth in Figure 4–2. These listings indicate the numerous steps employed in programming and testing. They are also indicative of the formidable task in systems implementation.

For the most part, programming and testing efforts for an interactive processing mode can be difficult. Even though conversion is from one computer system

1. Define the problem.

2. Prepare the program flowchart(s) and/or decision table(s).

3. Enter the computer program at the terminal. If the program is complex, the computer program is generally written prior to getting on the system.

4. Make corrections to the program as indicated by the system.

5. Test the program with sample transactions.

6. Correct program errors found with sample transactions.

7. Test the program using systems testing.

8. Test the program using parallel operations.

9. Convert to daily operations.

10. Documentation throughout the preceding steps.

FIGURE 4-1. Problem analysis, programming, and implementation for an operational computer program—interactive processing mode.

1. Define the problem.

2. Prepare the program flowchart(s) and/or decision table(s).

3. Write the computer program at your desk.

4. Desk-check the program.

5. Prepare (keypunch and key-verify) program cards.

6. Compile for an object program.

7. Correct program errors as indicated by the system.

8. Recompile for an object program.

9. Test the program with sample transactions.

10. Correct program errors found with sample transactions.

11. Test the program using systems testing.

12. Test the program using parallel operations.

13. Convert to daily operations.

14. Documentation throughout the preceding steps.

FIGURE 4-2. Problem analysis, programming, and implementation for an operational computer program—batch processing mode.

to another, there are basic differences between a batch processing mode and an interactive processing mode. Many programs must be started from scratch because there is no counterpart available in the previous system for emulating, simulating, or revising present programs. The steps enumerated in Figure 4-1 will add time to the systems implementation phase. However, the next change should not be so difficult.

As with any project, programming supervision is essential to meet the new installation deadlines. Too often, programmers take the most difficult route first instead of taking one that is relatively simple and straightforward. Invariably, they try their talents in utilizing the new features of the equipment. This level of sophistication can be undertaken at a later date when time is available to increase the program's throughput performance. Programmers must be content to get the system on the air and leave intricate programming until a later time if it is not fully understood. Only in this manner can the systems implementation schedule be met.

Systems Testing

Before parallel operation is undertaken, it is recommended that systems testing be employed, inasmuch as programming testing is rather limited. Systems testing involves utilizing old files so that the system can be tested with past data (primary objective). Such an approach introduces "realism," because testing is done with previous live data. Normal transactions and exceptions are tested against the computer program for reliability. Testing under real-world conditions should lessen the problems encountered with parallel operations. Depending on the type of system, this phase could be short or somewhat lengthy.

Systems testing is concerned with training the company employees in the operation of the new system as well as maintaining it (secondary objective). Employees must learn to operate what is being turned over to them. This can be accomplished by formal classroom sessions, seminars, on-the-job training, and computer-assisted instruction. Operating manuals for training, operating, and maintaining the system are necessary for efficient systems testing.

File Conversion

Because there are files of information that must be converted from one medium to another, this phase should be started long before programming and testing is completed. The cost and related problems of file conversion are significant whether they involve on-line files (distributed data bases) or off-line files. Present manual files are likely to be inaccurate and incomplete where deviations from the accepted format are common. In a similar manner, present punched card files tend also to be inaccurate and incomplete. Both files suffer from the shortcomings of inexperienced and, at times, indifferent personnel whose jobs are to maintain them. Computer-generated files tend to be more accurate and consistent. The formats of the present computer files are generally unacceptable for the new system.

Besides the need to provide a compatible format, there are several other reasons for file conversion. The files may require character translation that is acceptable to the character set of the new system. Data from punched cards, magnetic tape, and comparable storage mediums may have to be placed on magnetic disk, magnetic drum, and/or other mass storage files in order to construct an on-line data base. Also, the rearrangement of certain data fields for more efficient programming may be desired. A new format that takes advantage of packed decimal fields may be necessary for conversion.

For the conversion to be as accurate as possible, file conversion programs must be thoroughly tested. Adequate controls, such as record counts and control totals, should be required output of the conversion program. The existing computer files should be kept for a period of time until sufficient files are accumulated for backup. This is necessary in case the files must be reconstructed from scratch when a "bug" is discovered at a later date in the conversion routine.

OPERATION OF DISTRIBUTED PROCESSING SYSTEMS

Even though new programs and procedures have been used to test representative systems data, there is no way to duplicate the actual flow of work with all its timing considerations and exceptions. The best way to prove the new system's reliability is to run parallel operations with the existing system.

Parallel Operations

Parallel operations consist of feeding both systems the same input data and comparing data files and output results. This is depicted as step 8 in Figure 4-1 and as step 12 in Figure 4-2 for interactive and batch processing modes, respectively. Despite the fact that the best test data possible were used during the preparatory work phase, related conditions and combinations of conditions are likely to occur that were not envisioned. Last-minute changes to computer programs are necessary to accommodate these new conditions.

For distributed processing systems using an interactive mode, the process of running dual operations for both new and old systems is more difficult than for a batch processing mode. The problem is that the new system has no true counterpart in the old system. One procedure for testing the new system is to have several remote input/output terminals connected on-line and to have them operated by supervisory personnel who are backed up by other personnel operating on the old system. The outputs are checked for compatibility, and appropriate corrections are made to the on-line computer programs. Once this segment of the new system has proven satisfactory, the entire terminal network can be placed into operation for this one area. Additional sections of the system can be added by testing in this manner until all programs are operational.

During parallel operations, mistakes found are often not those of the new system but the result of the old system. These differences should be reconciled insofar as it is feasible economically. Those responsible for comparing the two systems should establish clearly that the remaining deficiencies are caused by the old system. A poor detail checking job at this point can cause undue harm later when complaints are received from customers, top management, salesmen, departments, and other parties. Again, it is the responsibility of the DP manager and staff to satisfy themselves that adequate time for dual operations has been undertaken for each functional area changed.

The DP group must keep the entire firm posted on parallel operations and conversion activities. Departmental personnel should be informed when they are to start on systems implementation and what specific activities will be required of them. Department heads should be informed before the actual date of conversion activities so that anticipated problems can be worked out before they occur. Ample time should be spent instructing personnel on parallel operations or conversion activities to prevent wasted motion and time and eventually a cost that will exceed the original study figures by a wide margin. Activities must be organized, directed, and controlled around the original plan, i.e., the feasibility study.

Conversion to New System

After on- and off-line files have been converted and the new system's reliability has been proven for a functional area, daily processing can be shifted from the existing system to the new one. This is step 9 in Figure 4-1 and step 13 in Figure 4-2 for interactive and batch processing modes, respectively. A cutoff point is established so that all data files and other data requirements can be updated to the cutover point. All transactions initiated after this time are processed on the new system. DP personnel should be present to assist and answer any questions that might develop. Consideration may have to be given to operating the old system a short time longer to permit checking and balancing the total results of both systems. Differences must be reconciled. If necessary, appropriate changes should be made to the new system. The old system can be dropped as soon as the data processing group is satisfied with the new system's performance. It should be remembered that it is impossible to return to the old system if significant errors appear later in the new system. The operation of the existing system provides an alternative route in case of system failure during conversion.

Provision for Necessary Changes

Before any parallel or conversion activities can start, operating procedures in the form of documentation must be clearly spelled out for personnel in the functional areas undergoing changes, as specified per the final step in Figures 4-1 and 4-2. This applies to both programming and operational procedures. Information on input, data files, methods, procedures, output, and internal control must be set forth in clear, concise, and understandable terms for the average reader. Written operating procedures must be supplemented by oral communication during the many training periods on the systems change. Having qualified DP personnel in the conversion area to communicate and coordinate new developments as they occur is a must. Likewise, revisions to operating procedures should be issued as quickly as possible.

Once the new system has been completely converted, the DP section should spend several days checking with all supervisory personnel about their respective areas. As with every new installation, the need for minor adjustments can be expected; the system as initially designed should be flexible enough to accommodate these changes. Channels of communication should be open between the DP group and all supervisory personnel so that necessary changes can be initiated as conditions change. Thus, the proper machinery for making changes must be implemented, thereby bringing the distributed processing systems project to a formal close.

Scheduling Personnel and Equipment

Scheduling DP operations for a comprehensive distributed system is a difficult task for the DP manager. As he or she becomes more familiar with the new system, the job becomes more routine. The objectives of scheduling both personnel and equipment are depicted in Figure 4-3.

Schedules should be set up by the head of data processing in conjunction with the departmental managers of the operational units. The master schedule for next month should provide sufficient computer time to handle all required processing. Daily schedules should be prepared in accordance with the master schedule and should include time necessary for reruns, program testing, special nonrecurring reports, and other necessary runs. In all cases, the schedules should be as realistic as possible because it is more difficult to schedule an interactive system than a batch processing system.

The time to assign remote batch programs at the local and regional levels under normal operating conditions is a problem because the number of interruptions that will occur at the headquarters level is generally unknown. One approach to this problem is to assign a time block each day for operation of remote input/output devices. If this arrangement is not feasible, the DP manager must look to past experience. When total random and sequential demands are not high, the

- Maximize utilization of personnel and equipment, in particular, "intelligent" I/O terminal devices to further the objectives of the firm.
- Produce timely reports and meet deadlines for output desired.
- Increase productivity of personnel by including time for training and on-the-job training.
- Facilitate the planning of proposed new applications or modifications of existing applications for new and/or existing equipment.
- Reduce conflicts of several jobs waiting for a specific piece of equipment. (Conflicts may result in delays of important outputs or unnecessary overtime.)

FIGURE 4-3. Objectives of scheduling personnel and equipment in a distributed processing environment.

central host processor will have sufficient capacity to complete all scheduled work even though batch processing runs will be stretched out by random system inquiries.

Just as the equipment must be scheduled for its maximum utilization, so must the personnel who operate the equipment. It is also imperative that personnel who enter input data and handle output data be included in the data processing schedule. Otherwise, data will not be available when needed for subsequent processing. It is essential that each person follow the methods and procedures set forth by the data processing group. Noncompliance with established norms will have an adverse effect on the entire distributed processing system. Effective supervision of personnel enhances compliance with established procedures and scheduled deadlines.

Alternative Plans in Case of Equipment Failure

Alternative processing plans must be employed in case of equipment failure. Priorities must be given to those jobs that are critical to the firm, such as billing, payroll, and inventory. These jobs can be performed manually until the equipment is functioning again.

Documentation of alternative plans is the responsibility of the data processing section. It should be a part of the company's systems and procedures manual, which should state explicitly what the critical jobs are, how they are to be handled in case of equipment failure (use manual methods or some other approach), where compatible equipment is located (includes service bureaus), who will be responsible for each area during downtime, and what deadlines must be met during the emergency.

OVERVIEW OF LOCAL PROCESSING OF SOURCE DATA ENTRY— FIRST-LEVEL SYSTEM

To be successful when implementing local processing of source data entry (first-level system), the feasibility study must have determined what data to transmit from the remote I/O terminals to the main computer. Distributed processing economics are based on the idea that the remote terminal can process and store locally much of the data that in the past had to be sent to the main computer. The more data that can be handled locally, the better a particular remote location is for distributed data entry. A central factor in distributed processing is the transmission of usable information that is preformatted and error-free. This is a significant departure from the old method of transmitting raw, error-ridden data from a "dumb" terminal to a central CPU where error checks, processing, and storage took place. Although this important factor is not discussed below per se, it is an underlying rationale for going distributed.

The first-level system of distributed processing centers around local processing of source data entry. Fundamentally, it is oriented toward distributed data entry systems whereby single or multiple data entry units are distributed at various

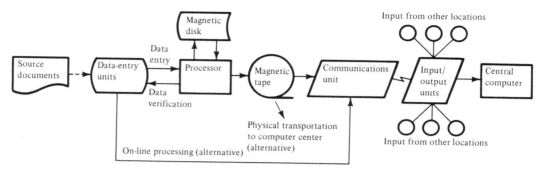

**FIGURE 4–4. Overview of the first-level system of distributed process-
ing—local or regional processing of source data entry.**

company locations for local or regional processing. As illustrated from an overview standpoint in Figure 4-4, data entry units are used to capture input data on
either magnetic tape or disk, which are then communicated on-line to input devices
of a computer system. To speed up the process, data from the key entry units are
communicated directly to the computer for on-line processing. A slower alternative
as illustrated is to transport physically the tapes and disks to the computer center
for processing. This first-level system of distributed data entry is capable of bringing
flexibility and economy to an organization's data entry operations. Hence, it is
capable of meeting specific user needs at the lowest level, i.e., the local or regional
processing level.

Based on the foregoing overview, there are several specific approaches to distributed processing at the first level. Two of the more popular ones are discussed
below. Additional variations will be illustrated in the next section on applications.

One of the most common types of source data entry at the local level centers
on key entry units which are under the control of a small processor—refer to
Figure 4-4. Data are entered through the keyboard, processed by the system's
processor, and stored on a magnetic disk in locations appropriate to the key
station of original entry. Once data are verified, completed batches can be transferred automatically from the disk onto a single reel of magnetic tape or another
magnetic disk. Finally, this tape or disk is the input for any computer batch processing run. In most cases, the data are communicated directly to the computer
center via a communications facility, or data are physically transported to the
computer center.

The use of data entry units, then, allows the collection of business data at
distributed field locations in an organization. Likewise, communication of distributed data (refer to Figure 4-4) is made to the centralized computer center. For
low cost, data are transmitted over standard dial-up telephone lines on an overnight basis. During the day, operators use the data entry units in an interactive
processing mode for storing data on magnetic media until an optimum time is
reached for transmission to the centralized computer center.

While the foregoing approach to local processing provides for processing during the day and transmission of data at night, the next approach allows for concurrent entry of source data along with other chores. Utilizing a processor that has a partitioned supervisor, the system can handle batch processing, communications, or other "background" chores while simultaneously servicing a number of data entry units. Users at the local level can perform all necessary day-to-day interactive data entry while other needs are being met. This type of equipment eliminates the need for shutdowns of local data entry units while batch processing communications work or other "background" chores are being handled.

APPLICATIONS OF DISTRIBUTED PROCESSING—
FIRST-LEVEL SYSTEM

Distributed processing systems at the first level, as indicated previously, center on data entry at the local or regional level. This is accomplished with a system offering computer capabilities that deal with data entry applications which are independent of the large computer and which communicate clean files to the main DP center. To illustrate this first-level approach to distributed processing systems, three applications are given below.

Motor Transportation Firm

A large motor carrier in the United States found that it had to change from a Teletype system which worked well when 4000 to 5000 freight bills were processed each day. At their current rate of 14,000 bills a day, a more effective and economical communications system was needed as well as one that would help minimize clerical billing errors caused by the pressure of preparing such a volume of documents within a very short time frame. In view of the increased volume, intelligent terminals with cassette orientation and communications facilities were selected and installed.

Each terminal checks to ensure that the biller completes the shipper's name and address; extends the weight of the shipment; multiplies the rate; totals the number of pieces, weight, and charges; verifies that all origin and destination codes are valid; checks minimum rates/weights tables and searches for the proper rates; and extends service charges for fluctuating items. In the past, most of such functions used to be performed manually by a rate clerk with completed information then retyped by a billing clerk.

At the end of the day, a switching device is used to sort all freight bills—by shipper and origin—and transmit a manifest to each origin and destination location. It then produces a tape which is communicated to the central computer, which produces freight bills for billing purposes and retains an image of all unpaid bills. Within this distributed processing environment, billing is performed at the local level and is, in turn, transmitted to the central office for further processing.

Medical Service Bureau

A medical service bureau performs patient billing for numerous medical groups in a large city. Formerly, clients mailed their information to the bureau's data processing center where it was keyed and processed on its computer. However, third-party billing, such as Blue Shield, Medicare, and Welfare, created bottlenecks as claims forms became more complex. As part of an expansion effort, the service bureau installed communicating processors as data entry terminals at the offices of 10 high-volume clients. For each of these clients, the system allows efficient "fill in the blanks" type of data entry. Formats appear on the CRT screen which prompt the user for all necessary information. As data are entered, the processor checks for mistakes, such as an operation date earlier than date of admission. Delays that used to occur in resolving such troublesome errors are now totally eliminated.

Data recorded on tape cassettes are the validated source files. All billing data are accumulated on reusable cassettes, and at the end of the day, these files are communicated via high-speed communications to the central computer (Figure 4–5). The central system spools files to magnetic tape that is in the proper format for final processing on the service bureau's computer. Billing is merely the first phase of a total medical system. Phase 2 will be medical records, while phase 3 will be diagnostics.

The main benefit provided by the communicating processors is reduced turnaround time. The system uses the most cost-efficient media, namely, tape cassettes. And most important for the service bureau, interactive processing power at their clients' sites means easy expansion of applications without extensive hardware changes.

FIGURE 4–5. Data entry system used by high-volume clients of a medical service bureau.

Agricultural Products Company

A large agricultural products company operates many terminals in 16 cities as part of a distributed processing environment. By and large, its distributed processing system is a hybrid. A few remote locations with the simplest requirements communicate with the central computer in the home office by Telex. Other remote stations use a keyboard/CRT with two diskette drives. Still other outlying sites use a clustered terminal with up to eight keyboard/CRT data entry stations operating from a common memory and disk storage.

Although none of the processing required by remote-site operations is carried out in real time, remote job entry from field locations is transmitted back to the inquiring location within two hours. Limiting personnel at the branch locations to specific daytime hours for remote job entry communications with the central computer and using existing WATS telephone lines for automatic nighttime remote data entry are some of the elements in the distributed processing system.

Referring to remote job entry, it is prohibited from 9:30 to 11:00 a.m., 12 noon to 1:00 p.m., and 2:00 to 3:00 p.m., central time. This limitation obviously translates into restrictions during different daytime periods at different time zones. This encourages remote-site operations to build up their files on disk, thereby reducing the number of remote job entry communications and mainframe computer overhead. During daytime hours when remote job entry is not taking place, data for home operations and data received from remote locations are processed. Hence, data collected in this manner are handled in a pure batch mode, and processed results are usually transmitted to outlying areas for printout at the beginning of the next working day.

From an overview, the present distributed processing system places computer power where it is needed. For the future, the company foresees no need for the installation of computers at the outlying branches because the clustered terminals take over part of the computer function. For example, in a large southeastern city, two clustered units, each with 64K memory storage and 5 megabytes of fixed disk storage, are used. Even though plans call for an upgrading of the central computer to a larger mainframe size, this is not necessary for the outlying areas.

OVERVIEW OF LOCAL PROCESSING OF SOURCE DATA ENTRY, TRANSACTIONS, AND MANAGEMENT REPORTS— SECOND-LEVEL SYSTEM

Building upon the framework of the first-level system, the second-level system goes beyond just source data entry and includes the processing of transactions and the preparation of management reports at the local or regional level. Also, like the first level, appropriate information is forwarded to central headquarters for further processing where deemed necessary.

Within this second-level system environment, a whole host of equipment configurations can be developed to fit the user's needs. To be an effective distributed processing system, generally it must be custom-tailored to user needs; i.e., an important measure of any system's success is the degree to which it meets those needs. Proper selection of the distributed processing equipment can put the precise amount of computer power exactly where it is needed. There is no reason to over- or underspecify when selecting the hardware.

When choosing the hardware, flexibility at this second-level system is a prime consideration. This flexibility can take many forms, such as upward flexibility—the ability to upgrade hardware through a manufacturer's line to meet expanded user needs at a particular location. Closely related to this is the ability of the terminal to operate with the line or message protocols of the host environment.

Thus, equipment considerations at this second-level system are more stringent than those found at the first level.

An overview of this second-level system is given in Figure 4-6, an elaboration of Figure 4-4. After source documents are entered and verified by some type of data entry units, the output of source data entry, namely, magnetic tape, becomes the input for the local or regional computer. Generally, the computer employed will be a minicomputer or a small business computer that operates in a batch processing mode. However, some computer systems will allow processing in both an interactive and a batch mode. Nevertheless, the on-site computer at the local level will allow transactional processing of source input data.

The output of the computer at the local or regional level can take many forms. First, it can be managerial reports that serve the needs of operating management. Second, it can be detailed and summary information that is being forwarded via a communications link or physical transportation to a higher level, that is, the home office level. Third, it can be updated data files that will serve as input for local or regional processing. Last, output may be just historical data that are being accumulated to serve some future need.

Referring to Figure 4-6, data can be communicated from the data entry units directly to the communications unit if they have the capacity. Normally, output from the local or regional computer is forwarded on a remote batch processing basis to the host computer. However, for those computers having the capability of computer-to-computer transmission, it is possible to transmit from the local or regional computer to the central computer in real-time.

Overall, this second-level approach to distributed processing can take many directions in terms of hardware configurations. Applications, to be found in the next section, are typical ones. However, they are not to be construed as encompassing all possibilities of the second-level system.

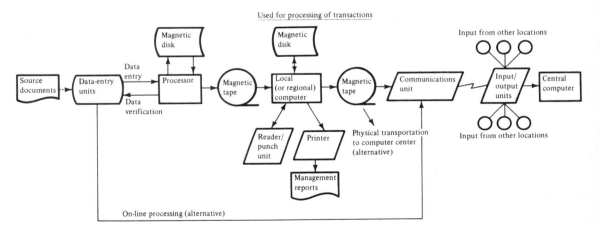

FIGURE 4-6. Overview of the second-level system of distributed processing—local or regional processing of data entry, transactions, and management reports.

APPLICATIONS OF DISTRIBUTED PROCESSING—
SECOND-LEVEL SYSTEM

Distributed processing at the second-level system involves more sophistication than at the first level. Basically, this is caused by more processing being performed at the local or regional levels instead of forwarding source input data directly to the central computer system. In view of this increased level of sophistication, three sample applications are presented for the second-level approach to distributed computing.

Major Oil Company

A major oil company maintains regional marketing centers which are responsible for order entry, invoicing, distribution, and sales analysis of the company's products. Previously, the manual system involved processing 400 orders a day. Invoices had to be typed and were then sent by manual Teletypes to 20 distribution centers within each region. Complex tax codes and pricing and product information compounded the need for some system of local file maintenance, computation, and high-speed transmission.

After instituting a feasibility study, a key-to-diskette data entry system was installed (Figure 4-7). It allows rapid data entry, and its diskettes provide unlimited storage, easy handling, and fast access to local files. After the operators key in the orders, the processor automatically verifies customer files and product codes. Likewise, it calculates price extensions and taxes, appends any special terms, and then stores the completed invoices on diskettes. In two hours of high-speed data transmission a day, all invoices are printed on remote receive-only teletypewriters. The complete invoice transaction file, in turn, is communicated to the corporate data center and is entered into the accounts-receivable system on the host computer. At the regional level, the processors accumulate managerial sales analyses for summary reports which were previously unavailable at this level. In this sample application, regionally installed processors serve as "intelligent" data entry systems for the central computer and act as transaction processing output systems for distributing a high volume of data to numerous field sites.

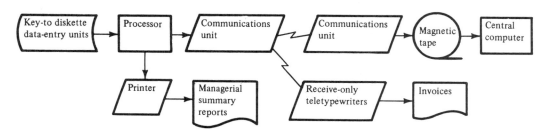

FIGURE 4-7. Combined data entry, transaction processing, and operational reporting system used by a major oil company.

Corrugated Container Manufacturer

A corrugated container manufacturer, operating 20 container plants across the country, has followed a progression from piecemeal recording and reporting systems of the past to a distributed processing system that gives both plant and corporate management a new degree of control over their operations. A few years ago, management foresaw growth in both the volume and sophistication of the packaging business and realized that the achievement of strong corporate direction and efficient plant operation was beyond the capacity of existing internal plant production and accounting systems.

Raw material inventory control, order entry and billing, and production monitoring and hourly payroll, to name the more important DP functions, relied on a combination of flexowriters, computypers, and manual procedures. Reordering of raw, roll-stock paperboard was difficult to schedule accurately because inventory data were rarely current. Assembly of summary information from paper records for accounting and forecasting at plant, regional, divisional, and corporate levels became an arduous task. Production information, indicating a need for corrective action, almost invariably became available too late to be of use. Finally, the flexowriters, computypers, and unit record equipment were aging physically and could not be replaced.

In view of these difficulties, a feasibility study committee was formed to evaluate the distributed processing concept. It was composed of representatives of plant management, corporate systems, and divisional staff under the chairmanship of an area vice president. Line and operational personnel on the committee made decisions regarding applications to be computerized and basic modes of operation. The systems group lent technical expertise and had responsibility for implementing the decisions. Within a short period of time, the committee recommended a move toward distributed processing with on-line, minicomputer-based, small business systems. Its real task, however, was to devise a distributed processing environment that would meet the actual needs of line management and also provide current input to the central computer processing unit.

Even though there was some controversy about the approach to be taken, the committee finally agreed upon three major areas for implementation. As mentioned previously, they include roll-stock inventory, order entry/billing, and production reporting and payroll. The first application, namely, *roll-stock inventory,* tracks raw materials for manufacturing and aids reorder scheduling. It was chosen as the first phase because of its relative simplicity of development. Each of the container plants processes roll-stock inventory as a stand-alone program; no communication is involved. The system assembles daily figures for rolls of paper on hand so that corrugating machine operation can be optimized. In addition, it maintains records of raw material receipts and consumption, compiles month-to-date totals for receipts and shipments, and extrapolates current inventory levels daily for operating management.

The second application—*order entry/billing*—involves maintenance of customer records, manipulation of specification files covering several thousand items at each plant, and printing customer acknowledgments, production orders, and sales invoices. An attractive feature of this program is the flexibility available to the plants to handle various customer order acknowledgment and sales invoicing requirements. Managerial summary data assembled by this program are transmitted by telephone link to the centralized computer system.

For the last application—*production reporting and payroll*—production reporting, machines and manpower utilization, plus machines and labor costs are processed, accumulated, and reported daily to local plant managers for review and control purposes. Payroll data on production employees are sent to the central computer, which calculates taxes to be withheld. After overnight processing, net pay and deductions are returned to the remote sites for printing of the checks and updating of local records.

Overall, the distributed processing system allows for local processing of data input, transaction processing, and the preparation of certain operating reports for line managers. Likewise, provision has been made to allow processing of selected data at the corporate level. In this manner, plant and corporate management get the information needed at their level. Additionally, it should be noted that this distributed processing system was implemented on the condition that it be operable by clerical personnel and that all programming and support be the responsibilities of the corporate systems group.

Public Warehouse Company

A warehousing company operates a chain of large public warehouses. In these facilities, which contain millions of square feet for the storage of assorted goods and articles, the company maintains many thousands of different items. Goods are moved out and in frequently. All these items have to be accounted for, both for billing purposes and to ensure that the goods are there when clients need them.

Distributed processing is currently installed and in operation at four of the company's scattered public warehouses. As illustrated in Figure 4-8, the A warehouse utilizes a processor and six data entry terminals. On the other hand, the B warehouse has a smaller processor with five input stations. Also, the C and D warehouses utilize the same size processor as the B warehouse; the number of CRT input stations is three each.

Each of these installations has a printer and associated data storage units. The configuration in the A warehouse can be accessed by up to 16 terminals with the processor and up to 8 terminals with the smaller processor in the other three warehouses. Terminals allow the operators to have full use of the storage and computing capability of the processors. They are equipped with a standard typewriter keyboard and 11-key numeric pad for data input as well as an 80-character by 24-line video display screen. The screen is used to display data being entered, which the operator can scan for possible errors.

Operators enter information relative to movements of inventory in and out of the warehouses and for associated billing purposes from source documents. The screens can be used by the operators to display a sequence of preprogrammed

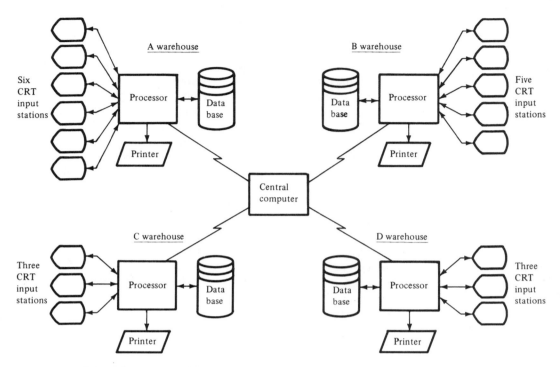

FIGURE 4–8. Combined data entry, transaction processing, and management reporting system used by a public warehouse company.

formats corresponding to the source documents being processed. The terminals are programmed to reject certain types of entries for a specific input application if the inputs fail to conform to preset range guidelines of symbol conventions. These equipment features have helped to reduce input errors in converting from source documents, which had been a cause for confusion and unnecessary cost in the past.

Terminal units are used to generate many critical documents and lower-management reports such as warehouse receipts and delivery orders. The systems are also used for account maintenance and item maintenance. Special instructions for stored goods handling can be introduced into the appropriate item or account file. Duplicate copies of delivery orders can be used as the basis for "picking" instructions for warehouse employees. The random access memory units allow each operator to have access to information on the location of every item stored in the warehouse, which lends itself to more efficient utilization of employee time and equipment.

Another inportant feature of the distributed processing system is the ease with which an operator can be trained to use the terminals. Based on the experience with the new system, it takes a typical operator about an hour and a half to learn the unit and to be able to work at about the rate of an experienced operator. In the past, training periods had to be measured in weeks. The basic reason for this reduction is the "menus" that are programmed into the system to guide the operator through the various phases of conversion and other applications as well. Programs for the systems have been written by the in-house programming staff. The language used for the creation of these programs is called Datashare, which is easy to use, maintain, and document.

Before installation of the terminal systems in the four warehouse facilities, the company had relied on a totally manual record-keeping system. Not only was employee cost high, but also an important hidden cost was the error rate that resulted and the time consumed in hunting down and correcting these errors. The capability of the distributed processing system has enabled the company to reduce the number of clerical employees required to handle documents on movements of inventories stored in its facilities and to prepare billing information. The clerical staff at the A warehouse was reduced by 35 percent and at the other locations from 10 to 20 percent. That magnitude of savings in a short period of time more than paid for the units. And this does not take into account the much greater capability of the distributed processing system, in particular, the daily operational reports for management.

CHAPTER SUMMARY

Systems implementation for a simple to a complex distributed processing environment begins after the formal signing of the equipment contract. It involves two steps: preparatory work and operation of the new system. Typically, systems implementation takes twice as much time as the feasibility study. The number of operating personnel outside the data processing group is substantially increased. Also, the organization will experience high costs during the systems conversion phase.

Although not discussed in this chapter, periodic review of the distributed processing system, which involves examination of new system approaches, new equipment, and cost factors, normally follows its installation. Often an evaluation of the existing system may signal the need for a new feasibility study, which means, in essence, that the system project cycle must start again. This allows for making changes that are necessary to accommodate environmental factors as well as the introduction of more advanced hardware and software. The feasibility study phase and systems implementation, then, are a continuous process of any organization desiring to have the best business information system for the times.

In addition to systems implementation discussed in this chapter, applications of distributed computing at the first- and second-level systems were treated. As demonstrated in the sample applications, great accent is placed on using a processor or minicomputer to perform the data entry editing tasks in an interactive mode and to accumulate information for transmission to the central computer for batch processing. This approach removes processing from a larger, more expensive, central system by putting it on the less expensive local or regional system. The main thrust, then, is placing computing power where it is needed as well as reducing total DP costs.

QUESTIONS

1. Distinguish between the preparatory work of a distributed processing system and the operation of such a system.

2. What are the critical factors in terms of preparatory work for a typical distributed processing system?

3. How important is scheduling for the operation of a new system?

4. Distinguish between a first-level system and a second-level system as found in a distributed processing environment.

5. a. Give at least one example of a first-level system for distributed computing.

b. Give at least one example of a second-level system for distributed computing.

6. Overall, what is the main thrust of first- and second-level systems in a distributed processing environment? Explain.

SELECTED REFERENCES

Business Week Special Report, "Glowing Prospects for Brainy Computer Terminals," *Business Week,* Oct. 25, 1976.

Computerworld Special Report, "Distributed Processing," *Computerworld,* March 28, 1977.

Feidelman, L. "Distributed Computing, It's a Small World," *Infosystems,* April 1977.

Kaufman, F., "Distributed Processing—A Discussion for Executives Traveling over Difficult Terrain," New York: Coopers & Lybrand, 1977.

Kelley, N., "Which Way—On-Line Batch or Interactive?," *Infosystems,* March 1977.

Kneppelt, L. R., "A Simple Distributed Systems Approach to Manufacturing Information Systems," *AFIPS Conference Proceedings* (National Computer Conference), Vol. 43, 1974.

LaVoie, P. "Distributed Computing Systematically," *Computer Decisions,* March 1977.

Lusa, J. M., "Distributed Computing, Alive and Well," *Infosystems,* Nov. 1976.

Masi, C., and MacDonald, A., "Wang on Distributed Data Processing," Lowell, Mass.: Wang Laboratories, Inc., 1976.

Severino, E. F., "Using Distributed Processing," *Computer Decisions,* May 1977.

Sycor, "Distributed Processing Helps Keep Michelin First" and "Distributed Operations Reduce Paperwork for F.A.G. Bearing," *Update,* March–April 1977.

Thierauf, R. J., *Systems Analysis and Design of Real-Time Management Information Systems,* Englewood Cliffs, N.J.: Prentice-Hall, Inc., 1975.

Trimpey, L., "Implementing a Distributed Processing System," *Infosystems,* Jan. 1977.

Yanigan, L., "Small Business Computers Give Management Information, Too," *Infosystems,* April 1977.

NETWORKS AND APPLICATIONS OF DISTRIBUTED PROCESSING SYSTEMS (THIRD LEVEL)

5

As presented in the previous chapters, distributed computing places a substantial part of the pre- and postprocessing of data and access to data at points where the data originate and are used. And at the same time, central control of the data communications network is maintained. Regarding the last item, emphasis in this chapter is placed on networks in distributed processing systems. Briefly, networks are systems of communication channels; they consist of a set of elements, commonly called *nodes,* that are interconnected in some way. Within this framework, network communications make it possible to establish contact when needed between any selected processors or terminals using common carrier or other low-cost data channels. Needless to say, endless varieties of network configurations are possible to meet the user's needs in a distributed processing environment.

Because networking is an area of technology that is contributing to the proliferation of distributed computation, its essential aspects are covered initially in the chapter. Specifically, dedicated versus dialed (switched) networks are explored along with the five basic types of network architecture. Distributed data bases in such an environment are discussed along with typical examples. Additionally, the need for and the function of a network control center are treated. As in the prior chapter, real-world applications are presented. Specifically, network distributed processing (third-level) systems are featured.

DEDICATED VERSUS DIALED (SWITCHED) NETWORKS

Before discussing (in the next section) the types of network architecture found in a distributed processing environment, we note that the most common arrangement in computer networks is a central processor surrounded by terminal stations (CRTs, Teletype, etc.), processors, microcomputers, minicomputers, and small business computers which feed in and out of it. The foregoing types of equipment can be located either near the central processor or around the country and can communicate with it over either dedicated lines or the switched trunks of a dialed network, such as the telephone service, Western Union's Telex, TWX, or a private branch exchange.

In a *dedicated network,* each unit of distributed equipment has a unique line associated with it which is permanently connected to the central processor whether or not the line is being used. In a *switched network,* a physical connection exists between the distributed equipment and the central processor only when a message is passing. In addition, a much larger set of terminals, processors, and similar equipment can be supported by a switched network than by a dedicated one. The basic mechanical difference, then, occurs in establishing a connection.

In a dedicated network, equipment is physically connected by transmission lines to the central processor all of the time, and whether or not characters are actually passing, they are always able to pass under control of the proper line protocol. Thus, the only way the central processor can tell one message from another or from none at all is by looking for special characters embedded in the message stream instead of by looking for different electrical or time states on the line. As illustrated in Figure 5-1 for a dedicated hookup, there may be one or more pieces of equipment on a line—if one, a single station or point-to-point line; if more, a multipoint line—but the total distributed units cannot increase indefinitely.

In either a dedicated or a dialed network, the first task of the distributed equipment is to tell the central processor that it needs service. The permanent line connections of a dedicated network lend themselves to a "polling" discipline for this task. To get a message going, the central processor sends each unit which is not busy a special character, at short intervals, asking if it has anything to send. It responds by indicating to the central processor either that it has something or nothing to send. If something, the central processor allows it to be sent; if nothing, the processor can then check if it itself has a message for the unit. If so, it delivers; if not, it waits a short interval before polling that same unit.

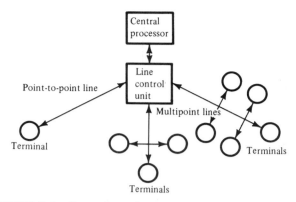

FIGURE 5-1. Examples of one point-to-point and two multipoint dedicated lines.

A dialed or switched network is represented in Figure 5-2. The terminals are physically disconnected from the central processor before and after a message is passing between them; hence, polling is impossible. To get a message going, the user dials the central processor (using data sets), thereby contending with all other dialed equipment or terminals which are trying to get service at that time. The dialed digits pass into the local telephone exchange, or end office, which then searches for an available trunk to the next exchange, and so forth until the end office attached to the central processor is reached. The call request causes an interrupt at the processor, which, servicing it, returns a ready signal to the terminal unit. This premessage interplay finally establishes a physical connection for data transmission. When the central processor has a message for the terminal, either one can originate the call. Either the terminal unit can dial and request the information when ready, or the central processor can originate the call by passing the

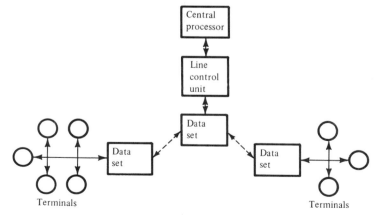

FIGURE 5-2. Examples of dialed or switched networks.

dial digits into an automatic calling unit, which transforms them into the proper signals for the switched network. As can be seen from the foregoing, the operating modes of dedicated and dialed or switched networks are different.

A scattered and a clustered terminal distribution may be designed as dialed or dedicated. If dedicated, then a further option exists for the clustered distribution only—to create a multipoint hookup by allowing groups of terminals to share one line. The purpose of multipoint is to save the cost of a separate line for each terminal unit to the central processor. It is only feasible when the sum of the individual terminal utilizations is kept quite low since this sum becomes the total utilization of the line. Another multipoint problem is that response time increases for each terminal added to the line because none will be polled until those ahead of it have received their share of service. To minimize response time, the line should be full duplex to eliminate modem turnaround time, the polling procedure should use minimum interplay, and the distributed terminals should transmit at maximum line speed. In summary, the factors that limit multipointing are geography, terminal utilization, and response-time requirements of the distributed terminal units in the system.

DISTRIBUTED NETWORK ARCHITECTURE

In distributed computing, *network architecture* refers to the combination of hardware and software that comprises the network. Fundamentally, a network is a complex of two or more interconnected computers. The hardware that supports it generally includes multiplexers, line adapters, modems, and computers with associated peripherals. On the other hand, software consists of modules in the host computer's operating systems, front-end processors, and remote processors that handle services provided to users.

The architecture of the networks designed around general-purpose mainframes is quite different from that of networks designed around minicomputers. The general-purpose computer networks evolved from centralized processing systems that use medium-to-large host processors to execute programs called by batch streams collected from remote and local terminals. In contrast, the minicomputer network grew from an interactive world where from the beginning the computer communicated with terminals.

General-purpose computer networks which are now primarily data communication networks are host dominated. This kind of network is often called a star network (refer to Chapter 2). On the other hand, the minicomputer networks usually consist of interconnected but independent computers. This type of network is commonly called a ring network (node-to-node) control network (refer to Chapter 2).

Based on the foregoing differences, an important design decision in building distributed networks is how to combine the minicomputers and general-purpose computers together in a network so that each one's best features are used. So far, the operating systems of general-purpose computers are imitating minicomputers, and the operating systems for minicomputers are imitating general-purpose computers.

One way of organizing a distributed network is to connect a series of self-controlled subnetworks. The subnets communicate with each other when the need arises, but otherwise each one operates autonomously. As indicated in Chapter 2, there are several different types of subnetworking available in a distributed processing system. They are

- *point-to-point network*—employs a communication line to link two minicomputers or general-purpose computers together
- *hierarchical or tree network*—links together minicomputers and computers that perform a dedicated function to another, usually, a larger computer
- *star network*—entails a heavy flow of communications between remote minicomputers and computers and the central computer (similar organizationally to a two-level hierarchy)
- *loop or ring network*—links several minicomputers and computers together to form the equivalent of a ring
- *fully connected ring network*—employs several minicomputers and computers where each unit can communicate directly with the others.

Although minicomputers and computers were used to describe the distributed processing environment, in actuality these networks can have processors of any size, including intelligent terminals as nodes. Generally, the node at the top is a large, general-purpose computer using a data base management system. The other nodes, for example, could be using local data bases for transaction processing with communication to the larger computer to update the data base or to execute certain large processing jobs. Thus, a wide range of hardware configurations (based on one of the above distributed networks) can be found in a distributed processing system, especially where the data base is distributed throughout the network.

For the distributed processing network illustrated in Figure 5-3, each computer node controls its assigned functions. Likewise, there is little interdependence between nodes, except that each computer has access to part or all of the files of others and backs them up as well. Although the nodes may be interconnected in any desired way, the network is configured as a fully connected ring so that the node computers can easily access each other.

As noted many times previously, the major objective in distributing functions, as in Figure 5-3, is to organize the data processing resources to support the remote applications, rather than to organize the system to satisfy the needs or constraints of a centralized site. These nodal functions can be assigned according to the following guidelines: (1) by operational departments within an organization so that each node handles a specifically defined set of departmental tasks, such as

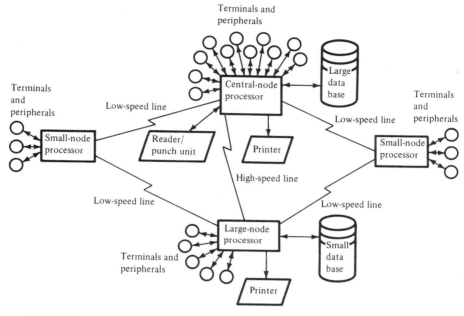

FIGURE 5-3. Distributed processing network—processors, terminals, and peripherals at local sites suit local needs; hardware and software are compatible with those of other nodes.

accounting or manufacturing; (2) by computing mode, such as interactive or batch; and (3) by application, such as order entry or inventory control.

From the foregoing, it should be evident that network design in a distributed processing environment is a challenge—more so in some cases than in others. The principal ingredient for success is sound planning for the distributed network based on careful analysis of the organization's systems and information needs, understanding of available hardware and software, and application of good design principles. For an effective distributed network, they include

- editing data as close as possible to the point where errors can be detected and corrected
- clustering processing requirements within organizational boundaries to the degree necessary to make processing equipment cost effective
- moving data from one place to another only if it necessary
- developing hierarchical data flows that will move upward only what is significant to the next level
- scaling processing, i.e., computing, power to the needs of each hierarchical level, that is, where it is best used

COMPARISON OF TWO NETWORK
ARCHITECTURES

Although five basic approaches can be found in distributed networks, there are two that have emerged more often than others in distributed data processing, namely, a hierarchical network and a fully connected ring network. In the *hierarchical network,* the lowest-level processor performs as if it had an extensive set of peripherals and an operating system. Actually, the local processor only has access to such resources through larger machines. In essence, processors, i.e., minicomputers, are hooked up with remote, centralized facilities that provide support. Both operations and development are available to the user through the processor, on demand from a shared pool.

In practice, the hierarchical network is made up of several levels of computing. In typical situations, it can be viewed as if it had three levels. At the bottom and under the control of the user are processors, i.e., minicomputers and small business computers, placed at any number of local or regional facilities. Above them are computers that store, concentrate, and forward messages. These intermediate systems are connected to the first-level computers by communications lines and are also connected to one or more host computers at the third level which provide interactive or batch processing on demand.

More flexible than a hierarchical network, on the other hand, is the fully connected *ring network* which does not depend on the proper operation of all components. Often, in hierarchical networks, failures spread to higher and lower levels. Because ring networks are made of processors, often all minicomputers and small business computers, connected by a common communications path, failure of any one processor or peripheral does not bring the whole system to a halt. The other systems are able to pass information around the affected node.

In this environment, software may be hosted by several or all of the processors in the network. Since each component machine is relatively small and inexpensive, the overall cost of ring networks is generally low. Generally, system software is inexpensive, and network expansion is simpler than in a hierarchical system. Additionally, resources may be more readily reorganized on a demand basis because there are no barriers between points on the network.

Technically and economically, computing power can be placed in the hands of the user through some type of a distributed approach. Building upon this distributed network concept, data bases can be distributed locally, much as processors are, while remaining available to all users. In the next section, this important part of distributed computing is discussed.

DISTRIBUTED DATA BASES

In its original meaning, distributed processing meant that processing power was dispersed among geographically separated sites which generally were linked by telecommunications lines. The meaning has evolved such that there is an implication that data are also distributed among geographically separate sites which are, for the most part, linked by telecommunications lines. Hence, data are distributed whenever more than one processing device is configured in a network.

Literally speaking, data stored at all relevant locations are considered to be the *distributed data base*. Practically speaking, however, a distributed data base exists only when the data elements at multiple locations are somehow interrelated or if one location requires access to data stored at another.

A distributed data base may consist of a single copy of a set of information divided into subsets that are stored at the various locations. This approach is called a *partitioned data base*. Likewise, a distributed data base may consist of a set of information all or selected parts of which exist at two or more locations. This storage scheme is called a *replicated data base*. A distributed system, then, may store data in either of these arrangements, and some systems may include data sets of both types. This gives an organization several ways to distribute processing power and data. For example, a network configured along hierarchical lines may support a replicated data base. Often, this is desirable when the master data base is used for summary analysis and periodic, scheduled reporting, while the local and regional data bases are used daily and are frequently updated. Also, the hierarchical distribution of power may support a partitioned data base. This approach is often useful for subdividing along corporate lines—headquarters versus geographically dispersed divisions.

There are still other possible versions. For example, a company with offices on both the east and west coasts may partition the master data base among horizontally configured processors. Within each of these horizontal processing configurations, the company can establish hierarchical structures with replicated data bases. The result is a *hybrid system*.

When determining whether multiple copies of the data will exist, whether the data base will be partitioned, or whether a hybrid will be implemented, the nature of the applications and the corporate organization are the key considerations. An additional consideration is the time value of the information, i.e., where information has to be and when it must be there in order to achieve maximum operational effectiveness. Last, hierarchical processors, intelligent terminals, microcomputers, minicomputers, and small business computers with local and regional storage capabilities currently provide the most effective means of distributing an organization's data base.

EXAMPLES OF DISTRIBUTED DATA BASES

In distributed processing network systems, there is a high probability that a distributed data base will be required. In view of this fact, two examples of distributed data bases are set forth below. The first one utilizes a partitioned data base, and the second employs a replicated data base.

As an example of a partitioned data base (a single copy of a set of information divided into increments which reside at multiple locations), a wholesale com-

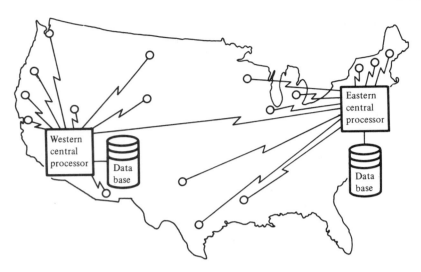

FIGURE 5-4. Example of a geographically partitioned data base.

pany has two central processors. The total data base is split into two partitions; one is attached to each computer. This separates both the processing load and the data base accesses between the two central processors. Since the company operates nationwide, the central processors are located as illustrated in Figure 5-4. It is logical to locate data base partitions heavily accessed by east coast users with the eastern central processor and locate those most accessed by west coast users with the western central processor. Accesses from intermediate locations must be equitably distributed between the two large computers. The important reason for geographical grouping of data is the cost of transmitting data to and from remote locations. Generally, the shorter the transmission distance, the lower is the cost.

An example of a replicated data base (a set of information all or selected parts of which is copied at two or more locations) is illustrated in Figure 5-5 for a complex banking system—formed by the interconnection of two hierarchies. In this system, the central processors maintain the master data base of customer accounts, with the total set of customer records partitioned between the two large-scale computers. Each satellite processor maintains a data base containing the accounts for its local customers. Each local data base is created by copying the necessary information from one of the partitions of the central data base. Essentially, the local data bases are work files, and they are updated each night from the master data base. On-line activity during the day is posted to the local data bases; these are used for withdrawal authorization and similar functions. At night, all activity is batched and used to update the master data base from which new local data bases are then created. The cycle is repeated for each working day. Within such a system, the replication of data at two locations is a way of maintaining a current distributed data base.

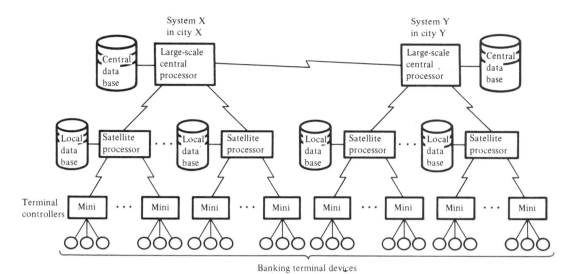

FIGURE 5–5. Example of a geographically replicated data base.

NETWORK CONTROL CENTER

Once the network architecture in relation to the distributed data base has been resolved via the feasibility study, consideration must be given to the network's reliability. How can reliability be achieved? A recommended approach to maintaining reliable operations is to centralize the performance monitoring, diagnosis, and repair functions into a single technical/managerial complex called a *network control center*. The sole function and responsibility of such a center is to keep the network operating reliably. Not only is it the single place to call with repair requests, but it also is responsible for sorting out the problem when users in a complex communications network point at each other and disclaim responsibility.

To be effective, the manager of such of center cannot hope to cope by simply responding to failures. Rather, the manager should anticipate problems where possible in a distributed network. To do this, the manager may be able to employ the facilities of the network itself to good advantage.

Various capabilities can be designed into the network to make the diagnosis and maintenance functions easier to perform. These facilities fall into the following classes: (1) reporting mechanisms, (2) diagnostic capabilities, and (3) recovery mechanisms. *Reporting mechanisms* provide the network control center with current information on the status of the network. Often, marginal components can be detected before they fail totally. *Diagnostic capabilities* enable one to isolate components to determine the exact source of a problem. *Recovery mechanisms* are the means by which repair is accomplished and the network restored to correct operation. Although hardware problems may require on-site repair crews, many software problems can be handled remotely.

Reporting mechanisms built into the network allow the network control center to monitor the performance of the network on a continuous basis. In systems, for example, with intelligent devices, information can be sent to the network control center at regular intervals about the number of retransmissions on each line required because of detected errors. In this way, the center can determine whether a particular circuit is deteriorating before it fails totally. A simpler reporting mechanism for a less sophisticated network is a toll-free WATS number that all network users can call when there is a problem of any sort.

Frequently, when an error occurs in a computer network, it is difficult to discover whether the failure is in the computer or communications portion of the system and whether it is due to hardware or software. One useful diagnostic technique is *loopback* whereby a probing message is sent by the network control center into the network and immediately back to itself. By successively involving more and more network components in handling the message, it may be determined which component is failing by noting when the message fails to return. Modern modems and switching equipment are being constructed to facilitate remote control of the loopback function.

Another useful diagnostic capability for software problems is a way to examine remotely the memory of intelligent devices in the network. Once a failure has been detected and isolated, it must be repaired. Most hardware failures require on-site attention—circuitry may have to be replaced. Many software failures may be remedied remotely or with a minimal amount of on-site assistance by untrained personnel following directions over the telephone.

The foregoing represent some of the ways in which a well-designed and well-managed network control center can improve the overall uptime of a distributed processing network. The need for maintaining a high level of service should be apparent in the distributed applications discussed later in the chapter.

OVERVIEW OF DISTRIBUTED PROCESSING NETWORKS—THIRD-LEVEL SYSTEM

The third-level system of distributed processing goes beyond source data entry, transaction processing, and producing operational and managerial reports at the local or regional level. Instead, its main thrust is directed toward a distributed network that ties together one operational area of an organization, some part of the total organization, or the entire organization. Depending on the level of sophistication within the network, the degree of management control to oversee operations will vary.

At the headquarters level, for example, a distributed processing network permits management to maintain a company-wide inventory and production control system, with the data base segmented according to physical location of materials and processing equipment. Not only is there a central computer to receive and send information to the plants, but also there is a computer at each plant to receive inputs from various operator input terminals, processors, or process sensors. The computer performs the file manipulations necessary to define processing performance, capabilities to fill orders, and the need for inventory replenishment. Communications among the plant computers would not only provide a total picture of corporate production but would also facilitate transferring raw materials and finished goods, smoothing loads and demands, and compensating for unexpected bottlenecks and shutdowns. Similarly, such a distributed network would allow critical information to be forwarded to the appropriate management level for analysis and review—employing the management by exception principle.

At the plant level, the distributed processing network generally implies dedicating small computers to specific tasks and interconnecting machines directly or through the network. Various configurations are possible for such distributed control, depending on plant requirements or preferences. Since distributed systems tend to be modular, each controller has well-defined and relatively restricted functions. Flexibility is high because a complex system can be implemented in stages, with computers integrated into the network as required. Within such a system, the evolution can be downward, beginning with a supervisory or management system and expanding through addition of more highly dedicated control devices. Upward evolution is also feasible by adding networking capabilities to a set of independent dedicated computers. After a network is operating, lateral growth is possible by increasing the amount of computation at diverse points. Thus, a distributed processing network is capable of meeting the needs of the user whether it is within one area or encompassing the entire organization.

An example of a distributed control network is shown in Figure 5-6 where a computer is dedicated to the monitoring and control of each manufacturing process. In operation, a minicomputer might detect that the tank level is too low and perform tests to deduce that the feed-stream valve has failed to close. The program in this minicomputer determines that the tank should be placed on hold by closing the outflow valve, thereby generating the necessary commands. This status condition is transmitted to the supervisory computer—where a scheduling and feedstock allocation program is initiated—to calculate how the remaining tasks should be operated to optimize performance under the given circumstances.

The supervisory computer sends a new set point to the control computer on one of the remaining tanks and down-loads an entire new program to the other. The supervisory computer also notifies the plant computer of the problem; this machine also schedules the necessary maintenance. While these commands are being exchanged, the operator interface computer displays data obtained from the other nodes, accepts and distributes any manual commands, and generates all logs and reports needed by supervisory and management personnel. In effect, the distributed processing network has performed the necessary functions to keep the plant running at a desired level of efficiency and, where necessary, has fed back necessary operational information for correcting problems in the manufacturing process.

While the foregoing approach has centered on optimizing one functional

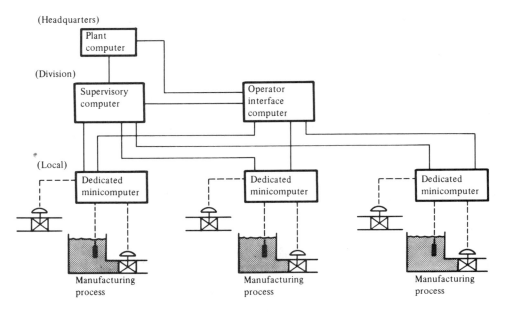

FIGURE 5-6. Overview of a third-level system—a distributed processing network at the production level. (Note: This same network is also applicable to a network for an entire organization—refer to items in parentheses.)

area, it can be expanded to include operations at the division and headquarters levels. As noted in the illustration (Figure 5-6), this distributed processing network, with some modifications, could be representative of the entire organization. Because many networks are structured from the local level to the headquarters level, the applications explored in the next section are presented on this basis.

APPLICATIONS OF DISTRIBUTED PROCESSING— THIRD-LEVEL SYSTEM

In typical distributed network applications, some minicomputers are employed to perform message switching, others to do input/output functions, and still others to carry out arithmetic calculations, and in a complex computer application, the designer configures a system to utilize the unique strengths of each minicomputer. Since a network results whenever two or more of these processors are linked by communication lines, a minicomputer network, in essence, distributes computer functions among its elements according to the most cost-effective arrangement in a specific application. In a similar manner, a computer system may also contain terminals and other input/output devices, but these can be considered network elements only if they possess integrated processors—the intelligent terminal. Other network elements include data concentrators, message switches, front-end processors, and remote job entry stations. Network software, of course, is the key to linking all of these elements. Likewise, it makes the difference between a cluster of computers that act independently and that same cluster integrated into an effective distributed processing system.

Within the third-level system, there are many hardware and software possibilities for a distributed processing environment. As will be seen in the sample applications, various types of equipment can be utilized in a distributed network. These range from intelligent terminals on up to large-sized computers utilizing various operational modes.

Motor Freight Carrier

In a large midwestern city, a motor freight carrier operates a central data processing center for the carrier's regional terminal centers in five large cities. Before the installation of the current distributed processing network, the payroll data had to be keyed in twice, once at the regional level and once at the headquarters level. Time slips had to be checked manually for accuracy of such data as drive time, miles, stops, load weights, and route codes. To eliminate multiple data entry, a processor was placed in each regional center as well as in the central DP center. Currently, payroll data are keyed daily into the regional processors for storage on diskettes; the daily files become the input for the weekly accumulations. The weekly data are then communicated to the central system and merged into a summary payroll file.

As shown in Figure 5-7, this multisite network system processes truckers' payroll at the regional level before transmitting the summary data to the central system. In turn, this system then stores the data on magnetic tape for further exception processing at the central processing center. Nothing is ever keyed more than once. Because the rekeying bottleneck at the central level was eliminated, attention is given to generating detailed reports for management, such as weekly summary reports, driver performance, equipment optimization, route loading comparisons, and overall productivity. With this current managerial information communicated to the operations data processing centers, performance data became available to the appropriate levels of management.

Of the five approaches to structuring a distributed processing network, this application takes a hierarchical approach; that is, the payroll function is linked from the regional processors to the central processor. Although a hierarchy of communications is highlighted in Figure 5-7, processing at these two levels allows operational data to be produced along with managerial reports. Such an approach, then, makes the integration of summary data convenient for both operating purposes and management control.

Medium-Sized Bank

A medium-sized bank, after an exhaustive study of its enitre DP operations, concluded that its current network of centralized DP operations is very expensive. At the hub of this communications system is a large computer system used for on-

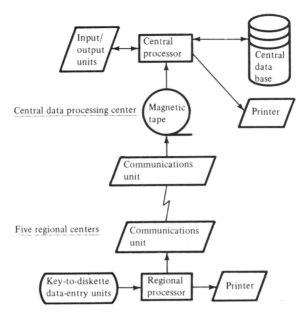

FIGURE 5-7. Hierarchical network of a distributed processing system implemented by a motor freight carrier.

line real-time processing by tellers in all of the bank's branch offices. When the first system fails, processing is switched to a second computer of the same size for continuous real-time processing by bank tellers. It should be noted that the second computer system is regularly used for batch processing until the first computer fails.

Recognizing the need for lower processing costs and reliability of processing for real-time operations by bank tellers, the bank decided to restructure its DP operations along the lines of a fully connected ring network. To achieve this, a software house, working in conjunction with the bank's systems analysts, decided to install a group of four minicomputers to service all banking operations handled by bank tellers. Each minicomputer services 40 bank-teller terminals. Not only can tellers inquire about the status of bank balances, but they also can enter deposit items or deduct items in real-time throughout the day. Thus, several offices will be linked to one minicomputer. In turn, all minicomputers are linked together. This linking of all minicomputers is necessary in order to enable a teller to interrogate the data base for a customer's account located at a location other than that for the one being used. Likewise, all minicomputers are linked to the central banking office. This communication arrangement allows the main computer to post all cleared checks as well as debit and credit items against each account at the end of the banking day, i.e., in the evening. During the day, however, the main computer is busy performing routine and special batch processing functions for the entire bank. Similarly, appropriate reports about bank operations are prepared daily and periodically to meet management needs.

If one of the minicomputers fails for any reason, real-time processing for this specific group of clustered bank terminals can continue by switching processing over to the main computer. Of course, batch processing time will be lengthened for the program being processed since the main computer must perform both real-time and batch processing operations. Although degradation is experienced by the main computer under these circumstances, the study group concluded that processing could be shifted to after hours without much difficulty.

An important benefit from this fully connected distributed network system is the bank's ability to grow without the need to upgrade the central computer system. With this new approach, several new offices can be brought on-line by adding a few more terminals. Since the bank is planning to go a step further and merge its operations with those of two smaller banks in the near future, two additional minicomputers can be added and linked with the other minis as well as to the main computer. Under either condition (growth or merger), the distributed processing network is able to handle the additional volume without degradation to the current system. This point alone has made the conversion to distributed computing very attractive to management. Overall, the network approach to distributed processing has the advantage of facilitating evolutionary development and orderly systems growth.

Consumer Products Company

A consumer products manufacturer found that its current DP system failed to produce timely management information. Based on this shortcoming and others, it decided to undergo a feasibility study which resulted in a decision to install a star network for a distributed processing system. The areas included are *sales, research and development,* and *manufacturing.* As illustrated in Figure 5–8, the communications network provides the mechanism for data communications between programs and devices on different systems and on computers running under different operating systems. And, most importantly, all three functional areas are designed to run on a single network using minicomputers, including a general-purpose computer at central headquarters.

Sales offices which perform sales order processing are widely dispersed. They need to access current inventory information and shipping data. Because individual telephone lines to a central computer are expensive, a communications network is used to reduce line costs. It contains terminal concentrators at local regional centers to send data over high-speed lines to the central system. These data are terminal input or data preinput on disk or tape. Processed sales information can be communicated back to the offices—to terminals or disk storage for later off-line printing, depending on the needs of the sales offices. However, at the highest level, weekly sales data (budget versus actual) are processed on Saturday and are avail-

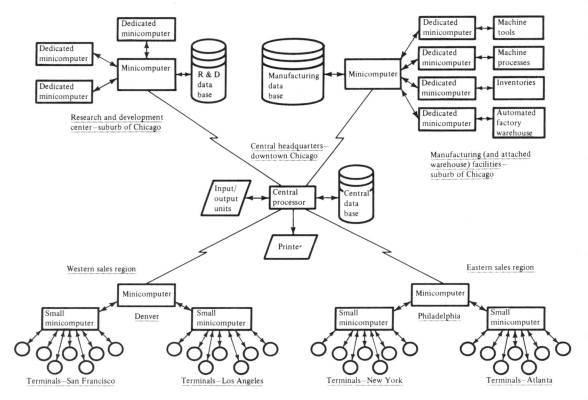

FIGURE 5–8. Star network of a distributed processing system for a consumer products company using minicomputers and a general-purpose computer.

able on Monday morning for evaluation by sales managers at the headquarters level. The ability of the distributed network, then, to provide timely sales reports gives the company "a handle" on where to focus its current sales efforts.

Scientists in the company's research and development center work on laboratory experiments and gather data for analysis. Each lab uses a dedicated minicomputer that includes a console terminal. Scientists use the terminal to edit, compile, and transmit data and programs for storage and execution. The output from these dedicated minis is communicated to the larger-sized minicomputer for processing. In turn, the output is returned to the dedicated minis. When large scientific programs are run, the larger minicomputer is used. In all cases, information on R&D projects at scheduled intervals are forwarded to central headquarters for periodic evaluation. In this manner, management has control from the standpoint of time and cost over R&D projects.

The manufacturing plant which has automated its plant operations controls raw material input, manufacturing machinery, and operations of an automated warehouse (attached to factory) for finished goods storage. Because management wants access to current inventories and stock levels, the star distributed computer network per Figure 5–8 distributes the tasks to individual minicomputers, each specifically designed to handle a function and each in communication with other systems. For example, real-time process control systems monitor the actual manufacturing operations, and these are linked to a supervisory system that controls the overall parts flow. In turn, the supervisor computer (large-sized minicomputer) sends critical manufacturing operational data for management control to central headquarters. Due to the size of the data base in such a distributed processing system, the central processor at headquarters utilizes a data base management system.

As indicated above, organizationally, the distributed star network entails a heavy flow of data back and forth between the central processor and those minicomputers for the three functional areas—sales, R&D, and manufacturing. However, for data that originate at a lower level, they must pass through another level before their summary contents are communicated to the central processor. When necessary, detailed and summary data are forwarded to the appropriate functional area from the headquarters level. Overall, the central processor acts as a receiver of data and a communicator of information as deemed necessary for the appropriate application.

CHAPTER SUMMARY

Networking within a distributed processing environment provides a great deal of flexibility for DP management. Distributed networks make it possible to substitute, add, or modify procedures by changing autonomous modules within a system at a low cost, thereby bypassing traditional risks encountered when altering monolithic structures. Networking also facilitates phased implementation. A system can accordingly be brought on-line gradually, in useful segments, each of which can be individually justified, tested, and operated. In addition, phased implementation protects investments in hardware and software since new configurations are extensions of existing systems. Almost any device with enough logic to recognize an address, accumulate data, and respond to simple digital commands can be made to act as a node in a distributed processing system.

The future of computer networks is particularly bright because LSI microprocessor chips are inexpensive enough to be integrated into a vast number of products and powerful enough to qualify as network nodes. Since the telephone network already extends into virtually every office and home in the country, the means is already at hand for business machines as ubiquitous as the typewriter or office copier to be integrated into vast intelligent reticular structures, i.e., to transmit status reports, to receive operating commands, and to bring previously unimaginable types of intelligence directly to the points of use. This mode of operation will be evident in Part IV, where we shall be dealing with future directions in distributed processing systems.

QUESTIONS

1. Under what circumstances should a dedicated communications network be used? Explain.

2. What types of network architecture are generally found in a distributed processing system? Why?

3. a. Differentiate between partitioned and replicated data bases.
   b. What is the major problem with each type?

4. How important is the network control center in a typical distributed network? Explain.

5. What techniques are available to managers of network control centers for maintaining reliable network operations?

6. Give at least one example of a distributed processing network at the third-system level.

SELECTED REFERENCES

Auberbach Editorial Staff, "What Is Network Architecture?" *Computer Decisions,* June 1976.

Bizarro, L. A., "Networking Computers for Process Control," *Chemical Engineering,* Dec. 6, 1976.

Booth, G. M., "Distributed Information Systems," *AFIPS Conference Proceedings* (National Computer Conference), Vol. 45, 1976.

Buckley, J. E., "Shared User Networks," *Computer Design,* June 1977.

Caswell, S., "Satellite Business Systems: The Start of Something Big," *Computer Decisions,* March 1977.

Chou, W., "Planning and Design of Data Communications Networks," *AFIPS Conference Proceedings* (National Computer Conference), Vol. 43, 1974.

Cotton, I. W., "Network Control Centers," *Computer Decisions,* Sept. 1976.

——, "Network Security," *Computer Decisions,* April 1977.

——, "Minicomputers in Networks," *Computer Decisions,* May 1977.

Doll, D. R., "Relating Networks to Three Kinds of Distributed Function," *Data Communications,* March 1977.

Fidlow, D., "System Trade-Offs: Dedicated and Dialed Networks," *Datamation,* April 1973.

Foster, J. D., "Distributive Processing for Banking," *Datamation,* July 1976.

Fotts, H. C., and Cotton, I. W., "Interfaces: New Standards Catch up with Technology," *Data Communications,* June 1977.

Foy, N., and Helgason, W., "Europe Claims the Lead in Banking," *Datamation,* July 1976.

Glover, R., and Klingman, D., "A Practitioner's Guide to the State of Large

Scale Network and Network-Related Problems," *AFIPS Conference Proceedings* (National Computer Conference), Vol. 45, 1976.

Held, G., "Sharing the Line: A Cheaper Way than Multiplexers," *Data Communications,* March 1977.

Hunter, J. J., "Distributing a Database," *Computer Decisions,* June 1976.

Jensen, F. J., "Centralization or Decentralization in Banking?," *Datamation,* July 1976.

Kallis, S. A., Jr., "Network and Distributed Processing," *Mini-Micro Systems,* March 1977.

Kaufman, F., "Distributed Processing—A Discussion for Executives Traveling over Difficult EDP Terrain," New York: Coopers & Lybrand, 1977.

Kelley, N., "Bank of America Goes Distributive, " *Infosystems,* March 1977.

Kershenbaum, A., "Tools for Designing and Planning Data Communications Networks," *AFIPS Conference Proceedings* (National Computer Conference), Vol. 43, 1974.

Levin, K. D., and Morgan, E., "Optimizing Distributed Data Bases—A Framework for Research," *AFIPS Conference Proceedings* (National Computer Conference), Vol. 44, 1975.

Lynch, A., "Distributed Processing Solves Mainframe Problems," *Data Communications,* Nov.–Dec. 1976.

Malhotra, R., "Interactive Monitors in a Distributed System," *AFIPS Conference Proceedings* (National Computer Conference), Vol. 44, 1975.

Martin J., *Principles of Data-Base Management,* Englewood Cliffs, N.J.: Prentice-Hall, Inc., 1976.

——, *Telecommunications and the Computer,* Englewood Cliffs, N.J.: Prentice-Hall, Inc., 1976.

——, *Computer Data Base Organization,* Englewood Cliffs, N.J.: Prentice-Hall, Inc., 1977.

Masi, C., and MacDonald, A., "Wang on Distributed Data Processing," Lowell, Mass: Wang Laboratories, Inc., 1976.

McKenzie, A. M., "Some Computer Network Interconnection Issues," *AFIPS Conference Proceedings* (National Computer Conference), Vol. 43, 1974.

Mills, D. L., "An Overview of the Distributed Computer Network," *AFIPS Conference Proceedings* (National Computer Conference), Vol. 45, 1976.

Newton, N., "What's the Word on Data Communications," *Computer Decisions,* Dec. 1976.

Ratner, S., "Arponet Concept Used at Citibank for Dedicated Net," *Data Communications,* June 1977.

Reiser, R., "Interactive Modeling of Computer Systems," *IBM Systems Journal,* Nov. 4, 1976.

Russell, R. M., "Approaches to Network Design," *Computer Decisions,* June 1976.

Schwartz, M., *Computer Communication Network Design and Analysis*, Englewood Cliffs, N.J.: Prentice-Hall, Inc., 1975.

Severino, E. F., "Database and Distributed Processing," *Computer Decisions*, March 1977.

Simonette, I., "Ring in Distributed Computing," *Computer Decisions*, Jan. 1976.

Swartwant, D. E., Deppe, M. E., and Fry, J. P., "Operational Software for Restructuring Network Databases," *AFIPS Conference Proceedings* (National Computer Conference), Vol. 46, 1977.

Taulbee, O. E., Treu, S., and Nehnevajsa, J., "User Orientation in Networking," *AFIPS Conference Proceedings* (National Computer Conference), Vol. 44, 1975.

Wyatt, J. B., and Polley, V. I., "Network Interface Systems—An Evaluation by Simulation," *AFIPS Conference Proceedings* (National Computer Conference), Vol. 45, 1976.

part three

CASE STUDY OF CURRENT DISTRIBUTED PROCESSING SYSTEMS

SELECTED DISTRIBUTED PROCESSING SUBSYSTEMS— AMERICAN PRODUCTS CORPORATION

6

As emphasized in Part II, distributed processing systems evolved from centralized systems, and they represent the ultimate in that evolution. In many organizations, large central computers have become unwieldy, and their efficiency is being undermined by the extent and complexity of the software required by the variety and complexity of applications. However, the availability of data communications facilities as well as the increasing capabilities and low costs of minicomputers and intelligent terminals are strong inducements for company management to deploy their processing resources out to the remote, i.e., local or regional, centers that generate and need the information. Thus, the application of distributed processing is quite feasible today.

Building upon these important aspects of distributed processing systems, in Part III we shall concentrate on the design aspects of selected functional areas or subsystems. Basically, the American Products Corporation—a typical manufacturing company—is utilized throughout this chapter and the next four chapters to exemplify what comprises the essentials of a distributed processing system at the local and central processing levels.

Initially, we shall present a brief background on the American Products Corporation before concentrating on the selected subsystems, namely, marketing, manufacturing, physical distribution, and accounting. In contrast, other subsystems could have been included, that is, corporate planning, research and development, engineering, inventory, purchasing, finance, and personnel. However, space does not warrant such a detailed presentation.

AMERICAN PRODUCTS CORPORATION

The American Products Corporation is a company specializing in the manufacture of products for the consumer market. The firm's sales are currently $95 million per annum and are projected to be about $120 to $125 million in five years. Its product line consists of 15 products which can be categorized into three basic product groups. Variations of these basic products are for specific customers whose requirements differ owing to the markets they serve. For large orders, products are shipped directly to retailers from the firm's manufacturing plants. All other orders are shipped from the firm's warehouses to the many retailers. Experience has shown that 20 percent of the firm's dollar volume represents direct shipments from the plants and 80 percent represents shipments through the firm's warehouses.

Corporate headquarters are located in St. Louis; manufacturing plants are found in Minneapolis, Philadelphia, and Los Angeles. Wherever a manufacturing plant is located, a warehouse is attached. The present employment level for the entire organization is approximately 2000 employees.

As shown in the organization chart (Figure 6-1), the president and chief executive officer reports to the board of directors and is assisted by the corporate planning group. The executive vice president, in turn, reports to the president. In a similar manner, nine vice presidents (marketing, research and development and engineering, manufacturing, purchasing and inventory, physical distribution, accounting, finance, personnel, and management information system) report to the executive vice president. Various corporate headquarters managers, plant managers, and warehouse managers report to their respective vice presidents.

The American Products Corporation has progressed through a series of data processing systems limited by the constraints of available equipment. Many years ago, manual systems were augmented by adding machines and calculators. Punched card equipment and tabulating machines provided expanded system capabilities. As electronic computers became available, the data processing system was adapted to utilize these machines, making the translation of data into information much faster. Also, the computer provided capacity for the development of new applications. Presently, the firm uses an integrated management information system (batch-processing-oriented) which is being converted to a distributed processing system (interactive-processing-oriented). The problem encountered with the integrated MIS was that information (for management and nonmanagement purposes) was not

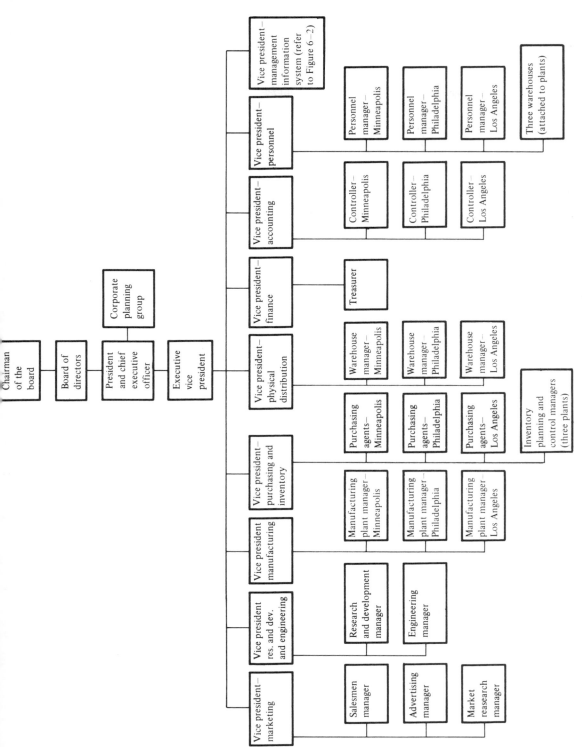

FIGURE 6-1. Organization chart of the American Products Corporation.

sufficiently timely to effect changes in the current operating environment. Too often, information was received too late by corporate headquarters to effect the necessary control over manufacturing and warehousing operations. Thus, the batch processing mode of the integrated MIS whereby data are collected for a period of time before being processed and summarized did not facilitate optimal day-to-day decision making.

Because of this problem with the integrated MIS, it became apparent that a company-wide information system had to be developed. What is needed is a forward-looking control system that promotes operational control in an interactive processing mode. Because a distributed processing system is capable of accomplishing such a goal, the MIS vice president initiated a feasibility study. The study disclosed the feasibility of distributed computing, i.e., an interactive-oriented management information system, after giving consideration to tangible benefits and, more importantly, intangible benefits. Specifically, the more important reasons for implementing a management-oriented distributed processing system that centers on an interactive processing mode are

- better customer service and improved selling efficiency
- more timely and improved management information analysis and reporting at the plant and home office levels
- improved coordination and control of the overall organization and its individual parts
- better opportunity to match demand with production
- on-line information available from a distributed data base for management analysis of the organization's operations and prospective operations

DATA PROCESSING ORGANIZATION STRUCTURE

The data processing organization chart in a distributed computing environment is illustrated in Figure 6-2 for the American Products Corporation. The systems and programming manager and the computer operations manager report directly to the vice president of the management information system. On the systems side, systems analysts and programming supervisors report to the systems and programming manager. Generally, the systems and programming positions are unchanged from the prior system, with the exception that program development and testing can take place in a user/machine mode by utilizing one of the many on-line CRT devices. From an operational viewpoint, the CRT terminal supervisors, the computer supervisors, and the internal auditor (from the accounting department) report to the computer operations manager. Unlike systems and programming, several organizational changes from the previous systems are applicable to the operations area. The CRT terminal supervisors control on-line CRT and hard-copy units at corporate headquarters, the plants, and the warehouses. The computer supervisors control the computer's operators, data entry personnel, and servicemen. Thus, the

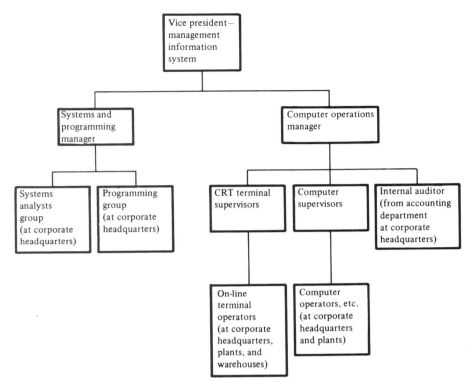

FIGURE 6–2. Data processing organization in a distributed processing environment for the American Products Corporation.

interactive capabilities of the new system involve more advanced equipment which must be supervised for effective control.

Although the specific positions and levels of systems work are clearly set forth (Figure 6-2), the systems project cannot be delegated completely to analysts who are asked to find "the answer." The firm's management must work closely with systems designers to create an awareness of value systems and premises used in planning and decision making. Top management must exert leadership, and operating managers must actively cooperate with computer specialists in order to form an effective team to implement the new distributed processing system. Only when the firm's managers get involved, cooperate with data processing specialists, and relate their problems to the computer's capabilities can objectives be fully realized for the American Products Corporation. Similarly, the firm's systems designers need to communicate and work with the operating people on the detailed methods and procedures of the new system. This is necessary in order to determine how exceptions and problems are to be handled. Also cooperation is needed to evaluate realistically the decision-making process at the local and the central head-quarters levels and the necessary information flow for that process. Systems analysts and programmers must work with people above or below them as well as on the same level for effective results because the firm's managers and operating personnel generally will accept only methods and procedures that they fully comprehend.

DISTRIBUTED PROCESSING SYSTEM ENVIRONMENT

Based on the feasibility study mentioned above, the company has selected a computer system that integrates satellite minicomputers at each of the three manufacturing plants, including the attached warehouses, with a centralized computer system. Within this hardware configuration, there is an environment of cooperating software, thereby allowing the organization to distribute its data base at the appropriate level and application programs among the remote locations.

An examination of Figure 6–3 indicates that a hierarchical or tree network is utilized by the American Products Corporation. Essentially, the central or host

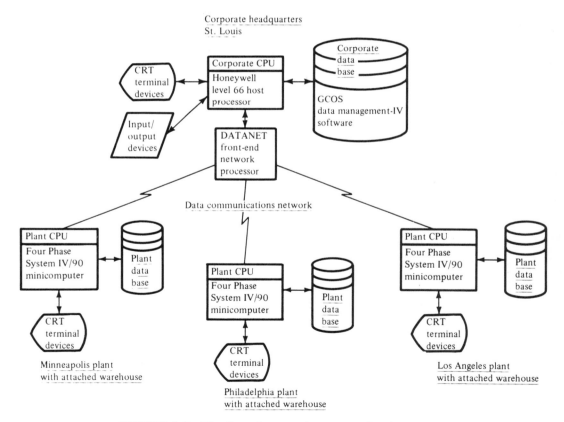

FIGURE 6–3. Distributed processing system for the American Products Corporation.

FIGURE 6–4. Honeywell Level 66 Computer System at corporate headquarters in St. Louis—American Products Corporation. (Courtesy Honeywell Information Systems.)

computer is a Honeywell Level 66 computer (Figure 6–4) that employs a DATA-NET front-end network processor for controlling all input from the three satellite minicomputers—Four Phase System IV/90, capable of supporting up to 32 video displays (Figure 6–5). Currently, at each of the plants with attached warehouses, 4 terminals are being installed for use by sales order processing plus 4 for accounting. In a similar manner, 14 are in the process of being installed for manufacturing and physical distribution. The employment of these CRT terminals, some of which have printers, is the subject matter for the next four chapters. A typical configuration of CRT display stations with printers is illustrated in Figure 6–6.

The executive software for the Honeywell Level 66 Computer System is GCOS (General Comprehensive Operating Software), which controls, schedules, and monitors all activities and adjusts processing activity to changing demands. Processing modes include transaction processing, data base inquiry, time sharing, interactive job entry and execution, and batch processing. These modes are available at the central site and remotely via Level 66 communication facilities, using the corporate data base.

For this distributed processing environment, the Data Management-IV (DM-IV) is used because the Level 66 data base management system is designed for high-volume on-line transaction processing and efficient, interactive remote query and

FIGURE 6–5. Four Phase System IV/90, capable of supporting up to 32 video displays, at each of the three manufacturing plants with attached warehouses—American Products Corporation. (Courtesy Four Phase Systems, Inc.)

reporting. It uses a common language for defining, managing, and directing data and provides a standard user interface that is simple and logical. Additionally, it allows a common file description to govern the structure of all data but is independent of that structure. In effect, DM-IV gives organizational personnel timely access to vital information and provides data integrity protection, security, and automatic recovery and restart.

DATA COMMUNICATIONS NETWORK

The data communications network for implementing a distributed operating environment was determined during the equipment selection phase of the feasibility study. It is a full duplex system that links all of the firm's plants, including ware-

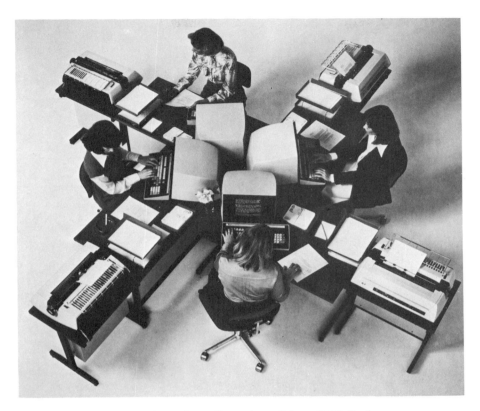

FIGURE 6-6. Typical configuration of four CRT displays with printers for sales order processing or accounting functions at each plant level with attached warehouse. (Courtesy Four Phase Systems, Inc.)

houses, to the corporate headquarters in St. Louis. The full duplex communication channels have the ability to transmit information in both directions simultaneously. In addition, all communication lines from and to corporate headquarters are full dedicated lines—that is, it is not necessary to telephone in order to reserve a communication line from the plants, including warehouses, to corporate headquarters or vice versa. This approach for relaying information back and forth simplifies data communications for the DATANET front-end processor.

OVERVIEW OF MAJOR SUBSYSTEMS

From an overview standpoint, the American Products Corporation can be described as a *materials-flow company*. This concept for the three manufacturing plants is illustrated in Figure 6–7, shown as a double-line arrow on the outer rim of the system flowchart. Purchased materials and manufactured materials for stock flow

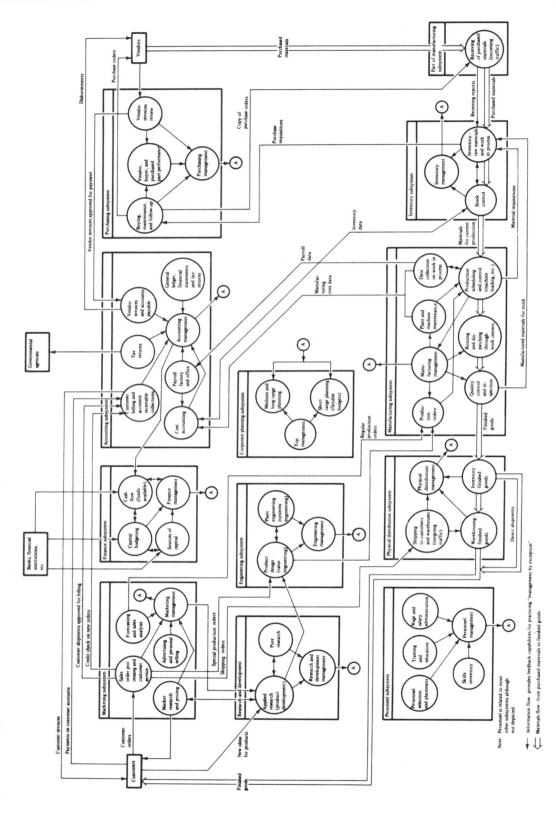

FIGURE 6-7. System flowchart depicting the major subsystems for the American Products Corporation—a typical manufacturing firm.

into the various stages of the production process; as they do, the materials take on a variety of forms and shapes until they become finished goods. Next, the finished products flow through the distribution system either directly via direct shipments or indirectly through company-owned warehouses until they reach the customer. Thus, in this materials-flow concept, several of the corporation's subsystems are involved, namely, purchasing, inventory, manufacturing, and physical distribution.

Coupled with materials flow is their corresponding information flow (Figure 6–7). Materials-flow information is a most important factor in coordinating the diversified activities of the three manufacturing plants and attached warehouses with corporate headquarters. It must be comprehensive, thereby integrating decision making throughout the entire materials-flow process—from purchased materials to shipment of finished goods. With this integrated flow of essential information, management and operating personnel can make adjustments swiftly and effectively in response to the ever-changing business environment. The materials-flow approach, then, is an essential part of the distributed processing system for the American Products Corporation (or any firm, for that matter).

The information flow is not restricted to the materials area only. In fact, there may well be more information being generated for activities that are not related directly to the materials-flow process. For example, many subparts of the corporation's corporate planning, marketing, research and development, engineering, accounting, and finance subsystems are not related directly to the manufacture of the final product. No matter what the source or need of information is, the overall distributed processing system must be "open-ended." This approach provides flexibility such that activities can be linked with one another at minimum cost and effort. But more importantly, the open-ended approach allows for changing the direction and speed of information flow in response to management and operating personnel needs. More will be said about the information flow for selected subsystems in the following sections.

To illustrate the concept of information flow, the quarterly sales forecast (marketing subsystem), based on external and internal factors, affects the quantity of finished goods to be produced (physical distribution subsystem), which, in turn, affects materials to be purchased from outside suppliers (purchasing subsystem) and to be manufactured within the firm (manufacturing subsystem) by future planning periods. Goods purchased or manufactured are procured on an optimum basis by using the economic order quantity (EOQ) formula and are eventually handled by the inventory section (inventory subsystem). Both are requisitioned to meet the manufacturing plan in accordance with the schedule of master operations (manufacturing subsystem). The operational or shop status of the final product, material, labor, and similar items is used for operations evaluation control at the manufacturing level. In some cases, operating information is significant enough for review by middle and top management. If this happens, feedback at this level of importance may make it necessary to review future plans (corporate planning subsystem). Also, it may be necessary to revise future sales forecasts. Finally, finished goods are shipped directly to the customers or through plant-attached warehouses.

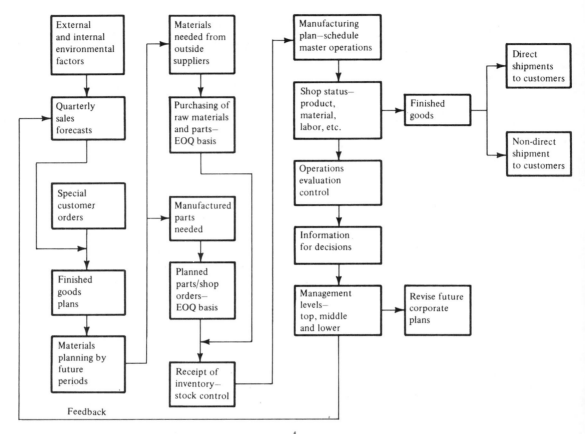

FIGURE 6-8. The integrated flow of information for the American Products Corporation from the external and internal environmental phase to actual day-to-day operations whereby output from one subsystem becomes input to another subsystem.

This foregoing flow of information from one subsystem to another—in particular, from external and internal environmental factors through shipped goods to customers or plant-attached warehouses—is depicted in Figure 6-8.

Due to space limitations, all of the major subsystems for the American Products Corporation, as set forth in Figure 6-7 and the above, are not explored in a distributed processing environment. Rather, only the basic subsystems found in the American Products Corporation are discussed below and in the following chapters, namely, marketing, manufacturing, physical distributions, and accounting. The analysis and design of these selected subsystems serve to highlight the interrelationships of local processing (plants with attached warehouses) to centralized processing (corporate headquarters).

MARKETING SUBSYSTEM

The firm's marketing subsystem consists of several modules (subparts). The more important ones are depicted in Figure 6-7 and are as follows:

1. forecasting and sales analysis
2. sales order processing and customer service
3. advertising and personal selling
4. market research and pricing

These major components are covered in Chapter 7 from a distributed computing viewpoint. Basically, quarterly sales forecasting was treated previously on an integrated subsystem basis. Similarly, sales order processing is treated below.

Common sales order processing problems are encountered when designing a distributed processing system. It should be designed to answer these questions:

- Can this order be accepted?
- Does the firm want to accept the order?
- When is the order actually a sale?
- Where is the order entered?
- When do the finished goods belong to the customer?
- How much is to be charged for finished goods and when?

Other questions of the same type must be asked relating to this area for effective systems design.

In Figure 6-9 (as well as Figure 6-7), orders are received from customers. Appropriate order forms are prepared and edited before the customer credit is checked. If the order is not accepted because of poor credit, it is returned to the customer and the reason is noted. Generally, the order is approved for order entry whereby appropriate files (customer, pricing, and finished goods) are referenced for preparing shipping papers. Shipping papers are forwarded to the appropriate warehouses for regular shipment or to a particular plant for direct shipment.

At this point, other major subsystems interact with sales order processing (marketing subsystem). Shipping papers provide the basis for preparing customer invoices which are eventually utilized for aging accounts receivable and processing checks received from customers (accounting subsystem). In addition, they are used for assembling goods at the warehouse and plant levels. If items are available for shipment as noted by the perpetual finished goods file during the sales order processing phase, the file is changed from "finished goods on order" to "finished goods shipped" (physical distribution subsystem). Engineering also comes into contact with sales order processing through the receipt of special customer orders (engineering subsystem).

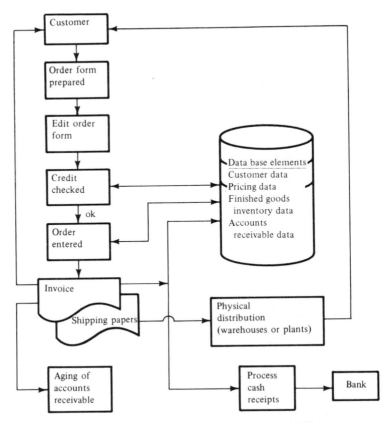

FIGURE 6-9. Sales order processing—an essential part of the marketing subsystem (American Products Corporation).

MANUFACTURING SUBSYSTEM

The next important subsystem for getting regular or special production orders produced is manufacturing. Its essential modules for the illustrated firm are the following (Figure 6-7):

1. receiving

2. production scheduling and control

3. manufacturing operations:
   a. machine shop
   b. assembly—major and minor
   c. plant and machine maintenance

4. quality control and inspection

5. data collection system

An analysis of these components within a distributed processing environment is presented in Chapter 8.

Common questions that must be handled by the distributed processing system are

- How much finished goods should be manufactured at one time?
- What raw materials are required where and when?
- What is the progress of job orders?
- How much work-in-process inventory is needed and where?
- What are the production schedules, and how are they being met?
- Have the finished goods been completed and/or shipped?
- What are the manufacturing cost variances?

Generally, these typical questions can be answered with relative ease by a distributed processing system.

The manufacturing process is a continuation of prior subsystems for forecasted finished goods marketing subsystem. As shown in Figure 6-10 (reference can also be made to Figure 6-8), raw materials are ordered on a quarterly basis (purchasing subsystem) and, upon receipt, are placed under the supervision of stock control (inventory subsystem). They provide input for the manufacturing plan of the production scheduling and control section, whose job is to schedule, route, and dispatch orders through the various manufacturing work centers. The quality control section is responsible for making appropriate tests of manufactured and finished products before forwarding them to the warehouse or customer (physical dsitribution subsystem). As illustrated, there is an interplay between physical activities and data files for operations evaluation, allowing feedback of critical information where deemed necessary.

PHYSICAL DISTRIBUTION SUBSYSTEM

The handling of finished goods after manufacturing is the responsibility of the physical distribution subsystem. Its modules (Figure 6-7) include

1. shipping to customers and warehouses (outgoing traffic)
2. warehousing—finished goods
3. inventory—finished goods

These principal areas will be presented in Chapter 9.

The manufacturing process culminates in having the finished goods transported from one of the three manufacturing plants to the customers directly (direct shipments) or to one or more of the plant-attached warehouses (nondirect shipments). To keep overall shipping costs for the firm at a minimum, the system designed must be capable of responding to these questions:

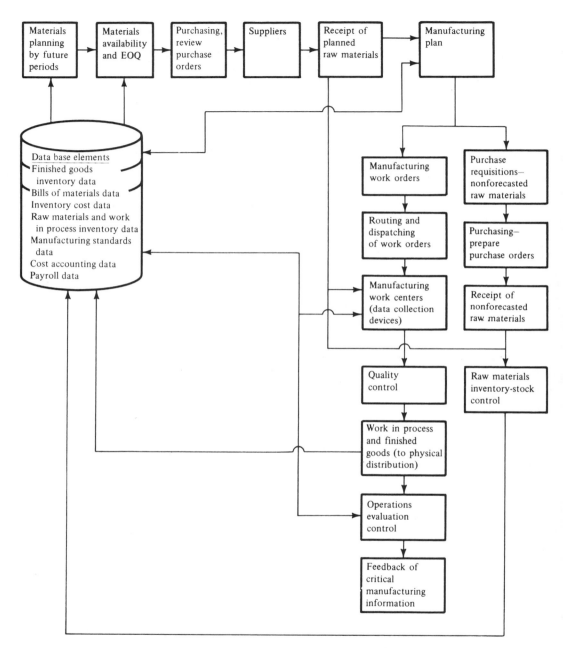

FIGURE 6–10. Manufacture of work in process and finished goods—important functions of the
manufacturing, inventory, and purchasing
subsystems (American Products Corporation).

- Can finished goods be allocated to warehouses such that customer orders can be filled promptly?

- Can procedures be devised such that the appropriate quantities desired by customers are in the nearest warehouse to reduce shipping costs?

- If goods are not available at the closest warehouse, are there procedures for locating goods at the next closest warehouse almost instantaneously?

- Does the physical distribution system keep overall costs at a minimum?

These sample questions can be answered with a well-designed distributed processing system.

The shipment of finished goods, whether they be direct or nondirect, must be reflected in the company's data files. Likewise, certain file data on routing finished goods are utilized in effecting the lowest total costs. In addition, these files, as shown in Figure 6-11, are referenced when finished goods are shipped to customers

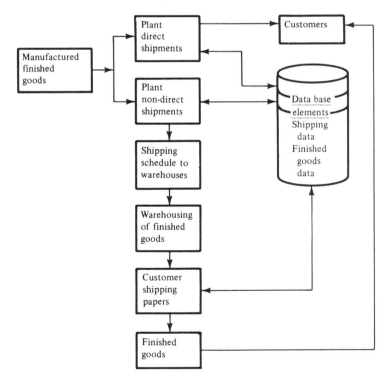

FIGURE 6-11. Distribution of finished goods from plants to warehouses and customers—the main function of the physical distribution subsystem (American Products Corporation).

via order processing (marketing subsystem). As shown in Figure 6-9 previously, shipping papers, initiated by the physical distribution subsystem, start the customer billing and collection process (accounting subsystem).

ACCOUNTING SUBSYSTEM

The sales and cost factors, generated by the previous subsystems, are accounted for and reported by the accounting subsystem. They provide the required inputs for the accounting modules (Figure 6-7), which are

1. receivables and payables
2. payroll
3. cost accounting
4. financial statements and tax returns

In Chapter 10, these accounting components are discussed within a distributed operating mode.

   The accounting subsystem, which involves keeping records, billing customers, arranging payments, and costing products, among others, is a myriad of details. For accounting information to assist other subsystems, it must focus on answers to these timely questions:

- Can actual cost data be compared to standard data for the various manufacturing work centers?
- Can information on the current status of customer accounts be obtained on a "now" basis?
- Is all accounting data in a machine-processible form for compiling current financial statements?

Such an approach is found in a distributed processing system for answering these typical accounting questions.

   Generally, accounting activities as set forth in Figure 6-12, center on those of recording and reporting sales and costs (expenses). Sales revenue and manufacturing cost data—raw materials, labor, and overhead—as well as marketing and general and administrative expenses provide the necessary inputs per the general ledger for producing periodic—overall and detailed—income statements. Cash, receivables, payables, and other accounts are recorded in the general ledger for producing the balance sheet. These financial statements provide inputs for intermediate and long-range analysis (corporate planning subsystem). In a similar manner, detailed income and cost (expense) analyses are helpful in determining future cash flow and capital budgets (finance subsystem).

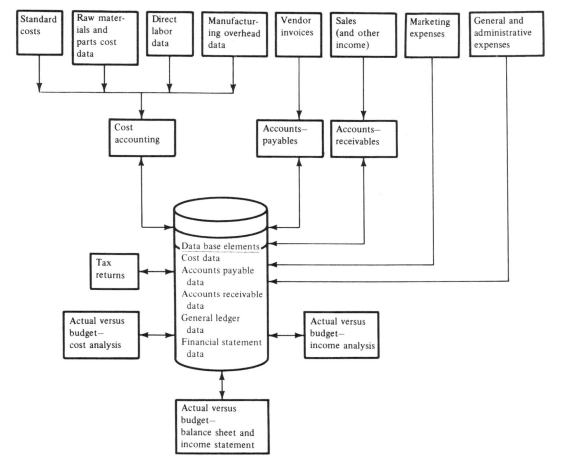

FIGURE 6-12. Sales and cost data—essential components of the accounting subsystem (American Products Corporation).

CHAPTER SUMMARY

Essentially, we have focused on an overview of the American Products Corporation in a distributed system environment. Selected subsystems were treated on an integrated basis, indicating the direction taken in subsequent chapters. From this viewpoint, the feasibility of implementing an effective distributed processing system is validated.

Distributed computing, as pointed out repeatedly in this chapter, represents the flow of information through the organization. It is structured such that information flows from one subsystem to another in order to provide the information when and where it is needed. In a real sense, distributed processing represents the internal communications network of the business, providing the necessary intelligence to organize, direct, and control according to corporate plans at the appropriate level. Stated another way, it is a reorientation of traditional information flow from a basic purpose of recording what happened to a new purpose of telling not only what happened but also how and why it happened at a particular level, the amount of deviations from the plans, and the effect on the plans. A history-keeping orientation is replaced by a management planning and control orientation at the appropriate level, i.e., local and central. Distributed processing, then, utilizes plans, policies, methods, procedures, and control guidelines; mixes these with people; adds integrated operating information; and comes out with the organized use of data for better decisions at the appropriate level.

QUESTIONS

1. Suppose the American Products Corporation was a much larger firm. Would the data processing organization structure change in a distributed processing environment?

2. Suggest an alternative way of setting up the hardware environment for the American Products Corporation in a distributed processing mode.

3. What problems are expected to be encountered by the American Products Corporation when it changes from an integrated MIS to a distributed processing system?

4. What characteristics are found in a distributed processing environment for the American Products Corporation that are not present in integrated MIS?

5. What changes from an integrated MIS must be undertaken to design an effective distributed processing system for the American Products Corporation?

6. Do the various subsystems and the component modules presented in this chapter differ in a distributed processing system from an integrated MIS for the American Products Corporation? How?

7. Suggest additional modules for each of the subsystems presented in this chapter for the American Products Corporation.

8. Can a distributed processing system be implemented for very large corporations, such as AT&T and General Motors?

SELECTED REFERENCES

Barlow, G., "Development of Online Processing," *Computer Decisions,* May 1974.

Cornish, F. B., "Management Information Systems—Cause and Effect," *Managerial Planning,* Jan.–Feb. 1971.

Couger, J. D., and Wergin, L. M., "Small Company MIS," *Infosystems,* Oct. 1974.

Gammill, R. C., and Shukiar, H. J., "An Interactive System for Aiding Management Decision Making," *AFIPS Conference Proceedings* (National Computer Conference), Vol. 46, 1977.

Gildersleeve, T. R., "Organizing the Data Processing Function," *Datamation,* Nov. 1974.

Haavind, R., "Adding People to the MIS Loop," *Computer Decisions,* July 1972.

Hansen, J. P., "Minis in Distributed Networks," *Infosystems,* Jan. 1977.

Head, R. V., "Real-Time Applications," *Journal of Systems Management,* Sept. 1974.

Hindman, W. R., "Integrated MIS: A Case Study," *Management Accounting,* Aug. 1973.

Hodge, B., "The Computer in Management Information and Control System," *Data Management,* Dec. 1974.

Huhn, G. E., "The Data Base in a Critical On-Line Business Environment," *Datamation,* Sept. 1974.

Jones, J. R., "Distributed Processing—Age of the Application Analyst," *Infosystems,* June 1977.

Karp, H. R., "System Network Architecture—Building Blocks to Support Future Business," *Data Communiation,* Jan.–Feb. 1976.

Kneitel, A., "DuPont Is Doing Things with MIS," *Infosystems,* Feb. 1977.

Lowe, R. L., "The Corporate Datacenter: Getting It All Together," *Computer Decisions,* May 1973.

Nolan, R. L., and Knutsen, K. E., "The Computerization of the ABC Widget Company," *Datamation*, April 1974.

Reside, K. D. and Seiter, T. J., "The Evolution of an Integrated Data Base," *Datamation,* Sept. 1974.

Sayer, W., "Galion: Blueprint for a Total Management System," *Modern Office Procedures,* Feb. 1970.

Seese, D. A., "Initiating a Total Information System," *Journal of Systems Management,* April 1970.

Tersine, R. J., "Systems Theory in Modern Organizations," *Managerial Planning,* Nov.–Dec. 1973.

Thierauf, R. J., *Systems Analysis and Design of Real-Time Management Information Systems,* Englewood Cliffs, N.J.: Prentice-Hall, Inc., 1975.

Zani, W. M., "Blueprint for MIS," *Harvard Business Review,* Nov.–Dec. 1970.

DISTRIBUTED PROCESSING MARKETING SUBSYSTEM— AMERICAN PRODUCTS CORPORATION

7

Initially, the essential parts of an integrated MIS marketing subsystem are set forth for the American Products Corporation. As will be evident throughout the first part of the chapter, data input for order processing are keypunched and key-verified at the corporate level. In contrast, order processing functions in a distributed processing environment are performed in an interactive processing mode at the local or plant level. Such a presentation gives the reader an opportunity to compare the prior batch-oriented system with a distributed processing system.

The chapter is structured using the marketing modules set forth in the prior chapter, namely,

- forecasting and sales analysis
- sales order processing and customer service
- advertising and personal selling
- market research and pricing

This approach provides a logical framework for reviewing the current batch processing system and designing the major marketing modules for the American Products Corporation in a distributed processing environment.

As will be apparent throughout the discussion in this chapter and succeeding ones, emphasis will be placed on processing data at the local or plant level, if possible, and forwarding summary data to central headquarters in St. Louis. However, in certain situations, data are processed only at the headquarters level.

OVERVIEW OF MARKETING ENVIRONMENT

The marketing subsystem, the prime source of determining what must be accomplished presently, is controlled by the corporate planning subsystem. Its major functional subparts, shown in Figure 7-1, are the same for integrated MIS as well as for distributed processing. They include forecasting and sales analysis, sales order processing and customer service, advertising and personal selling, and market research and pricing. However, their design for distributed processing will take on an added dimension because of the interactive processing ability. Marketing data will be stored on the appropriate data base, retrievable as is or manipulated depending on the user's needs. This added dimension to obtain current and exception marketing information via an I/O terminal device means information will be available much sooner. From this user/machine operating mode, corrective measures deemed necessary can be effected faster because of immediate feedback. Thus, interactive design requirements for such an environment are more stringent and difficult to coordinate than in a batch processing operating mode.

From an overview standpoint, both the integrated management information system and the distributed processing system will process forecasting, sales analysis, advertising, personal selling, market research, and pricing data at the corporate level only. However, sales order processing and customer service will be off-loaded from the corporate level to the plant level in a distributed processing environment. In this manner, an improved level of customer service will result from faster shipment and more accurate handling of customer orders.

INTEGRATED MIS MARKETING SUBSYSTEM

Input for the integrated MIS marketing subsystem of the American Products Corporation is from the firm's customers. Not only are orders received from customers, but marketing efforts are also focused on them, as illustrated in Figure 7-1. The firm's marketing executives derive their information about customers and the marketplace through marketing intelligence, formal market research, and company accounting information. *Marketing intelligence* activity describes the continuous effort to keep informed about current developments among customers, competing products, and the marketing environment. In a similar manner, *market research* centers on a more formal approach to current developments—in particular,

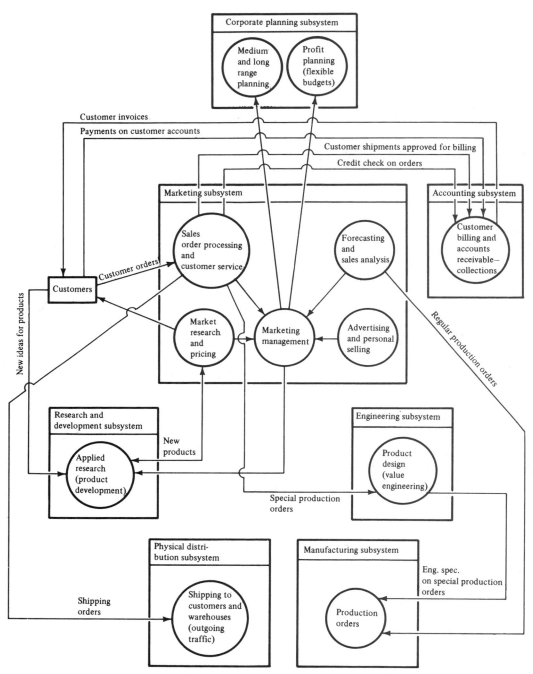

FIGURE 7-1. Marketing subsystem flow to and from other subsystems—American Products Corporation.

project-oriented research. The *company accounting system* generates sales and cost information in order to complement marketing intelligence and research.

The primary job of the marketing department is to contact potential customers and sell merchandise through advertising, personal selling, and special promotion. If products are sold, a multicopy *sales order* is originated by a salesman or the order section of the marketing department. Copies are distributed as follows: original copy to customer for acknowledging order, duplicate copies to the salesman and other departments as needed. The marketing department prepares other forms, such as *contracts, bids, back orders,* and *change orders.* No matter what form is involved, the marketing department starts the product information flow in the firm.

The basic procedures, devised in an integrated MIS environment for daily sales order processing, include checking on the customer's credit as well as preparing computer outputs—customer shipment orders (printed output) as well as a sales order file (magnetic tape file). The latter output is used in preparing a daily sales analysis. In addition, processing procedures include warehouse shipment orders—forwarding finished products from one location to another to handle out-of-stock conditions. Thus, order processing procedures for the marketing subsystem focus on accepting or rejecting orders. If orders are accepted, they are forwarded to the physical distribution subsystem for further processing. Special orders are routed to the engineering subsystem during order processing.

FORECASTING AND SALES ANALYSIS

Integrated MIS forecasting efforts of the American Products Corporation at the corporate level center on projecting upcoming quarterly sales demand for three basic product groups. Within each of these there are several specific products, resulting in 15 products manufactured by the three plants. The present method employed to forecast quarterly sales is the *least-squares* method.

In projecting future marketing information based on past and present data, there are many straight lines that can be constructed as possible trend lines, showing the movement and pattern of sales of the firm's products. A most useful trend line for each product is one that "best fits" the sales data under study. There is only one such line of best fit, and it is called the *line of least squares,* which can be defined as the trend line for which the sum of the squares of differences between the actual values (of the dependent variable) and the estimated values (for the dependent variable) is the least. In reality, we are trying to find an average line that minimizes errors between the trend line and the actual values.

As shown in Figure 7-2, there is a printout of forecasted demand for each product that is forwarded to the manufacturing manager. A tape containing this demand is forwarded to the manufacturing subsystem for producing the forecasted products.

After several years' experience with the least-squares method, the firm has found that conditions in the past do not always continue without change in the

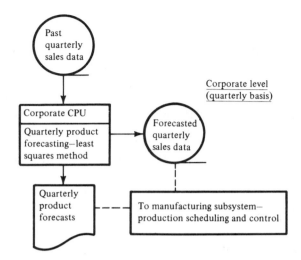

FIGURE 7-2. Quarterly product forecasting data flow for an integrated MIS marketing subsystem.

future. Thus, the least-squares or the trend-extension method, which looks to the trend factor, is not the only dominating factor in predicting demand; the seasonal factor is also important. For this reason, the firm has investigated other statistical methods and has decided to use exponential smoothing formulas when implementing the new distributed processing system.

Before product forecasting of any kind can be undertaken, there is need for sales analysis on a daily basis. From a longer viewpoint, the accounting subsystem supplies monthly and quarterly sales data as well as yearly information based on the firm's financial statements. Typical sales analyses include total sales (in dollars and units), sales by basic product groups, sales by customers and salesmen, and sales by geographical territory. Also, they encompass sales trends, market shares, and gross margins (contributions).

SALES ORDER PROCESSING AND CUSTOMER SERVICE

The activities performed by the forecasting system, as indicated above, trigger the generation of regular production orders on a quarterly basis. On the other hand, sales order processing at the corporate level initiates and provides the basis for control of daily activities that result in filling customer orders. It is of utmost importance that the information on the sales order form be complete and accurate. Otherwise, the sales order processing and warehouse shipment information, shown at the bottom of Figure 7-3, may be incorrect when forwarded to the firm's plants and warehouses.

Once the sales order is received—by phone, Teletype, mail, or hand—the first major activity, aside from detaching proceeds on a few orders, is the credit check—

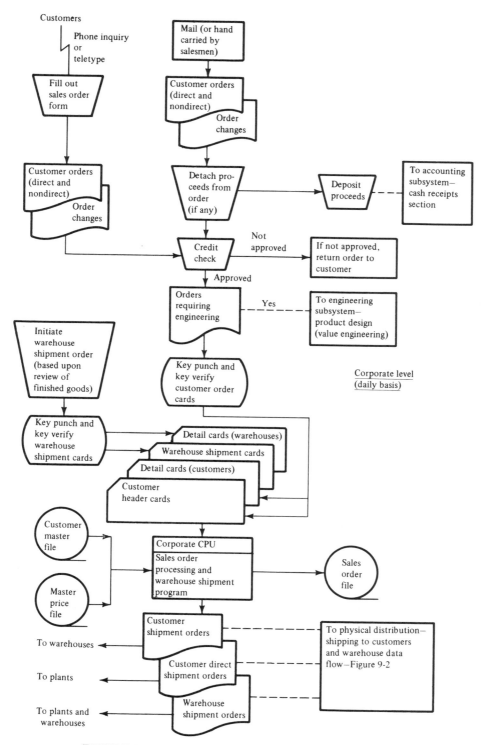

FIGURE 7–3. Sales order processing and warehouse shipment data flow on a daily basis for an integrated MIS marketing subsystem.

that is, is the customer capable of paying the ordered amount? In those cases where the credit of the customer is in question according to the accounting department, the order is sent to marketing management for further checking and a decision. In most cases, credit clearance is obtained and the order proceeds to the next step in Figure 7-3, which is to see if there is need for product design (applies to special orders). If engineering is required, the order departs from the normal sales order processing flow; otherwise, the appropriate customer header card and detailed item cards are keypunched and key-verified. Also merged with customer order cards are warehouse shipment order cards, which represent the finished products to be shipped from one warehouse to another. These shipments are made to take care of out-of-stock conditions.

The customer order and warehouse shipment cards are processed against the master name and address and price files, necessary for producing the three types of output shown in Figure 7-3. These outputs are forwarded to the respective plant or warehouse, depending on the type of order. Order processing stops here for the marketing subsystem at the corporate level and resumes at the plant or warehouse level through the physical distribution system for regular sales orders.

In conjunction with sales order processing, the level of customer service is considered. If the order can be filled from inventory or from current production, the order processing cycle continues with the development of shipping documentation and the scheduling of warehouse withdrawal and transportation. When the order cannot be filled from either source, the customer is notifed through the marketing subsystem. Hopefully, the customer will allow the order to be back-ordered and filled at a later date. If not, an alternative source of supply will probably be used, and the order at the American Products Corporation will be canceled.

ADVERTISING AND PERSONAL SELLING

The selling function of the firm's integrated MIS focuses on three specific areas—advertising, personal selling, and sales promotion. Because it spends the most on the first two, these areas will be explored at the corporate level.

Selection of the best set of national magazines plus audio and visual media to communicate its advertising message to present and potential customers is a many-faceted problem. The important variables influencing the media selection process are the availability of time or space in each media, the advertising budget, whom the firm wishes to reach with a given message, the value of each repeat exposure, the quality of the advertising medium, and the discounted cost of running a selected media. Consequently, it is not a simple task to formulate an effective advertising program by identifying the key variables and quantifying the relationship among them.

To solve the advertising media problem, the American Products Corporation turned to linear programming. The linear programming advertising media model chooses the advertising mix that will maximize the number of effective exposures subject to the following constraints: the total advertising budget, specified mini-

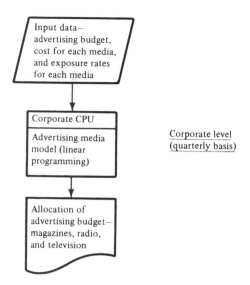

FIGURE 7-4. Advertising media model on a quarterly
basis for an integrated MIS marketing
subsystem.

mum and maximum usage rates of various media, and specified exposure rates to
the different market segments. The flowchart for this advertising approach on a
quarterly basis is shown in Figure 7-4.

After two years' experience with this approach the firm has found several
shortcomings. The model assumes constant effects of repeated advertising exposures, which is, in fact, rarely true. Media costs are not always constant. In
addition, there is no allowance for audience overlaps among media, nor is there any
indication of the best scheduling for the chosen media. Criticism of the linear
programming approach focuses on the amount and kinds of simplifications of the
real world needed to adapt the complex problem to the rigid form of the algorithm[1] and to keep the size of the problem small enough to fit the memory
capacity of the firm's computer. As a result of these shortcomings, the firm has
decided to use a simulation approach when the distributed processing system is
installed.

Personal selling, another important method of selling, is unique in that the
resources involved are people. The salesmen and their supervisors interact with
customers, who respond to selling effort in a complex and variable manner. This
makes it extremely difficult to computerize for effective control or to run controlled experiments and to shift salesmen around, except on a slow, evolutionary
basis. As a result, using a computer-based mathematical approach can be both risky
and expensive to simulate changes that may or may not result in a more effective

[1] Algorithm—a series of well-defined mathematical steps that are followed in order to obtain a
desired result.

sales strategy. For best results, selling strategy decisions should be made within the constraints of the present organization and with changes in organizational resources taking place over long periods of time.

MARKET RESEARCH AND PRICING

Market research at the corporate level plays a major part in developing new profit opportunities in the form of new products. The rationale is that the rate of product innovation, the rate of new product failures, and the cost of bringing out new products are all extremely high and continue to rise. To survive in such dynamic markets, the American Products Corporation must develop a sensitivity to changes in consumer behavior and in the conditions that influence behavior through effective market research. It is meaningless to talk of new products without considering, at the same time, the related marketing decisions that will have to be made. This consideration centers on the formulative role of research, suggesting that market research is really a coordinating agent. Each marketing decision should be thought of as an input, and research should be employed to coordinate these inputs before the actual product design begins.

Market research activities for the American Products Corporation center on the systematic gathering, recording, and analyzing of data about problems relating to the marketing of goods. To carry out these research functions, current and past data must be fed into the batch-oriented computer and analyzed by an appropriate research program before meaningful output can be produced (Figure 7-5). Generally, one of the current techniques in market research is employed, such as multiple regression, multiple correlation, and sampling theory. As noted in Figure 7-5, these techniques are stored on magnetic tape for immediate referencing by the market research program being processed. Computer output can be in the form of potential market size, product pricing, and other factors deemed important for the product under study.

For many of the computer's research studies, large data files are rarely used as are. Generally, the research analyst first retrieves and summarizes information from computer-processible files before beginning an analysis. For example, if he (she) wishes to utilize a stochastic[2] model of brand choice, he first retrieves the sequence of brands chosen by each household. Whether the ultimate analysis is the development of a stochastic model or another model, he develops a programming system to transform the edited data into a format appropriate for his statistical treatment. For models and statistical procedures used in marketing research, a system for retrieval and summary of data is developed in order to reduce the technological, time, and cost barriers to efficient market research.

In conjunction with developing needed market research data, exhaustive market research is undertaken with the possibility of attaining high unit volume as an objective. The selling of many units can bring both short- and long-run benefits

[2]Stochastic—ability, but not with absolute certainty, to know what will likely take place in the future.

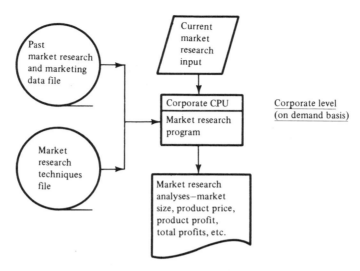

FIGURE 7-5. Market research data flow for an integrated MIS marketing subsystem.

to the firm. High unit volume can be sustained by many components of the marketing mix. Good product design, attractive packaging, and effective selling and advertising play leading parts. But more importantly, price often exercises a powerful influence on unit volume and the ultimate success of the new product. Because of the prime importance given to price, a relationship between potential demand and varying prices is determined by the market research analyst. The combination of demand and price that yields the highest profits is generally the basis for price determination. Likewise, consideration is given to prices charged at the break-even points at low and high volumes so as to indicate upper and lower price ranges corresponding to certain annual sales. Thus, marketing management is appraised of probable market volumes at various price levels for an overview of the proposed product.

DISTRIBUTED PROCESSING MARKETING SUBSYSTEM

Design consideration for the marketing subsystem are somewhat different from the firm's other subsystems. The marketing subsystem captures information about the external environment in terms of market forecasts and customer orders. It is the prime mover from which all other subsystems either directly or indirectly receive instructions on what must be accomplished. Its data base includes consumer sales forecasts, orders, shipments, product data, media data, advertising and promotion budgets, and other data, which must be designed carefully by the firm's system analysts. An important part of their job focuses on the data base elements themselves—specifically, what they are, what the validity is for storing them on-line, how they can be stored for easy retrieval, how they can be combined with data from other subsystems, and what type of output they can produce for an interactive operating mode.

To proceed with the design of the marketing subsystem (as well as any other subsystem), the systems designers must order their priorities in terms of what information and calculations are most valuable to plant and headquarters management. Ranking informational priorities, in particular, requires creative thinking and intuitive judgment of the highest order. Hard work is involved not only during the design phase but also in estimating the benefits of possible actions resulting from the new information. For effective results, there is an obvious need for systems personnel to interact with marketing personnel, especially marketing management, for concrete results. From these joint efforts, the most valuable informational opportunities can be pursued and developed to maturity for mutual benefit.

MARKETING DATA BASE

The marketing data bank (magnetic tape files), an essential part of the integrated MIS, must be converted to data stored on-line for the new distributed operating mode. Data base elements should be structured by major categories, as demonstrated in Figure 7–6 for the corporate and plant levels. This approach to the marketing data base assists the systems designer not only in effecting a logically structured design but also in programming data for instantaneous display or printed output.

The real test of effectiveness for the marketing data base revolves around how well and, in some cases, how fast marketing information can be retrieved to explain the dynamics of the markets in which the firm is operating. If marketing data elements cannot be correlated and subjected to factual and statistical manipulations, they will be of little help to marketing personnel—in particular, management and market research. It is in the grouping of data in new and different ways that marketing management is likely to find new and better answers. Also, the use of exception reporting from the data base will relieve marketing of scanning masses of numbers in the hope of finding meaningful ones. Thus, the systems designers must ascertain those combinations of marketing data and statistical manipulations which are the most valuable to the marketing subsystem.

Data as shown in Figure 7–6 for forecasting and sales analysis at the headquarters level consist of such items as past forecasting amounts, forecasted data for the coming period, present and past sales data, and past and present sales orders. By and large, these data revolve around the dynamics of the marketplace—that is, present and future sales. At the plant level, the current sales orders are input to sales order processing, whose basic data elements consist of the customer master file, shipping data, back order data, and similar items. Essentially, the level of current orders is dependent on the advertising and salesmen efforts, the next group of data elements stored on-line at the corporate level. All of the foregoing marketing data elements, in the long run, center on the developments of market research. Market

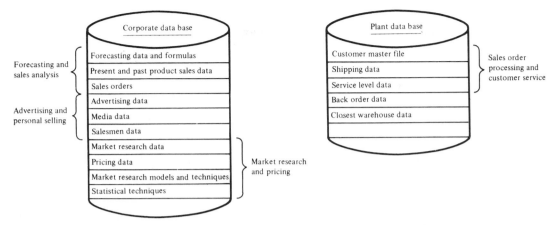

FIGURE 7-6. Typical marketing data base elements at the corporate and plant levels.

research—which connotes product-oriented research that usually begins with a consumer need and ends with a product recommendation—must, by its very nature, have certain data elements in a retrievable mode. In other cases, large magnetic tape or disk files of past data may supplement on-line market research data. The foregoing major marketing elements, then, comprise the marketing data base needed in a distributed processing environment for timely marketing information.

FORECASTING AND SALES ANALYSIS MODULES

Sales forecasting for the American Products Corporation in a distributed processing environment, as in integrated MIS, focuses on quarterly projections of the firm's products. Also, provision is made for interrogating the marketing data base at any time for utilizing the exponential formulas in conjunction with current sales data. The basic concept of *exponential smoothing* is that next quarter's forecast should be adjusted by employing weighting factors for current sales and the current forecast.[3] In a sense, the weighting factors update the upcoming forecast in light of what has happened most recently to actual demand. From this viewpoint, they are smoothing constants that are derived by examining past sales experience patterns. In addition, they allow seasonal and trend adjustments to be built into the forecasting formulas.

A CRT terminal, illustrated in Figure 7-7, is used to trigger on-line processing of exponential smoothing formulas quarterly in conjunction with the marketing data base. For interactive processing to begin, current sales, sales forecasts in the current period, and weighting factors for each product are read in from the data

[3] Refer to Robert J. Thierauf and Robert C. Klekamp, *Decision Making Through Operations Research,* 2nd ed., New York: John Wiley & Sons, Inc., 1975, Chap. 11.

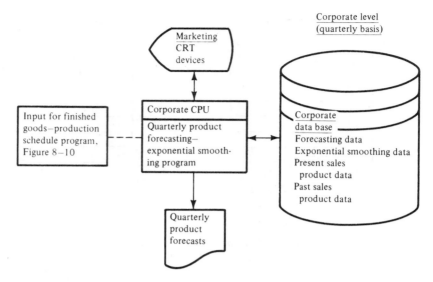

FIGURE 7-7. Quarterly product forecasting data flow for a distributed processing marketing subsystem.

base and manipulated by the exponential smoothing equations. The resulting output from the quarterly product forecasting-exponential smoothing program is the printed quarterly product forecasts. But equally important in terms of output is the storing of these forecasts on the data base at the corporate level.

Although it may appear that processing stops with a forecasted product printout and on-line storage of data, actually the forecasting program is just the beginning of a series of on-line processing operations. Output of the quarterly product forecasting-exponential smoothing program is input for the finished goods-production schedule program, which determines the number of finished products to manufacture after considering goods on hand and on order. This output becomes input for the linear programming program, one used to determine what quantities of each product should be made at which plants. It should be noted that each plant can make all 15 products. Based on this allocation of finished products by plants, the next program—materials planning by periods—"explodes" bills of materials for the finished product's component parts and determines to what planning periods the component parts apply in order to have them available at the proper time for manufacturing operations. The program on the next level—materials availability and EOQ (economic order quantity)—evaluates the component parts in terms of requirements by planning periods after considering what is on hand and on order. Generally, it will be necessary to buy large quantities of raw materials and parts from the outside as well as to place production orders for parts to be manufactured. To keep inventory costs at a minimum, orders from within and outside the firm are placed on an optimum basis by using EOQ formulas. Manufacturing orders are scheduled daily by plants using a production scheduling-linear programming program. Thus, the sales forecasting program triggers a whole series of programs which are the basis for daily manufacturing operations and buying from outside vendors. This interaction of programs will be continued in the next chapter.

The foregoing integrated programs do not end here in an on-line processing mode. Additional programs, such as plant attendance and recording of work in process for cost and factory payroll, are utilized. It should be noted that the latter programs are used for controlling activities as they occur in the manufacturing departments, while the sales forecasting through the economic ordering programs are processed at one time each quarter.

The forecasted sales stored on the corporate data base serve another purpose. They allow marketing management via an inquiry I/O terminal to compare projected product sales to actual sales activity (updated on a daily basis) for some specific time period. To make this information available to the proper marketing personnel, it is necessary to program different inquiry formats for maximum flexibility and ease of inquiry from the system. For the American Products Corporation, the systems designers have decided on a three-part division of inquiry formats:

1. total sales

2. detailed sales

3. exception sales

The highest level of marketing inquiry, or *total sales,* is the overall performance summary that describes the month-to-date or current month, last month, year-to-date, last year-to-date, and other data pictured in Figure 7-8. A sample

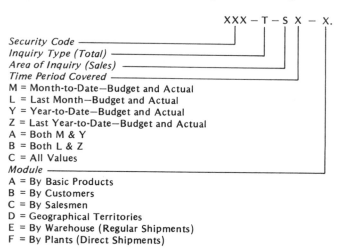

FIGURE 7-8. Total sales inquiry format in a distributed processing marketing subsystem.

Basic Products	MTD BUD	(000) ACT	LTD BUD	(000) ACT	YTD BUD	(000) ACT	ZTD BUD	(000) ACT
Group 1	1415	1450	1375	1379	4,292	4,095	4,252	4,242
Group 2	2040	2035	2100	2140	5,954	5,875	6,010	5,990
Group 3	1594	1505	1652	1695	4,753	4,852	4,852	4,950
Total	5049	4990	5127	5214	14,999	14,822	15,114	15,182

Question: What are the budget and actual month-to-date, last month-to-date, year-to-date, and last year-to-date total sales for the firm's three basic product groups?

Code: XXX−T−S C−A (based on Figure 7-8).

FIGURE 7–9. Total sales inquiry format example.

inquiry display for the firm's three basic product groups is shown in Figure 7-9. A review of this illustration indicates that the function of this level is to provide further inquiry and analysis in an area that is over or under budget forecasts. If a given sales performance is deficient compared to the budget figures, control can then be transferred to successive levels of detailed reports relative to the area of interest.

The second level of inquiry, or *detailed sales,* contains many modules of optional levels of detail. Normally, the inquiries requested of this structure are triggered for further analysis by the total sales inquiry. As with the prior level, data are available for the same time periods and by the same sales categories at the detailed level. Also, this inquiry format is so programmed to enable the user to format his (her) own report structures because marketing management might be interested in certain sales ratios or sales-to-expense ratios.

The last inquiry level, or *exception sales,* is more complex and flexible than the prior two. The exception inquiry is structured to highlight a certain condition or conditions. A sample inquiry is, "Which products are above 110 percent of forecasted sales and below 90 percent of forecasted sales?" Another inquiry example is, "Which salesmen are below their sales quotas?" In essence, this inquiry level provides the user with the ability to ask basic questions about the efficiency or lack of it in terms of the firm's marketing effort.

SALES ORDER PROCESSING AND CUSTOMER SERVICE MODULES

In the previous integrated management information system, all customer sales orders were received and processed at the corporate headquarters in St. Louis. In keeping with the concept of distributed processing, customer sales orders presently arrive via mail, telephone, and Teletype or are hand-carried by company salesmen to the three manufacturing plants. These preliminary activities are illustrated in Figure 7-10. A CRT terminal used in order processing includes a credit check of the customer's order. Initially, the CRT terminal displays a request for customer identification. The customer number is entered unless the transaction is

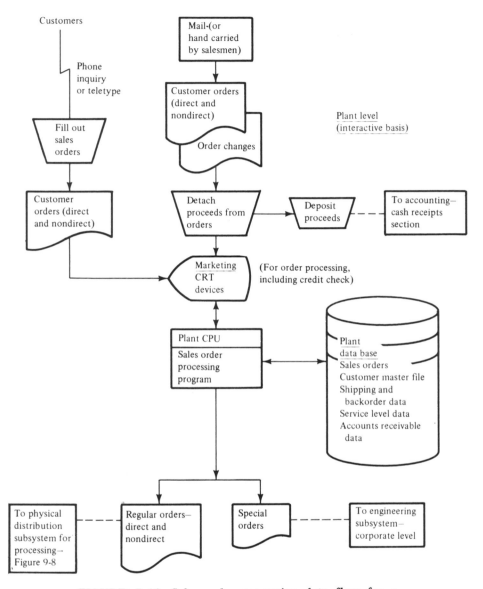

FIGURE 7-10. Sales order processing data flow for a distributed processing marketing subsystem.

for a new customer, in which case the customer name, address, and other information are entered. If the customer number is unknown for an established customer, the name is entered and the system displays a list of "sound-alike" customers from which a selection is made.

The system then displays successive requests for the entry of the data pertaining to the order. Flashed on the CRT screen are a series of questions pertaining to the following:

- customer order number (the customer's purchase order)
- "ship to" number
- date of order
- mail, phone, or Teletype
- tax code (the customer's tax type)
- salesman number
- number of items ordered of each product and catalog number
- job control number

Questions are projected on the operator's screen in a list. New questions are flashed in a pagelike sequence, and can cover up to 30 items on a single order. Sets of questions continue until the operator enters an L for "last." Each keyed-in answer appears on the screen opposite the question. At that point the computer summarizes each series of answers and "plays back" the information for visual review. There is only one edit check for each item on order, and the operator verifies that an entry is correct by keying in OK (okay) or NG (no good). After an NG, the operator redisplays the particular item in question and enters changes. An editing program stored in the computer checks the answers against preestablished facts, and question marks are flashed on the screen when the program finds an answer unacceptable. For instance, if the operator fails to include the number of items ordered, the program will flash a question mark. Or if the number of items ordered is present but the catalog number is not, another question mark will remind the operator that this information is missing. When all the questions on an order have been answered, the computer then checks the customer's credit and either approves the order for filling or, if there is a credit problem, holds it up and automatically prints out a warning message in the credit section of the accounting department on an I/O terminal unit.

Once the order has passed the credit check, the interactive sales order processing program accumulates finished goods requirements of the order for sales analysis and finished goods inventory. Finished goods items are not deducted from their on-line balances at this time but are deducted by the physical distribution subsystem (finished goods updating program) later. Awaiting shipment by the PD (physical distribution) department, finished goods along with their order numbers are stored on-line. The rationale for this approach is twofold. First, because there are discrepancies between what is physically on hand and the perpetual inventory on the plant data base, the systems designers have found it better not to deduct amounts that could result in misleading balances on-line. Second, at the end of the day, a computer program can be run to trigger all unposted finished goods of the prior day, indicating errors in orders not processed and billed. Thus, the sales order processing program makes a memorandum on the plant data base concerning finished goods, which are checked against the actual items shipped before being deducted from the finished goods quantity.

Although not shown at the plant level in Figure 7-10, a customer billing program is run at the end of each day whereby customer invoices are printed and mailed to customers (refer to accounting subsystem in Chapter 10, Figure 10-8). Similarly, a sales register is printed at the end of the customer billing run and serves as a record of daily sales. These summary sales data are forwarded to St. Louis.

The order operations described above take about 5 to 20 minutes, depending on the complexity of the order from the time the operator starts with the customer order number. By and large, the time in which orders can be pulled after entering them in an interactive processing mode ranges from one to several hours. When these two times are added together, the customer service level is very high, indicating that orders, in many cases, can be shipped the day they are received. However, owing to unforeseen operating conditions, it is possible for order service time to be longer.

ADVERTISING AND PERSONAL SELLING MODULES

The method that has been used in the past to solve the advertising problem for the American Products Corporation is linear programming. (As noted under the integrated MIS, there are deficiencies in this approach.) The ideal goal of any advertising media model at the corporate level is to provide the optimum exposure in terms of potential consumers to be reached, frequency of exposure desired among various prospective consumer segments, and other relevant decision rules. The more promising approach, which comes closest to this goal and minimizes the deficiencies of linear programming, is a custom-made advertising simulation model that incorporates probability elements.[4]

The need for probability factors enters into the model because of the time problem. For example, assume that a monthly magazine will be utilized, reaching the consumer directly. If the consumer was exposed (meaning that he or she noticed and read the advertisement) on the average of 9 out of 12 issues, then the probability of exposure to the average issue would be .75; if the exposure was 6 out of 12, the probability would be .50; and so forth. However, this approach fails to take into account the fact that the consumer's first exposure makes a greater impression than later exposures. The problem of how to treat additional exposures is solvable by ascertaining the effect of each additional exposure, given certain time intervals between exposures. Thus, the first month's exposure for a new product might be rated .9, the second month also .9 because of the newness of the product introduced, the third at .75, and so on.

[4]*Ibid.*, Chaps. 14 and 18.

The advertising simulation model, which evaluates alternative exposures to potential customers over time as submitted by the advertising manager, consists of procedures discussed below.

1. The use specifies the target customers by indicating their characteristics.

2. The media schedule to be evaluated is inserted—that is, each advertising medium and advertisements by time periods are listed. As noted above, the user inputs different weights for the first and successive exposures.

3. The time units (periods) to be used, say weekly or monthly, are stated.

4. The number of advertisements to be used during time period 1, 2, and succeeding periods are listed This instructs the computer when to move from one time period to the next.

5. The program selects an individual from the target customers. The individual is asked if he (she) was exposed to each of the specific media under consideration. Because it is not known which particular advertisements are seen by an individual, a random process is used to determine which advertisement he does see. For each advertising medium, a random number is generated. If the individual's probability for that particular media is, for example, .75 and if the random number is less than .75, the program considers that he was exposed to that particular advertising message. If, on the other hand, the random number is greater than .75, the program considers that he did not see the advertising, and the next advertisements are analyzed in similar fashion with respect to the same individual.

6. The data score obtained in step 5 is recorded as part of the individual's record for first, second, and following exposures so that they can be appropriately weighted over the time period under study. The score consists of exposure multiplied by the value assigned to that particular exposure.

All further computer looping procedures are essentially the same process as in steps 4 through 6. All individuals selected are scanned with respect to their exposure to the time period for the advertising medium included in the model. The output consists of the individual's scores and a target audience exposure distribution.

The advertising simulation model can be employed at any time. As depicted in Figure 7-11, advertising personnel can utilize a CRT terminal for appropriate output. For example, the advertising manager can call the above program or a comparable media selection program. Depending on the program, he or she can type in information, such as the size of the advertising budget, the number and size of important market segments, media exposure and cost data, advertisement size and color data, sales seasonality, and other information. The computer will return a media schedule that is calculated to achieve maximum exposure and sales impact in the desired customer segment(s). Thus, advertising media models lend themselves to interactive responses.

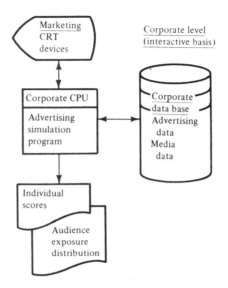

FIGURE 7-11. Advertising media model for a distributed
processing marketing subsystem.

Personal selling, like advertising, can benefit greatly from the capabilities of
the computer system. From the viewpoint of sales management, interactive models
permit the manager via an I/O device to examine systematically the consequences
of alternative selling strategies. By allowing the manager to work in a simulated
environment, interactive models can provide important insights about "what
would happen if . . ." without the difficulties inherent in experimenting with a real-
world sales force. They do not make decisions for the manager per se but provide a
basis for analysis and decision. In a similar manner, programs for monitoring sales
strategy and reporting potential marketing problems as soon as they begin to
develop, on an "exception reporting" basis, are an integral part of the system.
For example, a sales manager can dial a sales redistricting program, type in data on
the work load and/or sales potential of various geographical areas, their distances
from each other, and the number of sales territories to be created. The computer
will evaluate this information and assign various areas to make up new sales territories in such a way that (1) the sales territories are approximately equal in work
load and/or sales potential and (2) they are compact in size, thus cutting travel
costs.

When personal selling is considered from the salesman's viewpoint in an interactive mode, a salesman can enter the catalog number of a desired item through the
terminal keyboard (followed by the character D for detailed). The CRT retrieves
information from the plant data base and flashes back a display, including description, availability for sale, in transit, and the quantity on order. Next to the description appears the name of the product and its catalog number. "Availability
for sale" represents the most current inventory as calculated and stored on-line by

the system. "In transit" refers to the orders released to the warehouses and the plants. Finally, "quantity on order" refers to orders received but not as yet shipped. Current finished goods inventory data, then, can be retrieved by salesmen using either stationary (on the firm's premises) or portable (in the customer's office) I/O terminal devices.

MARKET RESEARCH AND PRICING MODULES

Throughout the development, introduction, and life of a product, the firm's marketing managers are faced with a number of decisions which require accurate market assessments. Frequently, substantial resources are committed for research and development, test marketing, and other related costs prior to the critical "go or no-go" decision. If the conclusion is to market the product, the marketing executive must decide on such matters as the amount of promotional expenditures, the allocation of these expenditures among different media, their allocation over a period of time, the amount of sales effort to be invested, and the duration of any special support for the product.

A chain reaction of other important decisions is initiated in other areas of the company, such as production and purchasing, because operations are geared to adjust to the new requirements. There may also be a substantial impact on research and development activities, because the potential success or failure of a new product could greatly affect the development of other similar or complementary products. In this regard, the success, or even the survival of a business firm depends on the ability of the company's executives to anticipate the future (or at least to anticipate it better than the firm's competitors do).

Because of the complexity of the phenomena to be predicted, the need for greater accuracy, and the dependency of outcomes on so many different variables, marketing management of the American Products Corporation has directed that its market research activities at the corporate level utilize venture analysis for the new product development phase only.[5] This approach directs the systems designers to structure a marketing data base which will be conducive to employing this mathematical technique.

Of paramount importance for venture analysis is the definition and evaluation of the specific variables, assumptions, constraints, and like items to be considered for inclusion in the model. For example, in terms of variables, an itemization of all candidate variables based on the subjective judgments of marketing research and other marketing personnel is necessary. Knowledge of the marketing environment and the relative importance of various factors is imperative. Then a cursory review is made of the sources of needed historical information. It is necessary to build a data base of historical data covering not only this company's new products but also all new products introduced in the industry over the past few years for which adequate source data are available. It is from these data that the mathematical relationships subsequently expressed in the model are derived. Thus, it is apparent

[5]*Ibid.*, Chap. 18.

that considerable pertinent data are needed before a new product can be effectively evaluated.

Essentially, venture analysis measures the relationships among many factors expressed in mathematical terms for the purpose of predicting the future. The underlying rationale is that if (1) for all new products introduced over a substantial period of time there is a strong relationship between demand levels and the specific variables considered during the early period of a product's life, and if (2) this relationship persists, the probable market activity for future new products can be estimated from corresponding early-period variables. From these interacting relationships, reliable output can be generated which includes aggregate demand, levels of demand at various points in time, prices throughout the product's life cycle, upper and lower limits of profits that can be expected over its life, and comparable analysis as programmed into the model.

It should be noted that as time passes the new product should be reevaluated periodically in light of new information and current market conditions. The marketing executive needs for decision-making purposes, during the critical first year after the product is introduced, include systematic reevaluation and possible revision of initial demand forecasts to reflect current knowledge. These analyses need to be generated at specific intervals after introduction.

Once the foregoing venture analysis program is operational, a market researcher can sit at a CRT device and call in the program (Figure 7-12). The researcher will then supply various estimates as they are called for by the computer, including the estimated size of the target group, recent product trial rates, repeat purchases, the promotional budget, size of investment, target rate of return, product price, and gross profit margin. The computer will process this information and print out a forecast for the next few years of the total number of customers,

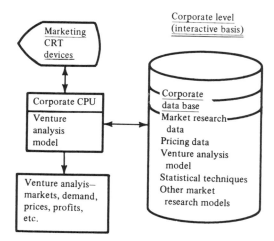

FIGURE 7-12. Market research model—venture analysis for a distributed processing marketing subsystem.

company market share, price(s), period profits, and discounted cumulative profits. The market researcher can alter various input estimates and readily ascertain the effect of the altered data on sales and profits. Also, the individual can perform the analyses deemed necessary for the new product under study.

Included in the venture analysis model is a determination of prices at various stages during the life cycle of the product. Utilizing a pricing model within venture analysis, the program relates a myriad of price, advertising, personal selling, and sales promotion combinations for the product under study and pertinent facts about competing products. Heuristically, the venture analysis model must hypothesize about the degree to which competitors will react to a price change and in what form this reaction will occur. It "guesses" on the basis of a hypothesis what blend of marketing decisions will go best with a given price. In turn, it determines what effect the given price will have on the sales of other products in the product line. Thus, the pricing aspects of a new product are included in the venture analysis model.

CHAPTER SUMMARY

The marketing subsystem of the American Products Corporation is the originating unit of order activities because it is the liaison between the firm and its customers' needs. Within this subsystem at the corporate level, forecasting centers on exponential smoothing formulas that combine past and current information in an objective manner, thereby providing a quantitative means to assist in making judgments about future sales levels to meet customer needs. Quarterly forecasts make "things happen" within the firm by triggering inputs to many of the other subsystems. In a similar manner, at the plant level, the customer order initiates action within and outside the marketing subsystem. Whether goods are produced based on a quarterly forecast or on special order, a prime concern of the marketing subsystem is fast and reliable customer service. Design considerations, then, for this type of environment represent a difficult undertaking.

The ability of the marketing subsystem to provide interactive responses applies not only to sales forecasting, sales analysis, and sales order processing but also to advertising, personal selling, and market research. Marketing personnel and their managers at the corporate level are capable of retrieving current data stored on the data base and combining them with appropriate mathematical (operations research) techniques for evaluating new products over their life cycle, determining appropriate prices, selecting the best advertising medium in terms of exposures and constraints, and comparable information. In essence, marketing information can be retrieved and manipulated on a "now" basis. This enables the firm to be forward-looking in its many marketing modules that require timely decisions.

QUESTIONS

1. In what ways is the distributed processing marketing subsystem superior to the integrated MIS marketing subsystem?

2. Referring to Figure 7–6, define the detailed data base elements for
   a. sales orders data
   b. advertising and media data
   c. salesmen data

3. Suggest an alternative method for forecasting the firm's sales each quarter.

4. If all order processing was handled at the corporate level rather than at the plant level, is the marketing subsystem truly distributed? Give reasons to support your viewpoint.

5. Define in some detail the major modules of the sales order processing master program at the plant level.

6. How is the simulation advertising model superior to the linear programming model?

7. Referring to the section on market research, design an ideal distributed processing environment for this marketing area.

REFERENCES

Berenson, C., "Marketing Information Systems," *Journal of Marketing,* Oct. 1969.

Cardozo, R. N., Ross, I., and Rudelius, P., "New Product Decisions by Marketing Executives: A Computer-Controlled Experiment," *Journal of Marketing,* Jan. 1972.

Chambers, J. C., Mullick, S. K., and Smith, D. D., "How To Choose the Right Forecasting Technique," *Harvard Business Review,* July–Aug. 1971.

Comer, P., "The Computer, Personal Selling, and Sales Management," *Journal of Marketing,* July 1975.

Cravens, D. W., Woodruff, R. B., and Stamper, J. C., "An Analytical Approach for Evaluating Sales Territory Performance," *Journal of Marketing,* Jan. 1972.

Falor, K., "Sales Prospecting Via the Computer," *Infosystems,* May 1975.

Fogg, C. D., and Rokus, J. W., "A Quantitative Method for Structuring a Profitable Sales Force," *Journal of Marketing,* July 1973.

Free, V. H., and Neman, T. E., "Market Research Matches Products to Consumers," *Computer Decisions,* May 1972.

Haavind, R., "Computer Shape Products, Aids Sales Effort," *Computer Decisions,* Jan. 1972.

Kelly, J. P., *Computerized Management Information Systems,* New York: The Macmillan Company, 1970, Chap. 4.

King, W. R., "Methodological Simulation in Marketing," *Journal of Marketing,* April 1970.

Kotler, P., "The Future of the Computer in Marketing," *Journal of Marketing,* Jan. 1970.

——, "Corporate Models: Better Marketing Plans," *Harvard Business Review,* July–Aug. 1970.

Lambin, J. J., "A Computer On-Line Marketing Mix Model," *Journal of Marketing Research,* May 1972.

Leitch, R. A., "Financial Implications of Marketing and Production Coordination," *Managerial Planning,* May–June 1976.

McNiven, M., and Hitton, B. D., "Reassessing Marketing Information Systems," *Journal of Advertising Research,* Feb. 1970.

Montgomery, D. B., and Urban, G. L., *Management Science in Marketing,* Englewood Cliffs, N.J.: Prentice-Hall, Inc., 1969.

Moyer, M. S., "Management Science in Retailing," *Journal of Marketing,* Jan. 1972.

Smith, P., "Unique Tool for Marketers: PIMS," *Management,* Jan. 1977, and *Dun's Review,* Oct. 1976.

Thierauf, R. J., *Systems Analysis and Design of Real-Time Information Systems,* Englewood Cliffs, N.J.: Prentice-Hall, Inc., 1975.

Treason, R. V., Jr., "MARKAD: A Simulation Approach to Ad Management," *Journal of Advertising Research,* Vol. 9, No. 1, 1972.

DISTRIBUTED PROCESSING MANUFACTURING SUBSYSTEM— AMERICAN PRODUCTS CORPORATION

8

The manufacture of finished products involves many operations. Not only must plant, equipment, and tools be provided, but appropriate personnel must also be hired and trained to utilize the manufacturing facilities. Raw materials and goods in process must be available when needed. Production must be planned, scheduled, routed, and controlled for output that meets specific deadlines. An effective system in this area, then, is a study unto itself.

Manufacturing informational needs vary from work center and production reports for operating management to specific operational machine data for in-plant line personnel. Pertinent information for those needs is extracted from common files and then is presented in a manner that permits timely and appropriate action. In this chapter we shall focus on various methods of obtaining needed information from these on-line and off-line files. Also, we shall specify the essential components of a typical manufacturing subsystem in both an integrated MIS and a distributed processing mode.

Initially, the manufacturing subsystem for the American Products Corporation, operating in an integrated MIS environment, is presented. After this brief review of present operations, considerations for a distributed processing system are explored for this functional area. This approach provides a sound basis for the design of important manufacturing modules, which include

- receiving
- production scheduling and control
- manufacturing operations
  machine shop
  assembly—minor and major
  plant and machine maintenance
- quality control and inspection
- data collection system

Basically, these major functional modules are the structure upon which the manufacturing subsystem is built for the American Products Corporation.

OVERVIEW OF MANUFACTURING ENVIRONMENT

The environment in which the manufacturing subsystem operates is illustrated in Figure 8-1. The information flow throughout the system is noted by a single arrow, while a double arrow denotes the physical flow of goods. Within this subsystem, management has the ultimate responsibility for coordinating manufacturing activities. However, the production scheduling and control section is the important coordinator of ongoing manufacturing operations. This group feeds back critical information based on a programmed response to plant foremen or to higher levels of manufacturing management as deemed necessary.

Because the current DP system allows for the processing of detailed manufacturing data at the plant level, the distributed processing system will make no change in terms of additional off-loading from the central site in St. Louis. In both systems, important summary data on manufacturing operations are forwarded via data communications to central headquarters. In this manner, management is appraised of results. However, as will be pointed out throughout the chapter, important manufacturing information is more timely within the distributed processing environment due to its interactive mode versus the older batch processing mode of the integrated MIS.

INTEGRATED MIS MANUFACTURING SUBSYSTEM

The firm's products can be produced in anticipation of demand, upon receipt of customers' orders, or some combination of the two. If goods are being produced to order, a sales order copy, in many cases, may be the *production order* (regular or

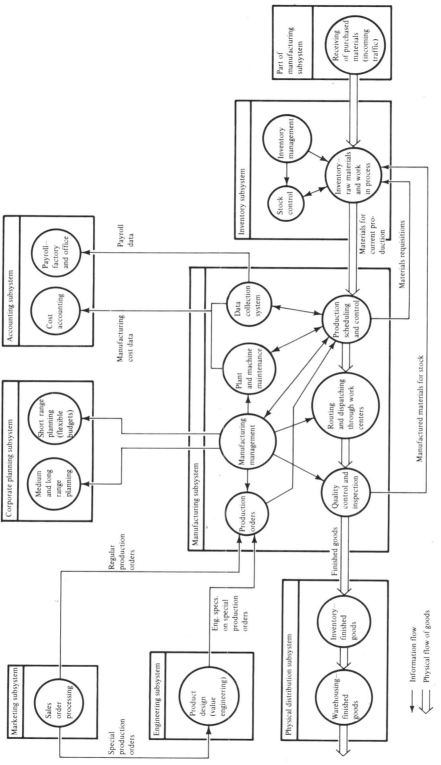

FIGURE 8-1. Manufacturing subsystem information and physical flow to and from other subsystems—American Products Corporation.

special). The usual arrangement is to have the production scheduling and control department initiate action on the order, which is then distributed to stock control, shipping, and accounting departments. The original copy is kept in the manufacturing plant files.

Manufacturing materials can be obtained from outside or within the firm. If a *purchase requisition* is prepared, it is forwarded to the purchasing department; otherwise, a *materials requisition* is prepared. Other typical records and forms found within the manufacturing function are *periodic production reports, tool orders, material usage reports, material scrappage reports, inspection reports, labor analysis reports, cost analysis reports,* and *production progress reports.*

The central point of the integrated MIS manufacturing subsystem is a magnetic-tape-oriented data bank. Entries are made at different intervals depending on the type of data. Each manufacturing plant employs punched card procedures in order to provide input for the data bank. The manufacturing plants in Los Angeles, Minneapolis, and Philadelphia utilize a remote batch operation to send data to the corporate office. All period data are accumulated on interim magnetic tapes. At the end of a period, such as a week or a month, sort/merge program routines are employed to combine the latest data with past records. At that time, cumulative and exception manufacturing reports (and new magnetic tape files) are produced for corporate management. Summation reports are forwarded to the three manufacturing plants. Periodic summation and exception reports are reviewed by the plant managers and corporate management in terms of past activities. In essence, historical reports are produced in order to review the status of budgets, orders, production, and comparable manufacturing information.

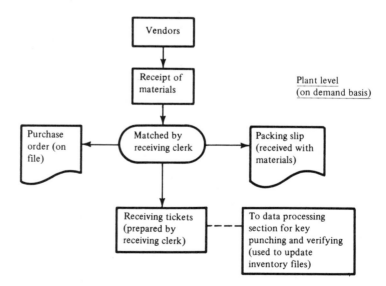

FIGURE 8-2. Receiving data flow for an integrated MIS manufacturing subsystem.

RECEIVING

As soon as goods are received from suppliers, the receiving department checks the enclosed packing slip against a copy of the purchase order (Figure 8-2). Once the receiving clerk is satisfied that the goods correspond to those on the purchase order, he prepares receiving tickets, noting any discrepancies between the order and actual material received. Sometimes an inspection record may be prepared by the receiving department along with the receiving tickets. Copies of both are sent to data processing (for keypunching and key-verifying), purchasing, stock control, manufacturing, and accounting. A carbon copy is retained by the receiving department.

Goods are delivered by the receiving department to the stock control department or to any other department that has ordered them. Generally, the individual or department that physically takes possession of the materials acknowledges receipt by signing a copy of the receiving report. In this manner, the receiving department is relieved of responsibility for the acquired materials and supplies.

PRODUCTION SCHEDULING AND CONTROL

Production scheduling and control is predicated upon quarterly sales forecasts for the three basic product groups (consisting of 15 individual products). As pointed out in the previous chapter on marketing, quarterly sales in an integrated MIS environment are forecasted by the least-squares method. These forecasts, in turn, are broken down by corporate manufacturing management as weekly production quotas for scheduling and control of each manufacturing plant.

The manufacturing operating function is based on a *production order* concept. Weekly production quotas are sent to the production scheduling and control departments (three plants) by corporate manufacturing management and are the basis for the next week's production. Production scheduling and control issues production orders to the various manufacturing departments and work centers based on exploded bills of materials (to be explored in a subsequent section), which are the basis for lay-up lists (detailed parts) which are sent to inventory stock control for parts procurement. The production order lists in sequence the departmental operations for each product to be produced. On completion in one work center, the parts are sent to the next work center in sequence. Expeditors and tracers follow the parts (Figure 8-3). Work center reports from production scheduling and control are issued weekly to corporate and plant manufacturing management.

The present system leaves much to be desired, because manufacturing work centers receive operational information at least a week after the work has been completed. Exception reports are generated and distributed but only after the critical time period has passed. The interaction of departmental delays is manually "guesstimated" and used to control the appropriate work centers. This approach leads to problems of human inefficiency—thus, an integrated MIS approach is not the most desirable one for controlling manufacturing operations.

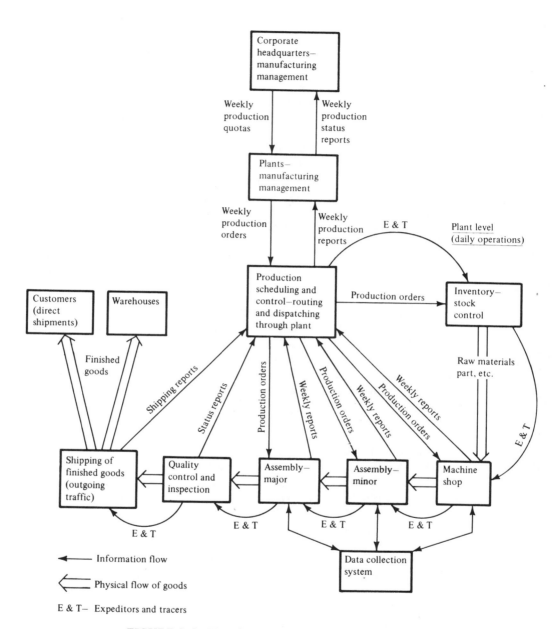

FIGURE 8-3. Manufacturing order processing flow in an integrated MIS environment under the direction of production scheduling and control.

MANUFACTURING OPERATIONS

All of the manufactured products for the American Products Corporation must pass through three manufacturing departments—machine shop, minor assembly, and major assembly—as illustrated in Figure 8-3. However, there are a number of manufacturing work centers within each department. Depending on the product itself, it may have to be processed through more than one work center before manufacturing is completed for that department. In addition to the foregoing three manufacturing departments, a plant and machine maintenance department is maintained to service all work centers for more efficient production.

The machine shop is the first department to initiate a production order. Once an order is entered and scheduled, the parts lay-ups are made. One lay-up proceeds immediately to the machine shop area, another goes to the minor assembly area, and a final one to major assembly. However, minor assembly cannot be started until the processed parts from the machine shop are received. The machine shop is the key to all assembly operations (Figure 8-3); completion dates from all succeeding departments depend on the availability of parts from the machine shop.

Before manufacturing activities of the various departments and work centers can begin, the weekly production order schedule (based on production quotas from corporate headquarters) must be keypunched and key-verified before being processed at the plant level. Basically, the bills of materials explosion program (Figure 8-4) determines what quantities of materials and parts are to be withdrawn from inventory as well as the dates when they are needed. It should be noted that the proper level of inventory on hand to meet production requirements is a function of the inventory and purchasing subsystems.

After exploded inventory requirements by periods have been prepared by the computer on a weekly basis, they are forwarded to departmental supervisors and work center foremen and are used to prepare material requisitions for lay-up lists. Completed materials requisitions are presented to the stockroom for forwarding of the materials as required. As illustrated in Figure 8-5, the materials requisitions form the basis for preparing punched cards. Later, these cards, which represent issues to production, are input to update inventory files.

Operational procedures for handling plant and machinery maintenance are basically on a manual basis within an integrated MIS operating mode. Machine failures are reported by work center personnel to their respective foremen, who, in turn, call for maintenance personnel to fix the required machine(s). (As will be seen in a distributed processing environment, the computer monitors machine functions and reports via CRT devices in the maintenance department the status of the machines. When failures are recognized by the computer system, a typed output alerts personnel to the situation.)

QUALITY CONTROL AND INSPECTION

The quality control and inspection department is an important control point in the manufacturing subsystem. It can have a profound impact on the firm's profits. The detection here of a bad part costing only $2 can save hundreds of

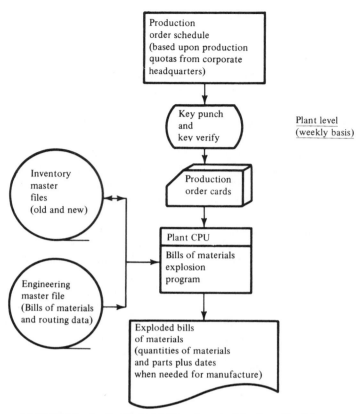

FIGURE 8-4. Exploded bills of materials data flow for an integrated MIS manufacturing subsystem.

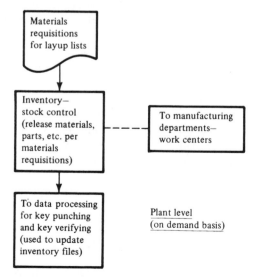

FIGURE 8-5. Materials requisitions data flow for an integrated MIS manufacturing subsystem.

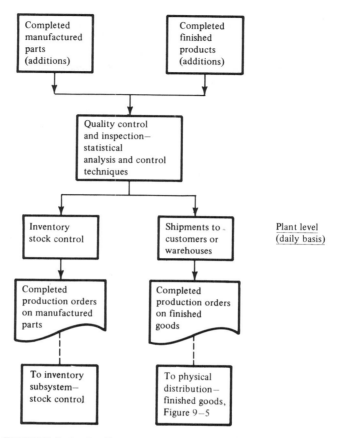

FIGURE 8-6. Quality control and inspection data flow of manufactured parts and finished products for an integrated MIS manufacturing subsystem.

dollars in manufacturing troubleshooting and rework. Statistical analysis and control techniques are employed to aid this department in evaluating the quality of manufactured parts and finished products. Although their outputs take different routes, as seen in Figure 8-6, manufactured parts and finished products are nevertheless additions to their respective inventory files. Eventually, corporate inventory files are updated via remote batch processing.

DATA COLLECTION SYSTEM

The data collection system at the plant level for the three manufacturing plants serves as a basis for paying employees as well as costing the firm's products. In the first case, weekly employee time attendance cards are punched in and out by employees on a time clock recorder. At the end of the week, these cards are reviewed by the appropriate foremen before being forwarded to the data processing section for keypunching and key-verifying. Immediately following this punched card phase, these time cards are the initial input for computerized payroll processing procedures found in the accounting subsystem. In the second case, separate weekly employee production order cards are utilized to record time on the various jobs. Plant employees ring in and out on a time recorder clock near their work place. Weekly, the manufacturing work center foremen check these cards against the time attendance cards to ensure that payroll records are compatible with cost records (Figure 8-7). Also at this time, production order cards are keypunched and key-verified before being merged on the plant computer in order to produce a labor cost file. As will be seen in the chapter on the accounting subsystem, the labor cost file is employed to produce a weekly work center, labor-cost analysis report for plant management.

DISTRIBUTED PROCESSING MANUFACTURING SUBSYSTEM

Design considerations for a distributed processing manufacturing subsystem are generally complex when viewed in terms of the data base. From this viewpoint, manufacturing activities are related to many other subsystems.. To produce meaningful information from the data base for controlling manufacturing operations, mathematical models are often employed. These models, which can access on-line data at any time, allow manufacturing management and line personnel to control their activities on a "now" basis, quite unlike that available in an integrated MIS.

MANUFACTURING DATA BASE

The data base elements of the American Products Corporation which are needed for the manufacturing subsystem are related directly to many other subsystems. Important data base elements from other subsystems, as seen in Figure 8-8, are processed from on-line operations, stored, and retrieved by the manufacturing subsystem. The data base at the plant level contains usable information for controlling current manufacturing operations. The real effectiveness of this data base approach is the fact that redundant manufacturing data are eliminated because all subsystems share the same manufacturing data elements.

For the manufacturing subsystem to operate effectively and efficiently, plant personnel utilize various CRT devices for desired data base responses. Data flow in and out of the data base according to the detailed design found in subsequent sections of this chapter. Before output responses can be operational, computer programs, many of which include mathematical models, are essential.

By and large, manufacturing management at the plant level of the American Products Corporation has need for a more detailed breakdown than that required for corporate manufacturing management. Whereas corporate management is concerned with flexible budgets, income statements, future production quotas, and summations and/or exceptions for all of its operations, plant management is more

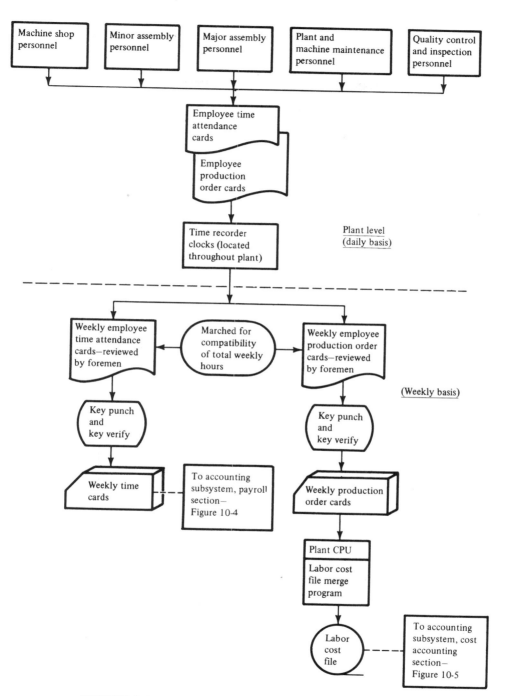

FIGURE 8-7. Data collection system for an integrated MIS manufacturing subsystem.

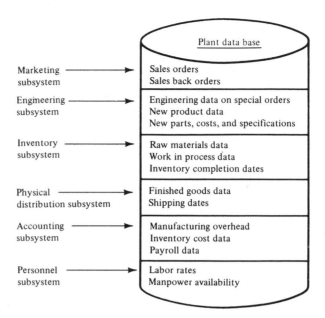

**FIGURE 8-8. Interrelated subsystem data base elements
for manufacturing operations (plant level).**

concerned with day-to-day operations than with possible future operations. This
plant operational mode lends itself to a separate and a more detailed data base
than that for corporate headquarters. Typical manufacturing data base elements at
the corporate and plant levels are shown in Figure 8-9. Additional information
regarding these two data bases will be given later in the chapter when each major
manufacturing module is analyzed.

MANUFACTURING SUBSYSTEM OVERVIEW

The procedure for determining next period's forecasts (three months hence)
after adjusting for finished goods on order and on hand were set forth in the prior
chapter. Although these procedures will not be repeated again, you will recall that
finished goods production requirements for the next three months provide the
necessary input for the manufacturing function. The operations research technique—linear programming program[1]—is utilized to determine what quantity of
each product will be produced in each of the three manufacturing plants. The
relationship of sales forecasts, forecasted finished goods, finished goods production
requirements is set forth in Figure 8-10.

Now that period requirement levels of on-line finished goods for each plant

---

[1] Refer to Robert J. Thierauf and Robert C. Klekamp, *Decision Making Through Operations
Research,* 2nd ed., New York: John Wiley & Sons, Inc., 1975, Chap. 6.

FIGURE 8-9. Typical manufacturing data base elements at the plant and corporate levels.

have been computed at the corporate level, the next phase is exploding bills of materials. The materials planning-by-periods program multiplies the quantity needed of each component times the number of final products that must be manufactured. Also, it places the component requirements in the appropriate planning period because some parts will be needed before others.

Continuing in an interactive processing mode, the output for the materials requirements by future planning periods can take two paths. One is the purchasing of raw materials and parts from outside vendors, and the other is the manufacturing of parts within the plant. The outside raw materials provide the basic inputs for manufacturing specific parts used in the assembly of the finished product. Likewise, outside purchased parts are used in the assembly of the final product. Before materials are to be manufactured or purchased, it is necessary to determine if present inventory and materials on order are capable of meeting the firm's needs for future planning periods. At this point, it is important to note that perpetual inventories stored on line have been adjusted to reflect physical counts in order to produce accurate output for the materials availability and EOQ (economic ordering quantity) program.

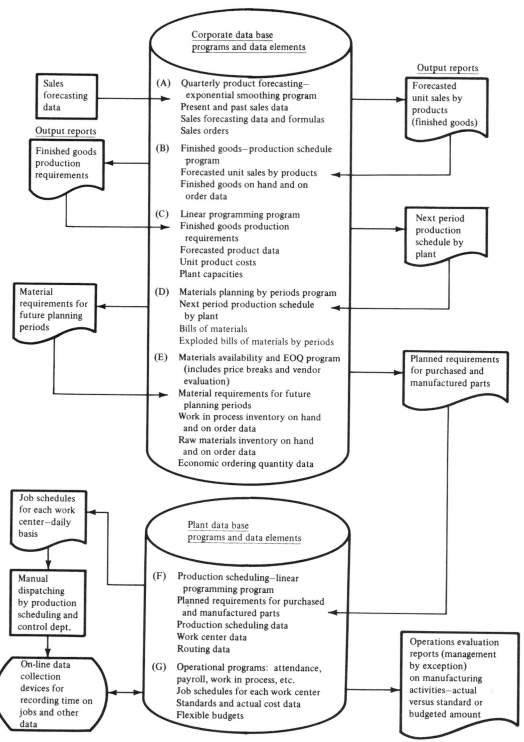

FIGURE 8–10. Corporate and plant data base programs
and data elements that control manufacturing activities in a distributed processing
environment.

The foregoing programs (Figure 8-10)—namely, (A) quarterly product forecasting-exponential smoothing, (B) finished goods-production schedule, (C) linear programming, (D) materials planning-by-periods, (E) materials availability and EOQ (includes price breaks and vendor evaluation)—have been handled by the corporate headquarters computer in an interactive operating mode. By no means does the integrated operating mode stop here for the period under study. The planned daily requirements, determined by the (F) production scheduling-linear programming program for all manufactured plant items, provide the means for scheduling production orders through the manufacturing work centers. Other (G) operational programs which are available to record and control daily activities include attendance, payroll, and work in process. The output of these programs provide operations evaluation reports on manufacturing activities.

In summary, programs (A) through (E) shown in Figure 8-10 do not operate individually but are integrated. Sales forecasting serves as input for finished goods product requirements, which, in turn, is input for the next period's production schedule by plant. In a similar manner, this output is input for exploding bills of materials, forming the basis for material requirements by future planning periods. In turn, this information is employed for manufacturing orders within the firm's plants and placing orders with outside suppliers. This input/output approach provides a basis for day-to-day scheduling and dispatching of the various manufacturing facilities.

RECEIVING MODULE

Receiving in a distributed processing system is somewhat similar to that in integrated MIS at the plant level. Upon receipt of materials from vendors, goods are checked and verified against the accompanying packing slip by the receiving clerk. In addition, the receiving clerk prepares receiving tickets, noting any apparent irregularities of materials received. However, before preparing receiving tickets, the clerk verifies on-line via a CRT terminal the shipment with the purchase order to ensure accuracy of incoming materials. Pertinent information is keyed in, and the system responds. If the shipment is valid, the materials are accepted and the inventory data base at the plant level is updated to include the shipment. Also, the system reduces the amount of goods on order in terms of outstanding purchase orders. On the other hand, if the system answers that the shipment is invalid and not due, the shipment is refused by the receiving clerk. The carrier returns the materials to the vendor. These procedures are illustrated in Figure 8-11.

Daily, the supervisor of receiving accesses the plant's data base (Figure 8-11). Expected shipments of the day, along with prices, specifications, originator's name, and similar items, are shown. The receiving supervisor or receiving personnel can update the order file from a CRT device (as noted above). Date received and quantity information are entered. By special function keys on the CRT device, plant personnel can notify the inventory control subsystem that goods have been received and can be initiated for routing.

The key to an efficient distributed processing system in this area is the

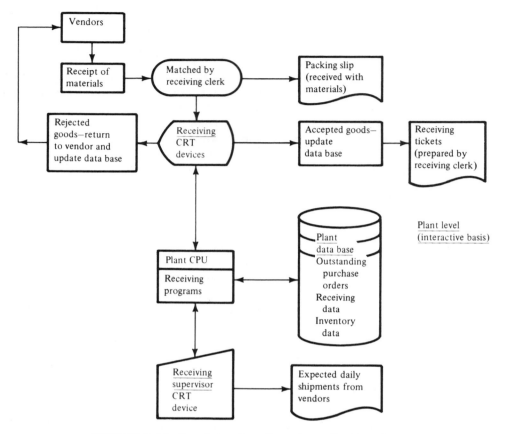

FIGURE 8-11. Receiving data flow for a distributed processing manufacturing subsystem.

subordination to a set daily routine. If the receiving supervisor did not review expected receipts daily, the production floor could sit idle, waiting for goods that are late. However, with CRT terminal capabilities, manufacturing departments can interrogate the data base and initiate requests to specific work centers for raw materials and purchased parts.

PRODUCTION SCHEDULING AND CONTROL MODULE

The production scheduling and control department at the plant level is responsible for all traffic among manufacturing departments and within their respective work centers. This important department coordinates all activities concerning a production order from its initial recording, through inventory lay-up and manufacturing, to shipping from the plant. This module relies heavily upon the plant's data base and its communications with all manufacturing work centers. But just as important for this department is the utilization of the production scheduling-linear programming program (Figure 8-10), mentioned in a previous section.

To utilize the above production scheduling program, all production control and scheduling data must be entered as they occur, thereby permitting creation of an up-to-date plant data base. Likewise, all production quotas for the present three-month period must be stored on line. It should be noted that periodically adjustments are made to period forecasts which are reflected on the data base. Before the start of each day (the program is actually run at the end of the prior day shift), the computerized scheduler first determines what products to make for the day based on the production quotas, stated on a daily basis, by utilizing linear programming. Next, the scheduler considers where jobs are backed up or behind schedule and where production bottlenecks are currently occurring. Based on these basic inputs, the computerized on-line scheduler simulates the activities of the plant for the coming day and determines what will happen as the day begins, thereby alerting supervisors and foremen about critical areas that need attention. Because all data affecting manufacturing activities are entered as they occur, the scheduler feeds back information in sufficient time to control upcoming manufacturing operations.

Many on-line recording techniques can aid the production scheduling and control department in its everyday operations. CRT devices, located in each manufacturing work center, enable the user to enter simple data regarding the name and location of goods in process. These keyboard entries, monitored on line by the plant computer, enable the production scheduling and control department to know when goods enter and leave a work center. Exception reporting alerts the department when goods are overdue from a specific work center. Delay reasons can also be entered from the individual work center CRT devices. Prolonged delays, resulting in possible shipment delay, are brought to the attention of manufacturing managers, supervisors, and foremen through exception reports. Figure 8-12 shows the data flow interaction with the production scheduling and control department.

On-line monitoring of goods enables the production scheduling and control department to eliminate most expeditors and tracers. Partial orders can be processed through a work center and sent to another with the assurance that production control knows the status of all parts. Reasons for delayed orders can be numerically coded and entered into the data base from CRT devices. Exception reports to the appropriate level will be converted from numeric codes to actual status reports.

The delay reports as entered onto the data base alert other manufacturing work centers about trouble areas. The work center(s) involved can enter "expected remedy" dates so that the rest of the line can make the necessary changes to the production schedule. In this manner, if noncritical parts are missing, such as power cords, the majority of the work can be performed with the part added later. Or, if critical parts are missing, such as the assembly shell, the complete order can be deleted from the daily run sheet until the part becomes available.

Once again, the adherence to set procedures enables the plant to operate in an efficient manner. Each work center must enter parts status when new lots are

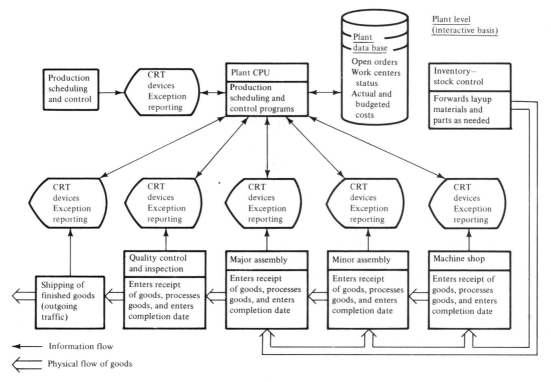

FIGURE 8-12. Production scheduling and control data flow within the distributed processing manufacturing subsystem— emphasis on exception reporting.

received and must clear the parts from the record of the work center when they move on to another work center. Other data, such as delay reasons, can be requested of the computer system when the expected hours within a work center exceed the normal time.

MANUFACTURING OPERATIONS MODULES

The manufacturing operations of the American Products Corporation comprises its physical manufacturing processes. Its major modules in a distributed processing environment, like in integrated MIS, are as follows:

- machine shop
- assembly—minor and major
- plant and machine maintenance

In separate sections that follow, each module will be explored in terms of its design.

Machine Shop

The machine shop, being the first department to start a production order in terms of the manufacturing process, requests parts from inventory-stock control. Completion dates from all other departments and work centers depend on the availability of parts from the machine shop. Scheduling of its operations follows the same path as through other manufacturing departments and work centers. The data base is updated when parts enter and leave the department, and the master schedule shows expected work loads and dates. Typical data flowing in and out of the machine shop area are illustrated in Figure 8-13.

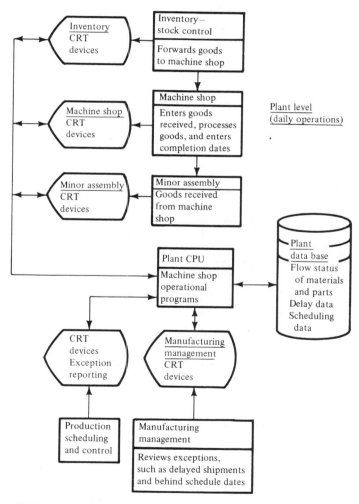

FIGURE 8-13. Machine shop (the first of the manufacturing operations modules) data flow in a distributed processing manufacturing subsystem.

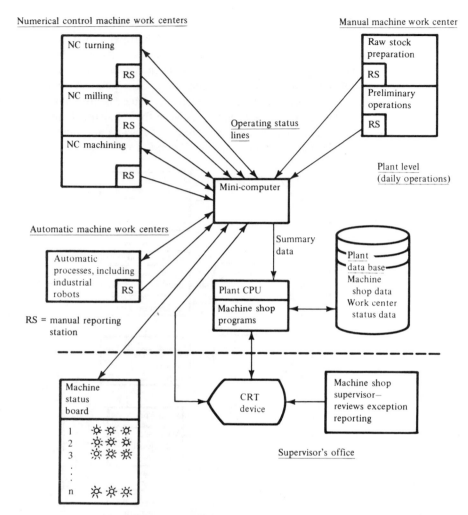

Numerical control machine work centers

Manual machine work center

Automatic machine work centers

RS = manual reporting station

Operating status lines

Plant level (daily operations)

Summary data

Supervisor's office

FIGURE 8-14. Minicomputer control of machine shop data flow in a distributed processing manufacturing subsystem.

The American Products Corporation utilizes many advanced manufacturing methods. Automated processes, numerical control machine tools, and computer-monitored processes are typical ones. With the feedback mechanism of these advanced techniques, machine utilization reports are no problem. A small mini-computer in the shop area monitors all processes and reports back to the plant computer (Figure 8-14). Exception reports are made available on-line by the mincomputer in order to assure immediate corrective action. When the storage capacities of the minicomputer are exceeded, this condition is reported to the plant computer throughout the day. Daily summary reports are produced for the supervisor of the machine shop. Weekly summary reports are sent to the superintendent of manufacturing operations and the plant manager. They are also transmitted to the corporate data base for future reference.

Because the machine shop is the heart of the manufacturing area, management has decided that it must know the status of all machines constantly. A "status board" has been installed in the supervisor's office under the control of the minicomputer. Through feedback lines attached to all plant machines, the computer knows if the machines are operating, idle, or in setup. Green, red, or yellow lights are illuminated, respectively, on the board for the proper condition (Figure 8-15). A manual key-in station, similar to the keyboards in the other departments, allows the machine operator to enter reasons for machine idle time.

The machine shop supervisor can monitor all machines. If a machine goes on "red" (idle) and no reason is received on the CRT device, attention can immediately be called to the trouble area. Missing tools, operator sickness, and machine maintenance are typical reasons for the red light. If the supervisor foresees any prolonged delay, revised completion dates can be entered via a CRT device to the plant data base. Other departments can then make their necessary adjustments.

The numerical control (NC) machine work centers have a great impact on the

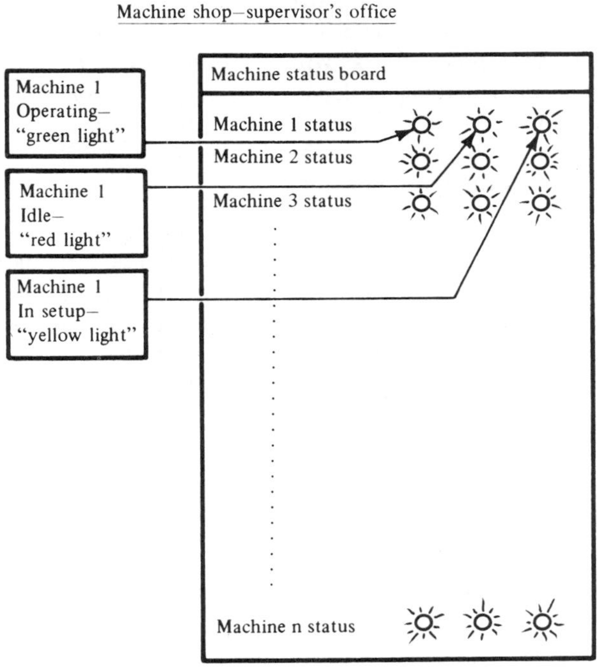

FIGURE 8-15. Machine status board (refer to Figure 8-14) in the machine shop supervisor's office.

manufacturing sybsystem. The advent of computer-controlled machine tools means the added efficiency of operations. Complete and accurate status reporting can be made without manual intervention and operator knowledge. This will eliminate "beat the game" tactics by operators and labor problems relating to "watchdog" activities.

The automatic processes in the machine shop consist of robot operations and fixed-cycle machine tools, such as plastic injection molding machines. By examining capital equipment utilization reports, the American Products Corporation has justified the use of robot operations for constant, large-lot-size, monotonous jobs. Past history showed that manual operations are boring, thereby adding to scrap problems and health hazards. The robots do these jobs with ease. The minicomputer monitors the robots and produces exception reports to the machine shop's supervisor and the foremen when operations go out of control.

Fixed-cycle machines are becoming more commonplace for this firm. They can do repeated operations without manual supervision. Parameters are input by dials on the machine, and the process begins. The minicomputer again monitors the actions of these machines and produces exception reports when tolerance limits are exceeded. The supervisor of the machine shop receives these exception reports by use of the status board and CRT device (Figures 8–14 and 8–15). This enables the supervisor to take corrective action before a complete parts lot has to be scrapped. Also, the minicomputer contacts other responsible people for corrective action at the appropriate times. With CRT devices in the tool crib and in the plant and machine maintenance department, exception reporting schemes allow for corrective action.

Assembly—Minor and Major

Even though the minor and major assembly departments constitute separate areas, they will be treated together because their data flow needs are the same. Their data flow is shown in Figure 8–16. As in the machine shop, a small minicomputer is used to monitor the automatic minor assembly and conveyor lines. Their status is reported on a "machine status board" in the supervisor's office. Exception reporting takes place via CRT terminals, as was illustrated for the machine shop.

Plant and Machine Maintenance

The manufacturing departments of the American Products Corporation place a high priority on keeping their equipment operating. This is exemplified by the installation of minicomputers in the machine shop and assembly areas. The plant computer monitors machine functions and reports via CRT devices in the maintenance department on the status of the machines. When failures occur, maintenance is immediately alerted to the problem machine or machines. In reality, corrective maintenance is an essential function of this manufacturing function.

But more importantly, there is preventive maintenance. As shown in Figure 8–17, the maintenance department requests maintenance schedule reports by work

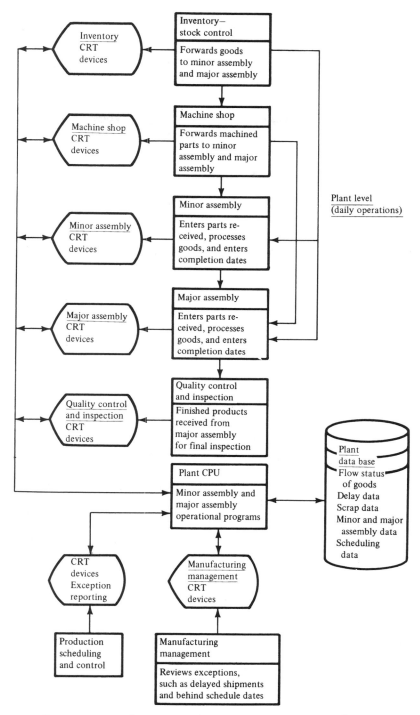

FIGURE 8-16. Minor assembly and major assembly (the second and third of the manufacturing operations modules) data flow in a distributed processing manufacturing subsystem.

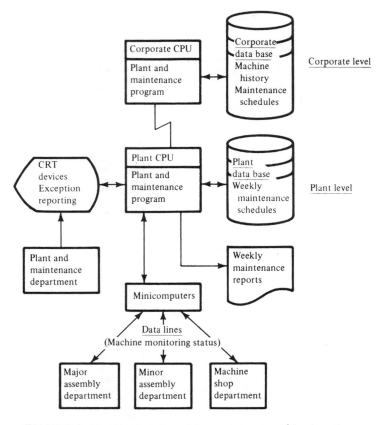

FIGURE 8-17. Plant and machine maintenance (the fourth
of the manufacturing operations modules)
scheduling data flow.

period from the corporate data base. These schedules are kept on the plant's base
but are divided into weekly schedules. Sufficient lead time for major maintenance
activities is always given.

The structure of the data base information is as follows:

1. task number

2. task description

3. time period between performances

4. location of task

5. coded skill requirements

6. date of last performance

7. time required for performance

8. crisis factor—importance of performance

This type of data base allows for both *task* and *time* maintenance reporting. Task maintenance is that performed in regular time periods. Time maintenance is that performed after so many operating hours of the machine. The minicomputer monitoring the machine can keep accurate records of hours in operation. The daily records are accumulated by the plant CPU and transmitted to the corporate data base, and, by means of a simple update program, the time records are adjusted.

Various simulation approaches can be employed to solve plant and machine maintenance problems. Mathematical models can define replacement times, payback periods, and expansion plans. Computer simulation of machine maintenance can be employed to predict failures. Also, it can be utilized for corrective maintenance so as to expedite location of problem areas and to suggest remedies.

QUALITY CONTROL AND INSPECTION MODULE

The quality control and inspection department is the most critical control point in a distributed processing manufacturing subsystem. The internal workings of this department are illustrated in Figure 8-18 for completed manufactured parts and finished products. Mechanical methods are employed to test the completed output. Sophisticated equipment is used to accelerate accurate checkout. However, the deadline of customer shipments and available labor make 100 percent sampling of the firm's output impossible. For these reasons, tools of statistical analysis and probability theory come into play.

To employ a statistical technique, a CRT device in the quality control and inspection department is hard-wired to the plant computer (Figure 8-18). By keying in the proper codes and part numbers, the statistical analysis model comes on-line and can direct the quality control section as to the number of parts to check, depending on the last part checked. The computer can relay the necessary information to the quality control and inspection department in order to make the decision on acceptance or rejection. This greatly relieves the manual burden of calculating the statistical probabilities by the quality control and inspection section.

DATA COLLECTION SYSTEM

At the plant level, a data collection system permits data to be fed directly into the computer system via data collection devices which are located conveniently for all job production personnel (Figure 8-19). When a factory employee starts a job, he (she) inserts his own plastic identification badge into a reader, which designates his work center and departmental number. He then places a punched card (a traveler card accompanies every production order as it progresses through the plant) into the same reader, which identifies the job being worked on. The data are transmitted to the computer. Upon completion of the job, the above procss is repeated, along with keying in the number of units produced. The data are automatically transmitted to the computer, where they are stored by job number for cost analysis, paying the employees, making the necessary adjustments to production

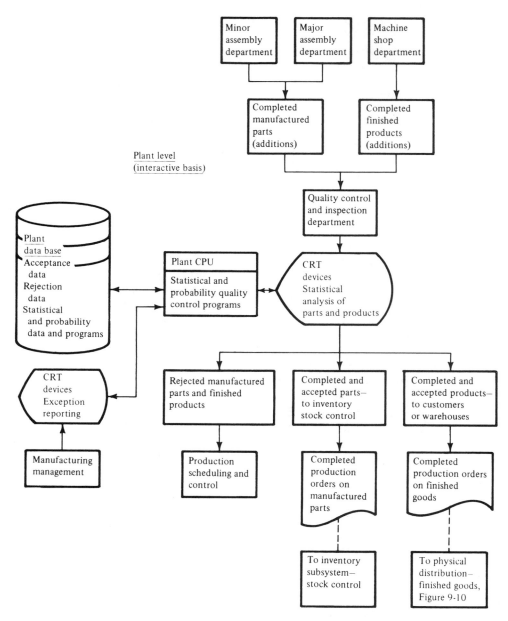

Plant level
(interactive basis)

FIGURE 8-18. Quality control and inspection data flow in a distributed processing manufacturing subsystem.

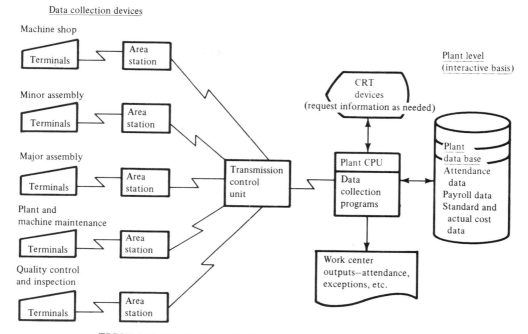

FIGURE 8–19. Data collection system informational flow for a distributed processing manufacturing subsystem.

schedules and inventory balances, and so forth. Actually, the data collection system makes informational data available to many subsystems.

The data collection system has a great impact on cost performance because it compares the results of expended labor hours against standards. Potential problems can be identified, thereby eliminating excessive costs. In a similar manner, because pertinent manufacturing data are available for on-line retrieval, shop foremen, supervisors, and managers can track the status and performance of individual parts at various levels of manufacture and act whenever exceptional situations arise. Thus, the system cuts through time-consuming manual data preparation steps and delivers timely information that tells what is happening and not what has happened, as with prior systems. Captured data are usable after entry by plant personnel.

CHAPTER SUMMARY

The manufacturing subsystem in a distributed processing environment has witnessed many exciting developments, such as numerical control machines and minicomputers. The automated factory, industrial robots, and other new processes are appearing on the production floor. In addition to the utilization of advanced manufacturing methods and machines, mathematical techniques have helped to bring an entirely new appraoch to the manufacturing subsystem. Numerous operations research techniques are capable of producing fast and accurate results for management; several of these techniques were discussed in this chapter.

For the foregoing hardware and technical advances to be operational in a distributed processing manufacturing subsystem, a data base must be accessible by various CRT devices, especially those on or near the production floor. The manufacturing data base must be structured such that it meets the needs of those that require timely responses, whether they be line personnel, operating management, or higher management. Only in this manner can the manufacturing subsystem operate in an interactive processing mode, representing a considerable advancement over the integrated MIS.

QUESTIONS

1. What are the essential differences between an integrated MIS manufacturing subsystem and a distributed processing manufacturing subsystem?

2. a. Enumerate the manufacturing data that should be stored on the corporate data base for centralized processing.
   b. Enumerate the manufacturing data that should be stored on the division data base for local processing.

3. State the various types of manufacturing information that can be and should be batch-processed in a distributed processing system.

4. Prepare a system flowchart for a manufacturing subsystem that depicts the information flow and the physical flow in a distributed processing environment.

5. Referring to the section on the operations of the machine shop, recommend improvements that reflect an ideal distributed processing operating mode.

6. Referring to the section on the operations of the major assembly area, recommend improvements that reflect an ideal distributed processing operating mode.

7. How important is a data collection system for a distributed processing manufacturing subsystem? Explain.

SELECTED REFERENCES

Anderson, R. A., "Programmable Automation: The Bright Future of Computers in Manufacturing," *Datamation*, Dec. 1972.

Arnold, J. G., "Online at the Factory," *Computer Decisions*, March 1975.

Benedict, G. A., "Time Sharing Keeps Machine Shop Production on Time," *Computer Decisions*, Feb. 1970.

Bevis, G. A., "A Management Viewpoint on the Implementation of a MRP System," *Production and Inventory Management*, March 1976.

Birmingham, D. J., "Factory Data Systems Smooth Production Flow," *Computer Decisions*, March 1972.

Bitran, G. R., and Hox, A. C., "On the Design of Hierarchical Production Planning Systems," *Decision Sciences,* Vol. 8, 1977.

Budzilovich, P. N., "Computers Prove Their Mettle in Manufacturing," *Computer Decisions,* June 1976.

Buffa, E. S., *Modern Production Management,* New York: John Wiley & Sons, Inc., 1977.

Campbell, G. J., "Tapping Your Plant's Hidden Capacity," *Industry Week,* Nov. 18, 1974.

Clark, J. F., and Cohen, D. M., "An Approach to Simulation of Multilevel Production Systems," *AFIPS Conference Proceedings* (National Computer Conference), Vol. 46, 1977.

Cogar, S., "Factory Management on a Mini," *Datamation,* Nov. 1976.

Conlon, J. R., "Is Your Master Production Schedule Feasible," *Production and Inventory Management,* March 1976.

Davis, K. R., and Leitch, R. A., "Improving Marketing-Production Coordination Through On-Line Modeling," *Production and Inventory Management,* Second Quarter, 1976.

Fischer, W. A., "Line of Balance: Obsolete After MRP?," *Production and Inventory Management,* Dec. 1975.

Frankovic, E. J., "Integrated Data Base Is Key to Production Control System," *Computers and Automation,* May 1970.

Fryer, S. J., "Minicomputers Speed Automation on the Factory Floor," *Computer Decisions,* Sept. 1970.

Infosystems Report, "Computers in Manufacturing," *Infosystems,* April 1976.

Kulerman, D., "Online in Real Time," *Tooling and Production,* June 1973.

Lee, W. B., and Khumawala, B. M., "Simulation Testing of Aggregate Production Planning Models in an Implementation Methodology," *Management Science,* Feb. 1974.

Leonard, L. V., "Improve Scheduling, Reduce Inventories with MRP," *Automation,* Aug. 1976.

Merchant, M. E., "The Inexorable Push for Automated Production," *Production Engineering,* Jan. 1977.

Miller, J. G., and Sprague, L. G., "Behind the Growth in Materials Requirements Planning," *Harvard Business Review,* Sept.–Oct. 1975.

Modern Data Staff Review, "Minis in Manufacturing," *Modern Data,* Nov. 1975.

Morris, R. G., and Cubbin, M. J., "Simulation of Material Handling Methods," *Industrial Engineering,* Oct. 1971.

Muther, "The Mag Count," *Modern Materials Handling,* Feb. 1974.

Peters, R. A. P., and Thumser, F., "On-Line Production Tracking Aids Integrated Management System," *Control Engineering,* Jan. 1970.

Plossl, G., "Opportunity and Mandate To Excel," *Production and Inventory Management,* March 1976.

Post, C. B., Jr., "Updating a Quality Information Feedback System," *Automation,* Aug. 1972.

Putnam, D. M., "MIS Sharpens Plant Maintenance," *Infosystems,* Sept. 1973.

Rickert, J. P., "On-Line Support for Manufacturing," *Datamation,* July 1975.

Riggs, J. L., *Production Systems: Planning, Analysis, and Control,* New York; John Wiley & Sons, Inc., 1976.

Special Report, "Minicomputers that Run the Factory," *Business Week,* Dec. 8, 1973.

Thierauf, R. J., *Systems Analysis and Design of Real-Time Management Information Systems,* Englewood Cliffs, N.J.: Prentice-Hall, Inc., 1975.

Thompson, F., "Tomorrow's Assembly System—Here Today," *Assembly Engineering,* April 1977.

Wagner, H. M., "The Design of Production and Inventory Systems for Multi-facility and Multiwarehouse Companies," *Operations Research,* March–April 1974.

DISTRIBUTED PROCESSING PHYSICAL DISTRIBUTION SUBSYSTEM— AMERICAN PRODUCTS CORPORATION

9

The introduction of business information systems has brought about an increasing emphasis on the importance of an integrated physical distribution (PD) system. The term *integrated* in this context means grouping together of those activities which have an impact on customer order service into a single subsystem, separate and distinct from other subsystems. Normally, a physical distribution subsystem includes the functions of handling shipping orders from sales order processing, finished goods inventory control, outgoing traffic, shipping schedules to warehouses and customers, warehousing of finished goods, and other order-service-related activities. The physical distribution subsystem discussed in this chapter for integrated MIS and distributed processing centers on these activities.

The subject matter of the chapter focuses initially on an integrated MIS physical distribution subsystem in terms of its major functions. After an examination of the present system for the American Products Corporation, distributed processing design considerations for the physical distribution system are examined, specifically those relating to data base elements and a routine for the next closest warehouse. In the last part of the chapter we shall present the design of the physical distribution subsystem in a distributed processing environment, focusing on these functions:

- shipping to customers and warehouses—outgoing traffic
- warehousing—finished goods
- inventory—finished goods

These functions form the essential parts of the physical distribution subsystem for the American Products Corporation.

OVERVIEW OF PHYSICAL DISTRIBUTION ENVIRONMENT

The physical distribution subsystem, depicted in Figure 9–1, consists of three major functions as set forth previously and is under the supervision of PD management. The quality control and inspection department at the plant level forwards goods for shipment directly to customers or through plant-attached warehouses to customers. The information flow for the warehousing operations begins when a customer shipment order is received from the marketing subsystem, specifically sales order processing at the plant level. A clerk enters the data via a CRT device for storage on the plant data base after checking and approving the customer's credit.

Basically, the customer order is pulled and shipped. In those cases in which finished goods are not available because of inventory errors, incorrect entries, and other factors, the unavailable items are not back-ordered. Rather, the *next closest warehouse* routine (to be explained in a subsequent section) is employed by the shipping clerk at the warehouse filling the order. In this manner, the customer order can be filled as soon as possible rather than having to wait for a replenishment of stock. This approach to finished goods speeds up the physical flow and improves service to customers.

In keeping with the concept of distributed processing, basically control over day-to-day operations has been moved from the corporate level under integrated MIS to the plant level. As explained in the chapter on the marketing subsystem, this local processing approach assists in improving the customer service level. Also, it aids in reducing errors and confusion involved at times with finished goods inventory. Thus, off-loading physical distribution activities from St. Louis has resulted in increased efficiency in this important subsystem, especially when viewed from the standpoint of the corporation's customers.

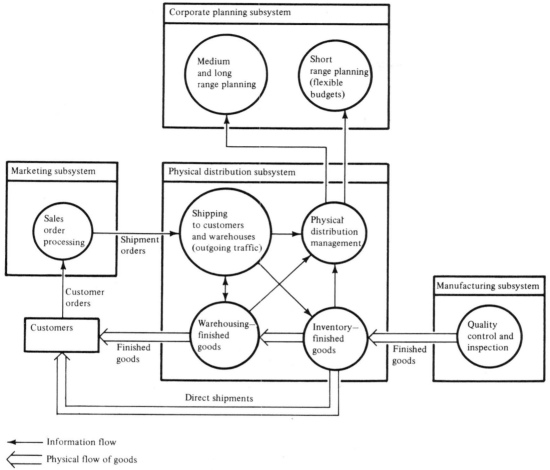

FIGURE 9-1. Physical distribution subsystem information and physical flow to and from other subsystems—American Products Corporation.

INTEGRATED MIS PHYSICAL DISTRIBUTION SUBSYSTEM

Once the goods for a customer order have been manufactured or the finished goods are available in the firm's warehouses, they are ready for shipment. The finished products must be packed, labeled, and transported to the customer. The *shipping order* which authorizes shipment is delivered with or in advance of the goods. If delivery is made directly to the customer, he will acknowledge receipt of goods by signing a copy of the shipping order, which is then filed in the shipping office. Shipments that are made via public carriers must be accompanied by a *bill of lading,* which is actually a contract between the consigner and the carrier. There is one copy each for the customer and the public carrier, and a third copy is filed by the physical distribution section as proof of shipment.

A physical distribution subsystem in an integrated MIS (or any other type of system) focuses on inventories interconnected by a transportation network. A finished product, moving from a quality control and inspection point in the manufacturing process, passes through several storage points before reaching the customer. However, for direct shipments to customers, the physical movement of inventories is reduced to a large degree. Nevertheless, the desired goal of a PD subsystem is to find the lowest-cost method of providing movement and storage services that create time and place utilities for the firm's products. Or, to state it another way, the firm wants a physical distribution program that operates at the lowest possible cost consistent with satisfactory customer service.

To achieve the foregoing goal, certain basic questions can be asked. These include

1. What customer service levels are desirable and at what cost?
2. Which products should be made at which plants and in what quantities?
3. Which markets should each warehouse serve?
4. How many warehouses should the firm use?
5. Should an additional plant be built to lower physical distribution costs?

Although these questions cannot be answered fully with an integrated MIS owing to the lack of readily available data and the need for advanced operations research models, a distributed processing environment is better equipped to answer them. But before doing so, current physical distribution operations are presented.

SHIPPING TO CUSTOMERS AND WAREHOUSES—OUTGOING TRAFFIC

The starting point for the PD system in an integrated MIS operating mode is found within the marketing subsystem. Customer shipments are initiated by this system at the corporate level—that is, customer shipment orders, including direct shipments, are forwarded to the appropriate warehouses and plants, respectively. Also, warehouse shipment orders are forwarded to the plants by St. Louis. As illustrated in Figure 9-2, goods are packed at the warehouse and plant levels for shipment to customers and warehouses. All shipment orders are converted to punched cards, which contain sufficient information for billing the customer and making the proper adjustments to inventory. This informational data will be utilized in the section on inventory—finished goods.

To route shipments to the appropriate destination, a visual card file with frequently used route and rate data for finished products is employed. A typical

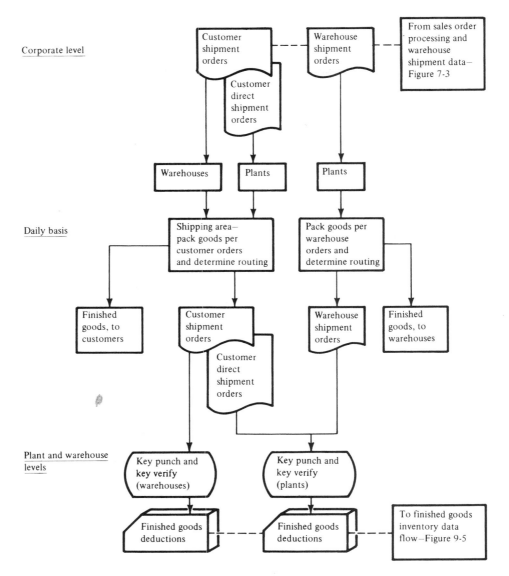

FIGURE 9-2. Shipping to customers and warehouses (outgoing traffic) data flow for an integrated
MIS physical distribution subsystem.

example of route, rate, and product information is shown in Figure 9-3. The
sample card indicates that several products are distributed by two transportation
modes plus appropriate weight breaks, among other factors. Routing information,
then, is obtained manually after searching the applicable route, rate, and product
information file.

RAIL R.B. 321 TRUCK R.B. 321 1 of 2

	PRODUCT 1	PRODUCT 2	PRODUCT 3	PRODUCT 4	PRODUCT 5	PRODUCT 6	PRODUCT 7	PRODUCT 8	PRODUCT 9	PRODUCT 10	ROUTE NO.
RAIL LCL	313	426	599	313	360						1
5m VOL.	361	410		361	349						1
CL 24 MR LBS.	174	333									3
CL 36 M LBS.	51½										3
TRUCK UNDER 1 M LBS.	386	475	667	386	386	386	520	452	475	400	5
1 M LBS. 2 M LBS.	372	453	630	372	372	372	495	432	453	384	5
2 M LBS. 5 M LBS.	362	439	606	362	362	362	478	419	439	374	5
5 M LBS. & OVER	337	411	672	337	337	337	448	392	411	349	5
TL 20 M LBS.				197		197					6
TL M LBS.											
FORWARDER											

RAIL	TRUCK	MIN. CHG.	FORWARDER
1 EL	5 H&S Motor Freight	7.86	9
2 NYC	6 LPC Express	7.86	10
3	7		11
4	8		12

EL Store door delivery 1.05¢ min. SDD $2.10

Atlanta, Ga.

FIGURE 9-3. Route, rate, and product information contained on outgoing traffic card.

WAREHOUSING—FINISHED GOODS

The major components for storing finished goods in the firm's warehouses are shown in Figure 9-4. In the receiving area of a typical warehouse, replenishment items arrive at the warehouse. The major functions performed in the receiving area are the unloading of the stock, verification of the unloaded quantities, inspection of the received materials for damage, and entering the received materials into the warehouse inventory. Typically, the handling required to move the received materials into the storage system involves the following functions: transferring to a palletizing area, palletizing the received stock, and transferring the pallet loads from the palletizing area into some relatively permanent location in the storage system. This movement into the storage system is accomplished by automatic conveyor.

The function of the storage area in Figure 9-4 is to hold the finished goods until they are needed for shipment. The layout of the storage area is fairly complex because items of differing shapes, sizes, and volumes are involved. Items which have the highest turnover have been located nearest the shipping area in order to minimize the amount of time expended in retrieving orders from the storage system. Thus, time required for handling between storage and shipping areas should be kept to a minimum.

At the shipping area, customer shipment orders (refer to Figure 9-2) are received which demand retrieval of goods from the storage system. The handling component from storage to shipping has several functions associated with it. There is the removal of the pallet from its storage location and its transfer to a depalletizing operation (unless full pallets are shipped). The depalletizing operation removes the required number of items from the pallet, deposits them onto a conveyor, and returns the partially unloaded pallet to the storage system. The depalletized items proceed directly either to the shipping area for loading or to an order consolidation area where an entire order is accumulated prior to movement into the shipping area.

The functions of the shipping area include checking off the quantities for each item as they are delivered from the storage system against the customer shipment order and inspecting the materials to be shipped for possible damage that may have occurred within the handling components of the warehouse. Also included is verification that the customer order has been properly loaded for rail or truck shipment.

INVENTORY—FINISHED GOODS

The finished goods deduction cards, prepared at the warehouse and plant levels, are forwarded via remote batch processing to the corporate headquarters at the end of the shift daily. On the other hand, finished goods additions are keypunched and key-verified by the data processing section from production orders completed, having been received from the quality control and inspection departments in the three manufacturing plants. These cards are forwarded via remote

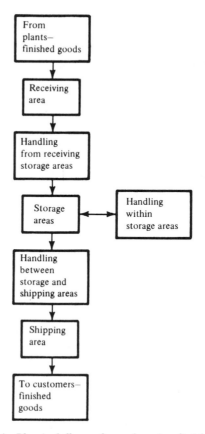

FIGURE 9-4. Physical flow of warehousing finished goods inventory in an integrated MIS physical distribution subsystem.

batch processing to the corporate headquarters daily. As illustrated in Figure 9-5, these finished goods inputs—additions and deductions—along with the customer master and finished goods inventory master files (magnetic tape) are utilized to update the finished goods inventory master file as well as produce a customer billing master file (magnetic tape) for preparing customer invoices daily.

The finished goods inventory master file provides input for preparing a weekly finished goods report. This printout is reviewed by physical distribution management in terms of what finished goods are stored at what warehouses. If there is an imbalance of stored products in one or more of the three warehouses, feedback is sent to those personnel in outgoing traffic at the plant level. Having been alerted to this condition, plant personnel alter the upcoming shipping schedules to rectify the specific warehouse overshipments made in the past. In this manner, too large as well as too small finished goods inventories at the various warehouses can be remedied.

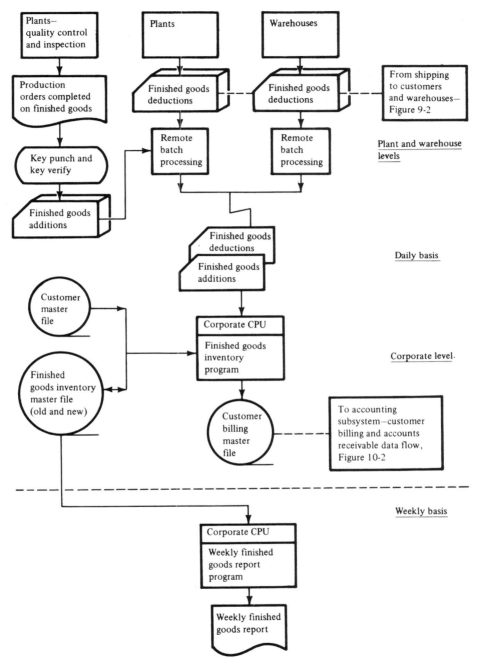

FIGURE 9-5. Finished goods inventory data flow for an integrated MIS physical distribution subsystem.

DISTRIBUTED PROCESSING PHYSICAL
DISTRIBUTION SUBSYSTEM

Although the design approach is somewhat complicated by the utilization of a computer to control warehousing operations, the physical distribution subsystem must be integrated with other subsystems. Specifically, marketing, manufacturing, and inventory must be designed with the physical distribution subsystem in mind. Likewise, PD must be designed in conjunction with the firm's other subsystems so that they will be logically related for an interactive processing mode. The design of the major physical distribution functions (namely, shipping to customers and warehouses, warehousing—finished goods, and inventory—finished goods) is examined in the remaining sections of this chapter.

PHYSICAL DISTRIBUTION DATA BASE

The design of a physical distribution subsystem, like the inventory subsystem, must have a standard coding system for finished goods inventory. This approach gives all other subsystems the ability to interact with finished goods inventory. For example, the sales order processing function must be able to interrogate the plant data base for appropriate data on goods available for shipment. In like manner, the quarterly marketing forecasts must be adjusted for finished goods on hand before determining product requirements. Thus, ready reference to current finished goods data elements is extremely important.

Finished goods inventory must be structured on an open-end basis, as are the raw materials and work-in-process inventories. The utilization of open-end files makes it possible to add new finished goods inventory items as well as delete old items. This open-end approach is not only applicable to finished goods data elements but also is an integral part of other physical distribution data elements, shown in Figure 9-6.

The physical distribution data base is constantly changing because of the type of data stored on-line. This statement applies to more than just finished goods inventory. Shipping costs from plants to warehouses, freight costs from warehouses to customers, and warehousing costs, to name a few, are in a constant state of flux. Within this type of environment, the plant data base must be accessible via CRT devices for updating changes as they occur. Systems analysts must consider these factors in their design efforts.

Next Closest Warehouse Model

The purpose of the next closest warehouse model is to maximize customer service. For the company to lose a sale because of a stockout at the warehouse getting the request is not good business. The shipment of a small quantity from a neighboring warehouse is justifiable. In such cases, air freight is an acceptable means of shipment to prevent losing a customer to competition.

The mathematical model, set forth in Figure 9-7, locates materials in the next

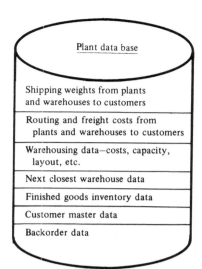

Plant data base

Shipping weights from plants
and warehouses to customers

Routing and freight costs from
plants and warehouses to customers

Warehousing data—costs, capacity,
layout, etc.

Next closest warehouse data

Finished goods inventory data

Customer master data

Backorder data

FIGURE 9-6. Typical physical distribution data base elements at the plant level.

closest (least expensive) warehouse. Although only two alternative warehouses are available, this generalized model sets up a hierarchy of closest warehouses in terms of air freight costs. Warehouses are queried in sequence for the short item(s). When finished goods are located, they are shipped directly to the customer. If an item is not available from the closest warehouse, the order is automatically routed to the closest plant capable of producing the item. The order can take one of two paths: It can be cancelled by the customer if delivery will be too late, or it can be manufactured by the selected factory. If manufactured, items are shipped directly to the customer. In either case, exception reports are generated to appraise management of the action taken.

SHIPPING TO CUSTOMERS AND WAREHOUSE MODULE—OUTGOING TRAFFIC

The shipment of finished goods is a multidimensional problem for the American Products Corporation. As information is received at the plant level from sales order processing (marketing subsystem), finished products are shipped in one of the following ways:

- to one warehouse from another for future sale—weekly basis
- to customers directly from the three manufacturing plants based on regular or special orders—daily basis
- to customers from warehouses based on regular customer orders—daily basis

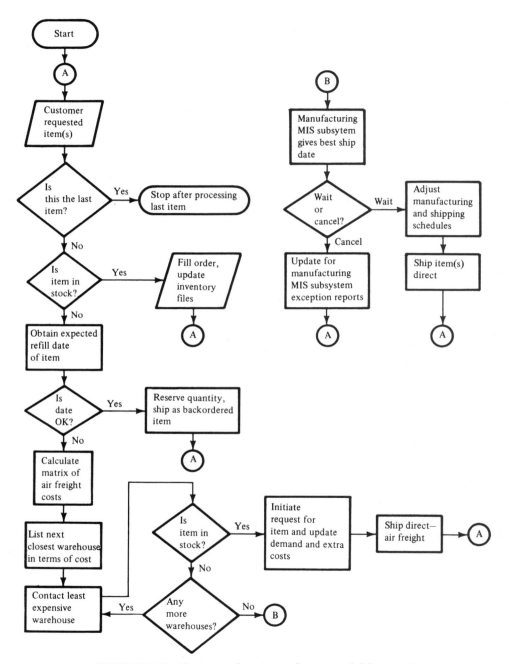

FIGURE 9-7. The next closest warehouse model for maximizing customer service.

Going beyond a daily basis, these data can be analyzed weekly in order to determine an optimum method for stocking the firm's warehouses. Shipping on these two time bases is discussed below.

Daily Basis

Direct shipments to customers present no real problem to distribution management because the warehousing function is circumvented (Figure 9-8). Basically, the PD clerk interrogates the computer for instant shipping information. Rate, route, and carrier information is made available via a CRT terminal. The outgoing traffic clerk selects the appropriate means of transportation, which is stored on-line for billing the customer later. The customer shipment order is completed with this information, and goods are shipped to the customer. The accounting subsystem takes care of customer billing at the plant level.

The procedures for customer shipment orders are somewhat the same as for direct shipment orders, except that goods are shipped from an attached warehouse rather than directly from one of the three plants (Figure 9-8). All outgoing traffic information is stored on-line for instant retrieval by the PD department via a CRT terminal. The best routing method is selected to keep the firm's costs at a minimum. These data are also stored on the plant data base—specifically, in the customer billing data file—for subsequent billing.

The second and last difference between direct and nondirect shipments is the employment of the next closest warehouse model. In those cases in which finished products are not available at the attached warehouse, the next closest warehouse in terms of lowest shipping costs to the customer is queried for available finished goods. If goods are available from this alternate source, they are shipped. If not available, the third warehouse is interrogated for an answer. As demonstrated previously (Figure 9-7), a factory order is initiated or the order is cancelled for the finished goods in question, depending on the circumstances.

Weekly Basis

The daily procedures for shipping merchandise from plants and warehouses to customers can operate best when goods are available at the right time and place for shipment. To be near this desired level, a mathematical multidistribution model is employed at the corporate level (Figure 9-8). Weekly, this model reevaluates past shipping data, comparing actual shipping costs to the lowest possible costs as generated by the model. Not only is the comparison made, but it is also used to help schedule future shipments, because the firm has found a high correlation between actual customer shipments and projected customer shipments. The output of the three plants, then, is distributed on the basis of projected shipments for the three warehouses. Of course, current finished goods on hand are taken into account in the development of the forthcoming warehouse shipping schedules.

Before the foregoing shipping schedules can be developed, certain distribution

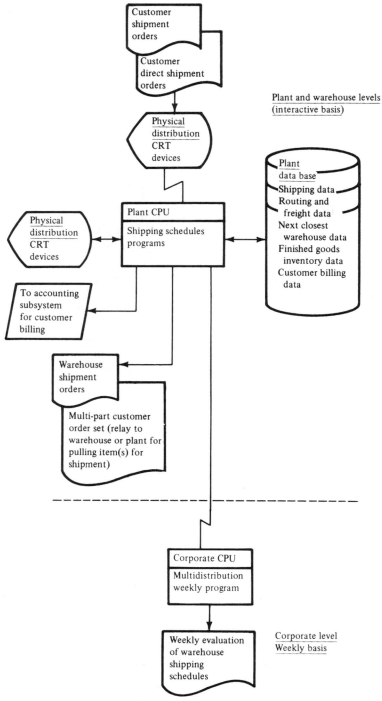

FIGURE 9-8. Shipment data flow at the corporate, ware-house, and plant levels within a distributed processing physical distribution subsystem.

factors must be determined and made available for computer usage. Among these are

1. size of the market in terms of the units of each product that is serviced by a particular warehouse
2. location of alternative warehouse
3. transit times and costs from each alternative warehouse to each market
4. product mix in each market and products made in each plant
5. average weight and size for each product as well as the pounds carried per rail car or truck
6. plant capacities for each plant and product class
7. unit manufacturing costs for each product of each plant
8. unit freight costs for less than carload lots (LCL), less than truckload lots (LTL), carload lots (CL), and truckload lots (TL).

In general, these data are stored on magnetic tape, because there is no need to keep them stored on the corporate data base.

Warehouse shipment data provide the necessary input for totaling actual weekly cost data. The multidistribution model relies on the foregoing listed file inputs plus rate and routing information from the originating plant through the warehouses and then to customers. In this way the output is an improved solution over the actual one, because it gives PD management precise knowledge about its efficiency.

WAREHOUSING—FINISHED GOODS MODULE

Warehousing of finished products in an advanced distributed processing environment revolves around the utilization of the computer for three levels of control. The first level is computer scheduling control, which is concerned with the management of the warehouse as a whole. This includes scheduled ordering, perpetual inventory management, and shipping schedules. The second level is directed toward the flow of goods through the warehouse. Here, the computer is involved in the decisions concerning the flow of specific items through the materials handling equipment into and out of the various storage system areas (Figure 9-9). The third level involves the computer as the controlling device for all operations in the warehousing system. Every move that is made by the materials handling equipment is initiated by the computer. In reality, the computer program defines the sequence of operations that are to be undertaken by the materials handling equipment.

The major components of control for the American Products Corporation and the role of the computer itself in directing materials handling control are depicted in Figure 9-9. Control components of an automated warehouse include materials control, information control, sensing devices, and command devices as

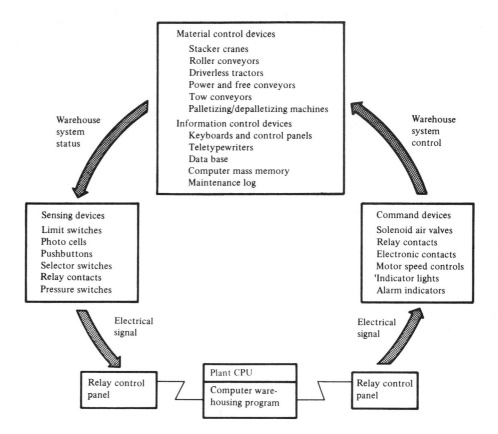

FIGURE 9-9. Control components of an automated warehouse for a distributed processing physical distribution subsystem.

well as relay control panels and computer control. In such a system, the computer can simultaneously monitor switches, relays, and materials-flow controls. Moreover, it contains within itself the definition of what constitutes a proper flow. It knows the sequence in which signals should be received in the relay control panels if they are to exercise proper control over materials flow.

Because the computer is monitoring individual relays and individual control points in the materials handling system, it prints a message when it diagnoses a failure within the system. The computer indicates to a maintenance man the particular relay or signal which led to the failure. In industrial applications of this concept of diagnostic monitoring, it has been found that troubleshooting time for the vast majority of system failures has been virtually eliminated. Also, the failure recognition time has been considerably decreased; it cannot, however, be completely eliminated because it does not make economic sense to monitor each single relay in the entire warehouse. The relays that are considered essential to operation are the ones that are selected for monitoring. Accordingly, until one of the critical relays is found to be in error, a failure which may have occurred in the noncritical area will go unrecognized by the monitoring system.

Referring to the foregoing three levels of control, computer scheduling control (the first level) can be employed to great advantage in terms of dollar savings. The computer can be used to detect shifting patterns of demand. Management can be alerted for the purpose of evaluating whether or not the shifting is a temporary or long-range phenomenon.

Scheduling (the second level) can be integrated so as to take advantage in the area of scheduled maintenance. The computer is used to maintain equipment failure histories; on this basis it can derive statistics, such as mean time before failure, on specific components of the handling systems. In addition, the computer can more efficiently utilize the time of maintenance personnel in systematically checking portions of systems that are expected to cause trouble in the near future.

The direct computer control of materials handling equipment (the third level) is really a question of machine design and operation. The companies that manufacture and market these machines obviously have the most experience in designing reliable equipment. Refitting an existing handling machine to run under computer control is likely to be more expensive than purchasing new machinery specifically adapted or designed with computer control in mind. This last level of control, then, is critical to the entire warehousing operation and must be designed as expertly as possible.

INVENTORY—FINISHED GOODS MODULE

The objective of finished goods inventory is to have the right amount of inventory available when required by the customer. Too little finished goods inventory results in a condition of poor customer service, while too much inventory ties up excess funds, resulting in a lower return on the firm's total assets. The approach taken below for distributed processing considers these important factors whereby customer service and finished goods cost are placed in their proper perspective for optimizing overall PD objectives.

The finished goods inventory subsystem, depicted in Figure 9-10, is on an interactive basis for all finished goods inventory transactions. Generally, additions to inventory are the result of the completion of production orders at the plant level, having been forwarded from the quality control and inspection department for updating the plant data base. Deductions from the finished goods data base are received via CRT terminals from the plant and warehouses, representing shipments to customers. These data plus the customer master file are utilized by the accounting subsystem for customer billing. Also, all information concerning back orders is stored on the plant data base for billing and further on-line analysis and reporting. In addition to introducing plus and minus values at the plant and warehouse levels, adjustments can be made to correct shipments, inventory, and other errors that have come to the attention of operating management. Thus, an interactive approach to finished goods keeps the plant data base up-to-date at all times.

Two important finished goods reports are prepared for controlling this large

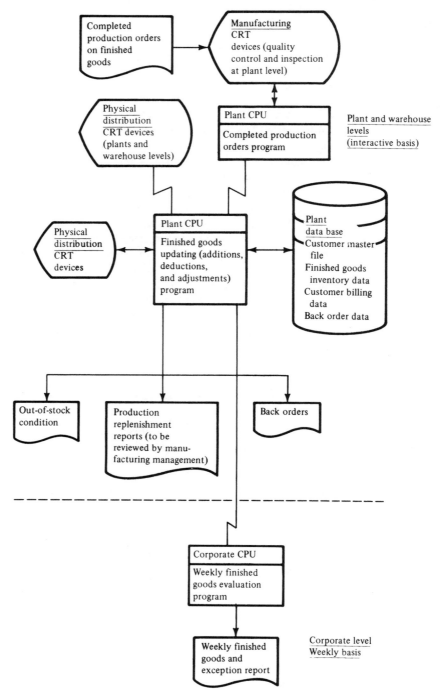

FIGURE 9-10. Finished goods inventory data flow for a distributed processing physical distribution subsystem.

financial investment at the plant level. Those finished goods that are out of stock are reported immediately to physical distribution, inventory, and manufacturing management. Management may find it necessary to issue a production order if goods of this type are not on order. At the corporate level, the weekly finished goods and exception report is not only a listing of items available for sale by warehouses; it also highlights out-of-stock conditions and what corrective action has been taken to remedy the situation. Those goods which are overstocked are starred for action by management. With such a summary and exception report, PD management can start corrective action, such as alerting marketing as to overstocked conditions of certain inventory items which can be candidates for special sales promotions. Likewise, the weekly finished goods and exception report can be reviewed to ensure that neither too little nor too much is tied up in finished goods inventory. This review is intended to ensure that customer service in relation to the finished goods inventory is properly balanced. These reports and others, then, are designed to maximize the firm's investment in finished goods in order to meet the firm's overall PD objectives.

CHAPTER SUMMARY

The distributed processing physical distribution subsystem is an improvement over the present integrated MIS subsystem. The ability to extract timely information allows the American Products Corporation to provide better customer service throughout its major modules. In the area of outgoing traffic or shipping to customers and warehouses (first module), past information can be evaluated in order to improve future shipping schedules. The utilization of computerized warehousing (second module) alerts management to shifting patterns of demand. Within the finished goods inventory function (third module), production replenishment reports are issued for appropriate action by manufacturing management. In essence, PD management is supplied meaningful and, in some cases, instantaneous information for maintaining and improving service to the firm's customers in a distributed processing environment.

QUESTIONS

1. What is the rationale for placing the finished goods inventory module with the physical distribution subsystem rather than with some other subsystem?

2. What are the important differences between an integrated MIS physical distribution subsystem and a distributed processing physical distribution subsystem?

3. Take the physical distribution data base elements in Figure 9–6 and define their detailed parts.

4. Referring to the section on warehousing of finished goods, suggest changes that reflect an ideal distributed processing environment.

5. Give two business situations where the next closest warehouse routine would greatly assist in improving shipments to customers.

6. Define in some detail the major modules of the finished goods updating program.

SELECTED REFERENCES

Ackerman, K. B., "Physical Distribution—A New Business Revolution," *Business Horizons,* Oct. 1974.

Armstrong, R. E., "Pushbutton Handling of Small Parts," *Automation,* March 1972.

Ballou, R. H., "Probabilities and Payoffs: Aids to Distribution Decision Making," *Transportation and Distribution Management,* Aug. 1969.

Benson, J. R., "The Intelligent Warehouse," *Datamation,* Sept. 1976.

Bickerton, R. L., "The Many Faces of Automated Warehousing," *Transportation and Distribution Management,* Feb. 1971.

Bowersox, D. J., "Planning Physical Distribution Operations with Dynamic Simulation," *Journal of Marketing,* Jan. 1972.

Bowman, D., "It Takes One to Move One . . . Computers, That Is," *Production,* May 1973.

Geoffrion, A. M., "Better Distribution Planning with Computer Models," *Harvard Business Review,* July–Aug. 1976.

Haavind, R., "Warehouse Without Men Acts as the Hub of a Production Information System," *Computer Decisions,* Nov. 1969.

Heskett, J. L., "Sweeping Changes in Distribution," *Harvard Business Review,* March–April 1973.

Hopeman, R. J., *Systems Analysis and Operations Management,* Columbus, Ohio: Charles E. Merrill Publishing Co., 1970, Chap. 10.

Hoppe, C. W., "Using Simulation To Solve Transportation Problems, *Management Controls,* Dec. 1970.

Klahr, J. M., Newbourne, M. J., and Thomas, R. R., "Physical Distribution and the Mathematical Model," *Transportation and Distribution Management,* Part I—Feb. 1970, Part II—March 1970, and Part III—April 1970.

LaLonde, B. J., and Grashof, J. F., "Computer Oriented Information Systems Provide Effective P. D. Management," *Handling and Shipping,* Oct. 1969.

MMH Special Report, "How Computers Can Run Your Handling Systems," *Modern Materials Handling,* April 1973.

Mueller, D. W., "Applying Computers to Warehousing," *Automation,* Jan. 1970.

Nelson, R. A., *Total Physical Distribution Management,* New York: AMACOM, 1975.

Rubal' Skiy, G. B., "On the Level of Supplies in a Warehouse with a Lag in Procurement," *Engineering Cybernetics,* Jan.–Feb. 1972.

Shapiro, B. P., "Improve Distribution with Your Promotional Mix," *Harvard Business Review,* March–April 1977.

Thierauf, R. J., *Systems Analysis and Design of Real-Time Management Information Systems,* Englewood Cliffs, N.J.: Prentice-Hall, Inc., 1975.

Zierer, T. K., Mitchell, W. A., and White, T. R. S., "Practical Applications of Linear Programming to Shell's Distribution Problem," *Interfaces,* Aug. 1976.

DISTRIBUTED PROCESSING ACCOUNTING SUBSYSTEM— AMERICAN PRODUCTS CORPORATION 10

The functions of accounting in a distributed processing environment are no different from the previous system. Basically, they center around recording, classifying, and summarizing transactions and events that are, in part at least, of a financial character and interpreting results thereof. Standard double entry is utilized to reflect the in- and outflow of cash and noncash transactions. However, accounting data are stored either on tape, disk, or some other machine-processible medium at the appropriate level, i.e., local or central. Accounting reports generated depend on the type of management information desired at the local and corporate levels.

Within this chapter, the essential elements of the batch processing system are explored before specifying the distributed processing accounting subsystem. Representative data base elements provide an underlying structure for designing this area's major components, which include

receivables and payables

- payroll
- cost accounting
- financial statements and tax returns

Essentially, the accounting subsystem for the American Products Corporation is structured on these four functions.

OVERVIEW OF ACCOUNTING ENVIRONMENT

The major functions found in the accounting environment are shown in Figure 10-1. They include receivables and payables, payroll, cost accounting, and financial statements and tax returns. However, the design of these functions will take on new dimensions because of the computer's interactive capabilities. Accounting data will be stored on the plant and corporate data bases, retrievable as are or capable of manipulation depending on the user's needs. The system will be capable of calculating accounting information on a current basis. Specifically, management will be able to retrieve current cost data, financial operating ratios, and cash balances.

In conjunction with the preparation of financial statements by the accounting subsystem, other subsystems can benefit from this timely information. The finance subsystem can analyze the current cash position for determining short-term needs. Likewise, the corporate planning staff can evaluate current trends in profitability for last-minute budget changes. Also, inventory management can evaluate its investment in light of current operating conditions. Purchasing management can appraise its overall ability to keep raw materials cost at a minimum. The ability to extract current financial information via a CRT terminal can indicate changes to the user as they occur. From this viewpoint, corrective measures can be effected much sooner.

As compared with the prior subsystem, the accounting subsystem will experience more changes in terms of off-loading from the central processing site. Specifically, receivables, payables, factory and office payroll, and cost accounting will be performed at the plant level for each of the three manufacturing plants, while processing was accomplished previously at St. Louis. The output from the accounting activities are transmitted for the preparation of financial statements and tax returns at the corporate level.

INTEGRATED MIS ACCOUNTING SUBSYSTEM

After the shipment of finished products, the accounting department prepares *customer invoices*. These not only serve as a record of charges but are also the basis on which the seller can legally claim payment for goods and services. Generally, the first two copies are sent to the customer, and remaining copies are distributed to the marketing department, the salesman, and the accounting department's billing files. Depending on the terms of the invoice, payments received from customers are

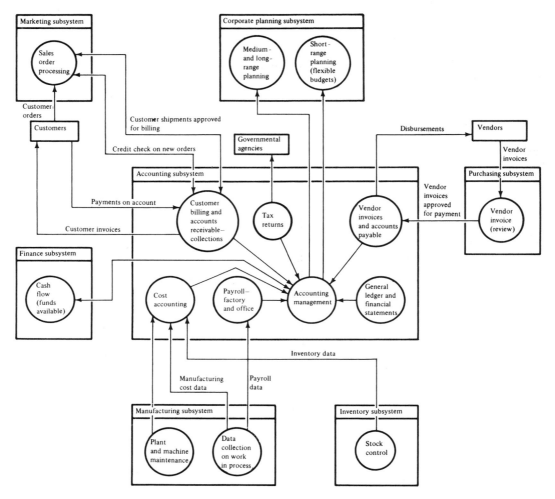

FIGURE 10-1. Accounting subsystem flow to and from other subsystems—American Products Corporation.

deposited in the firm's bank account. These payments are recorded in the *cash receipts journal* as documented evidence of their receipt. Periodically, *statements of accounts* are mailed to inform customers of the status of their accounts.

In addition to billing and collecting, the accounting department is concerned with disbursing funds, the major types being for payroll and for goods and services. *Time cards* are the originating source for paying salaries and wages. They may also be used for making labor distribution charges to various departments. *Payroll checks and earnings statements* are the output of payroll procedures.

The second type of disbursements involves checking the vendor's invoices against the purchase orders and receiving reports initially. Upon approval of payment by the purchasing department, *voucher-checks* are prepared. A voucher-check is a check with an attached voucher that contains sufficient space for date, purchase order number, vendor number, description, amount, discount, and net payment. The first copy is mailed to the payee on designated days of the month according to stated terms on the vendor's invoices, and duplicate copies are used for data processing. When processing is complete, they are filed.

The foregoing accounting functions are not complete untill all legitimate governmental forms have been prepared and the proper voucher-checks drawn for the respective amounts due. Federal, state, and local governments require the preparation of specific tax forms, ranging from *federal income tax returns, reports on social security taxes withheld (employer and employee), federal and state unemployment compensation returns, state income tax returns, personal property tax returns,* and *city income tax returns.* Other governmental information returns that form the basis for statistical data on the United States are also required. In the final analysis, government requirements can place a substantial load over and beyond the normal data needed for the firm's internal operations.

RECEIVABLES AND PAYABLES

The data processing flow for accounts receivable is an extension of the physical distribution subsystem—in particular, the finished goods inventory function (see Figure 9-5). The customer billing master magnetic tape file plus payment and adjustment cards provide the daily input for updating the accounts-receivable master magnetic tape file and producing customer invoices per Figure 10-2. Also, this program produces a sales-register and cash-receipts magnetic tape file that is used to print a daily-sales register and a cash-receipts register during two separate computer runs.

While the foregoing receivable activities center around daily operations at the corporate level, there are, at this level, two other accounts-receivable computer processing runs on a monthly basis (Figure 10-2). These include aging of accounts receivable and printing customer statements. The first output breaks down the balances due by past time periods—that is, by 30, 60, 90, and over 90 days. The other output is an itemized statement of each customer's account, which is promptly mailed to expedite payments on accounts.

Accounts payables, the reverse of accounts receivables, are concerned with paying vendor invoices when they become due on the corporate level. Generally, vendor invoices are reviewed by the purchasing department for prices and quantities before they are forwarded to the accounting department. Those invoices which are found to be incorrect by the purchasing agent are reviewed with the appropriate vendor.

Vendor invoice cards are prepared to update the accounts-payable master magnetic tape file twice a week. The output of the accounts-payable and voucher-register program is a new accounts-payable master file and a printed voucher regis-

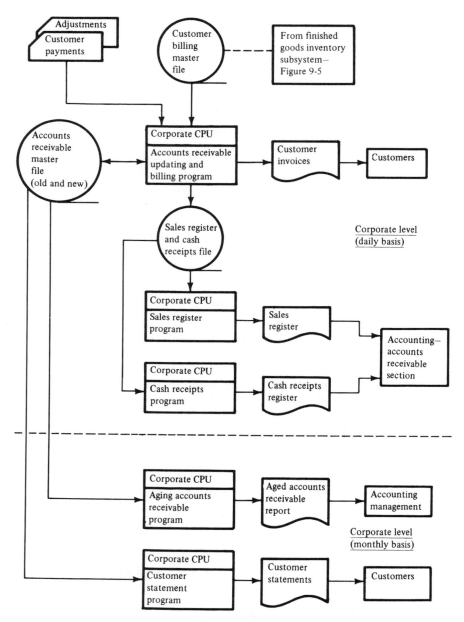

FIGURE 10-2. Customer billing and accounts-receivable data flow for an integrated MIS accounting subsystem.

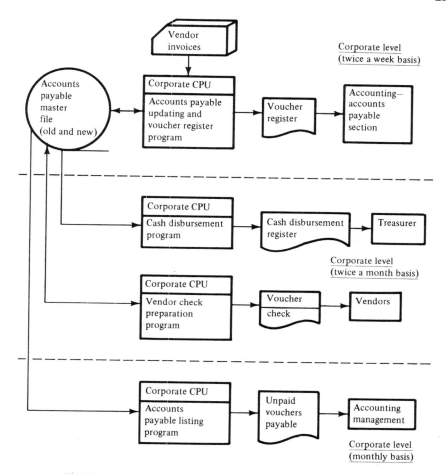

FIGURE 10-3. Accounts-payable and cash disbursements data flow for an integrated MIS accounting subsystem.

ter. As shown in Figure 10-3, on the 10th and 25th of each month, at the corporate level, a cash-disbursements register is prepared initially on the computer, followed by the printing of the vendor checks, which are mailed to vendors. At the end of each month, a listing of unpaid invoices by vendors is prepared for analysis by the controller and treasurer.

PAYROLL

Payroll, like receivables and payables, must go through a series of preliminary steps before checks can be issued on the plant level. As illustrated in Figure 10-4, weekly time cards are the input, along with the payroll master file for the gross pay

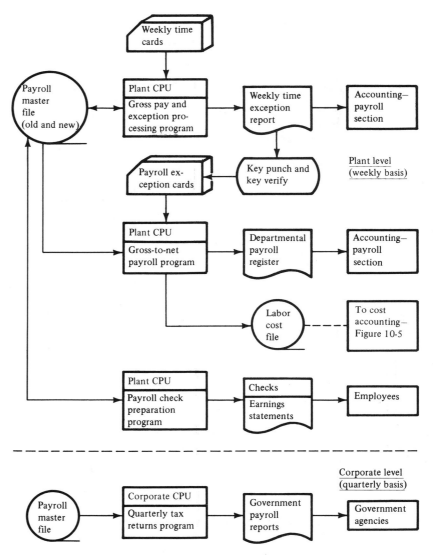

FIGURE 10-4. Payroll data flow for an integrated MIS accounting subsystem.

and exception processing program. The output is the weekly time exception report, containing excessive hours worked by employees, missing weekly time cards, and comparable exception items. After all exceptions have been investigated by the accounting-payroll section, exception cards are prepared. The payroll master magnetic tape file, including these cards, are computer-processed for preparing the weekly payroll register and the labor cost file for cost accounting. The succeeding computer processing program produces the weekly payroll checks, which are then distributed to plant employees.

The preceding weekly processing steps are directed toward plant and ware-house operations. Comparable payroll processing occurs at the corporate level for corporate officers and their staff. Whether they are on the plant or corporate level, governmental reports are prepared each quarter for reporting federal withholding and FICA taxes (required by law).

COST ACCOUNTING

Payroll and its distribution, like raw materials and work in process, are vital to cost accounting. A labor cost analysis processing run at the plant level, as shown in Figure 10-5, has as its output, a work center labor cost analysis. The report is

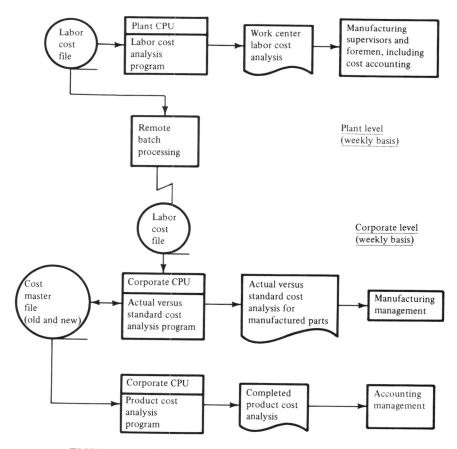

FIGURE 10-5. Cost accounting data flow for an integrated MIS accounting subsystem.

reviewed by plant supervisors and foremen as well as by the cost accounting section. These data, per the labor cost file (magnetic tape), are forwarded via remote batch processing to corporate headquarters for producing overall cost analysis reports.

Cost analysis at St. Louis is concerned with taking management action where costs have exceeded standards by 5 percent. The first of the two cost reports is actual versus standard costs for manufactured costs. The second one is a completed product cost analysis. Both reports contain raw materials, direct labor, and manufacturing overhead for actual costs versus standard costs. Weekly, these reports are scrutinized by accounting management. Where unfavorable results are reported, the appropriate level of management is called upon to explain unfavorable deviations. Only in this manner can unfavorable operating conditions be corrected.

FINANCIAL STATEMENTS AND TAX RETURNS

The input for the integrated MIS accounting subsystem of the American Products Corporation often originates in other subsystems. Marketing, manufacturing, inventory, purchasing, and physical distribution, to name the more important ones, forward data that are summarized onto magnetic tape for accounting. As illustrated in Figure 10-6, sales, payroll, receivables, payables, inventory, and cost data are direct input for the accounting subsystem. No matter what the sources are, these data are combined with existing accounting files for producing desired accounting output.

At the corporate level, the end result of all accounting activities is the preparation of financial statements, including tax returns. Before these outputs can be produced, detailed accounting transactions must have been compiled and accessible for computer processing. By and large, for this phase of accounting, these data will have been stored on magnetic tape, providing input as depicted in Figure 10-6. Also, accounting master magnetic tape files which include the general ledger will be an essential part of input for producing a general journal and a trial balance for the current month. The updated accounting master file is computer-processed in order to produce the following:

- general ledger balances
- monthly balance sheet
- monthly income statement
- detailed product statements
- cost analysis reports

In like manner, periodic tax reports, also shown in Figure 10-6, are computer-prepared when the accounting master file and selected governmental tax cards are the source input. Thus, an integrated MIS does provide for a wide range of managerial reports. However, as is the case with many other functions, there is

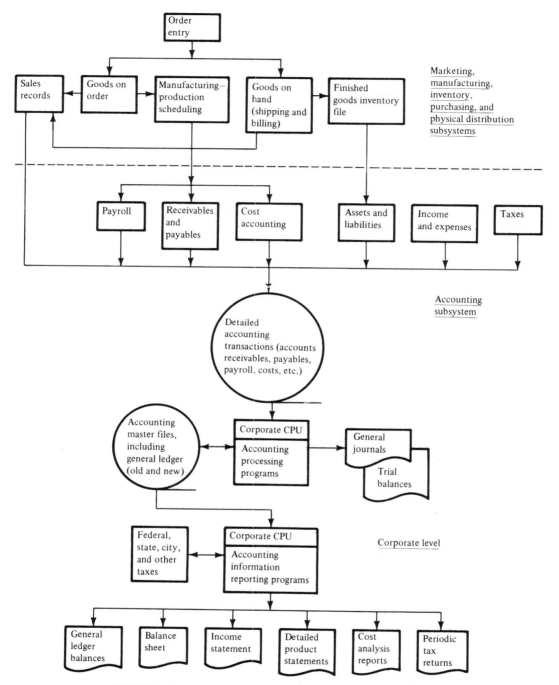

FIGURE 10-6. Accounting data flow within an integrated MIS system for producing financial statements and tax returns.

a time lag in receiving critical information needed to correct current operational deficiencies.

DISTRIBUTED PROCESSING ACCOUNTING SUBSYSTEM

Design considerations for the accounting subsystem in a distributed processing environment go beyond its own subsystem, as is the case for the integrated MIS. Customer billing is initiated by marketing, while vendor invoices are received from purchasing. Payroll, whether it is factory or office, originates outside the accounting subsystem. Similarly, feedback of product cost data is forwarded from the manufacturing work centers and inventory. The only real accounting functions that are generated within their own module are financial statements and tax returns. The former are forwarded to all subsystems for management review as well as for appropriate corrective action. The latter, on the other hand, are mailed to the various federal, state, and local tax agencies. Thus, design considerations must take into account most other subsystems for developing an effective distributed processing accounting subsystem.

ACCOUNTING DATA BASE

The accounting data bank (magnetic tape files in an integrated MIS) must be converted to data stored on-line. The accounting data base should be structured by the type of data, shown in Figure 10-7. But of equal importance, critical information should be easily accessible for instantaneous display by a CRT terminal.

Data at the plant level for accounts receivable and payable consist of such items as customer billing, accounts receivable, collection, vendor invoice, and accounts payable. Some of this information originates in other subsystems, while other are an integral part of the accounting subsystem. Ultimately, receivables and payables data elements are utilized in producing the firm's financial statements. In a similar fashion, payroll data base elements are received from the factory and office departments and are the basis for preparing weekly payrolls at the plant level as well as periodic statements within the accounting subsystem.

Cost accounting relies heavily on data compiled by manufacturing, inventory, and payroll functions at the plant level. Current input on operations is capable of being extracted and compared to standard cost data elements for meaningful analysis of operations. In addition, cost data at the corporate level are employed in the preparation of financial statements, the end result of all accounting activities.

The data base necessary to produce financial statements contains not only actual figures but also budgeted figures from the corporate planning subsystem— in particular, those for income and expenses on a flexible budgeting basis. Current tax rates for calculating estimated taxes are stored on the corporate data base for preparing periodic statements as well as for determining taxes due on the federal,

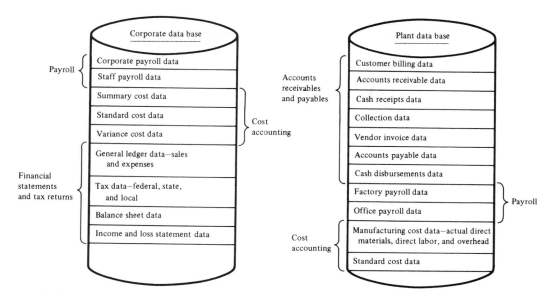

FIGURE 10-7. Typical accounting data base elements at the corporate and plant levels.

state, and local government levels. Basically, these data elements comprise the accounting data base needed in a distributed processing environment for timely accounting and finance information at the plant and corporate levels.

RECEIVABLES AND PAYABLES MODULES

The data flow for customer billing does not originate with the accounting function but rather with the sales order processing function. By way of review, a sales order clerk enters the customer order via a CRT terminal. The individual checks the customer's credit and then interrogates the finished goods inventory file and/or enters the production order for the desired items not available from any of the firm's warehouses. Data are accumulated on the plant data base regarding warehouse shipments and back orders. Each day at the plant level, a customer billing program is triggered and customer invoices are printed on the high-speed printer and mailed to customers. Likewise, a sales register is printed immediately following the customer billing run. The foregoing procedures form the basis for charging the customer accounts at the plant level, as shown in Figure 10-8.

The CRT terminal is also employed to post customer payments, only this time they are entered by the accounts-receivable section of the accounting subsystem. All legitimate complaints on customer accounts are handled as received and appropriate adjustments made to the plant data base, thereby reflecting the correct (current) accounts-receivable balances. Daily, a cash-receipts program is initiated

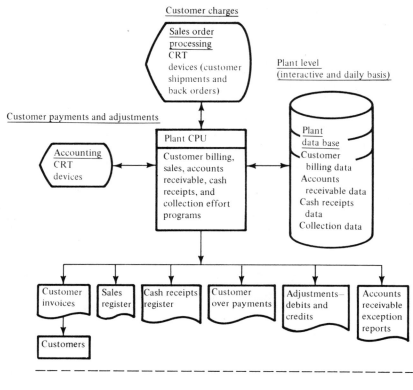

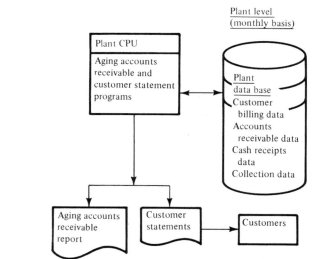

FIGURE 10-8. Customer billing and accounts-receivable data flow for a distributed processing accounting subsystem.

after all customer payments have been posted, resulting in a cash-receipts register. In addition, daily exception reports are triggered at the end of the day, including customer overpayments and adjustments—debits and credits. Entries are automatically made to the general ledger stored on the plant data base.

Just as with integrated MIS, reports are prepared on a monthly basis (Figure 10–8). These include aging of accounts receivable and the preparation of customer statements. Although an aging list is printed once a month, a terminal device can be used to retrieve information on accounts, thereby making customer account data available on an interactive basis.

Although the basic accounts-receivable functions are handled on a daily basis, the same time basis is not necessary for all accounts-payable activities. Basically, vendor invoices are entered by the accounts-payable section of the accounting department (Figure 10–9) at the plant level after review by the purchasing subsystem. Daily entry is via a CRT terminal for storage on the data base. Twice a week, a voucher register is prepared for invoices recieved since the preparation of the previous register.

The American Products Corporation, which pays its bills on the 10th and 25th of the month, schedules cash disbursements and voucher-check runs on these days. The cash-disbursements register is a listing of checks to be paid and those which will take advantage of cash discounts offered. After a brief review by the accounts-payable section, voucher-checks are computer-prepared. At the end of the run is a listing of prior overpayments to specific vendors.

Monthly, a list of unpaid vouchers is prepared at the plant level. Also, a vendor overpayments/credits listing is printed for review by the accounts-payable manager. It should be noted that current accounts of individual vendors, like customers, can be interrogated for current information at any time from a CRT device.

PAYROLL MODULE

Payroll within a distributed processing environment does not operate alone but relies on input from other subsystems. Factory payroll is an essential part of the data collection system found within the manufacturing subsystem. When a factory employee enters his work center in the morning, he enters his plastic badge into a badge-reader remote terminal. As shown in Figure 10–10, such terminals are connected to an area station, which, in turn, is connected to the plant CPU through a transmission control unit. When it is time for the employee's shift to begin, his foreman activates the area station to receive a printout of work center attendance.

Depending on the employee's current work assignment, the job being worked on is entered via the terminal. The employee makes a setting on the terminal to indicate the type of transactions he is entering (work assignment). Next, he enters his employee badge number in the selector dial and inserts a prepunched job card in the card-reader slot. He presses the entry level, and the data are recorded on the data base. As the employee changes from one job to another, entry via the remote terminal is used to indicate the end of job. Likewise, the new production order to

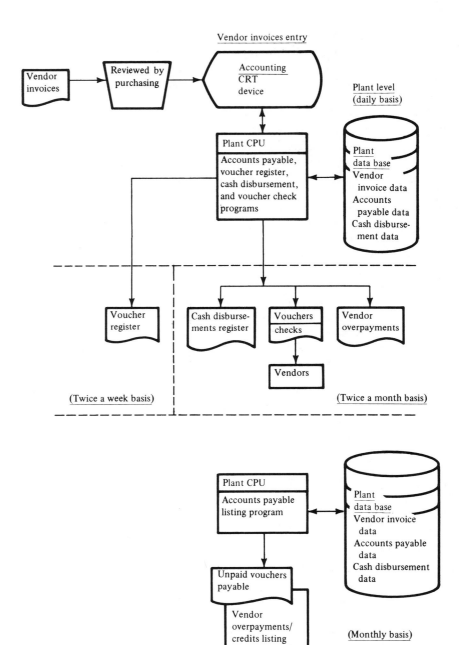

FIGURE 10-9. Accounts-payable and cash-disbursements data flow for a distributed processing accounting subsystem.

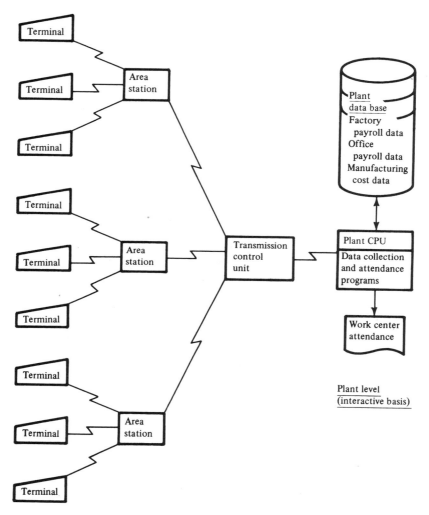

FIGURE 10-10. Factory payroll data flow for a distributed processing accounting subsystem.

be worked on is also entered. In this manner, the plant data base contains data for weekly payroll processing as well as for the costing of production orders.

Daily production-time data base elements are accumulated on a weekly basis and are summarized to produce a weekly time, gross pay, and exception report, as shown in Figure 10-11. Approved payroll changes are made via a CRT terminal in accounting before final processing occurs. The payroll register and checks, including earnings statements, are then produced and distributed to factory employees.

Payroll activities do not end with weekly processing at the plant level but

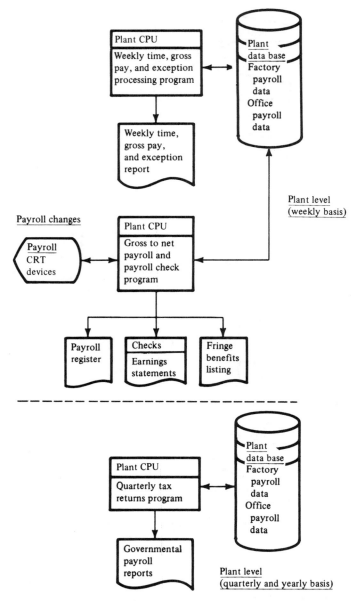

FIGURE 10-11. Overall payroll data flow for a distributed processing accounting subsystem.

must be carried forward for quarterly and yearly reports (Figure 10-11). Weekly figures are automatically forwarded to the general ledger stored on-line at the corporate level for producing monthly statements. Quarter-to-date earnings are used in preparing quarterly reports on federal income and FICA taxes withheld. Finally, year-to-date figures are the basis for preparing W-2s.

COST ACCOUNTING MODULE

Cost accounting in a distributed operating mode depends on data generated throughout the work day at the plant level by other subsystems. As indicated in Figure 10–12, usage of raw materials and parts is recorded by the inventory sub-

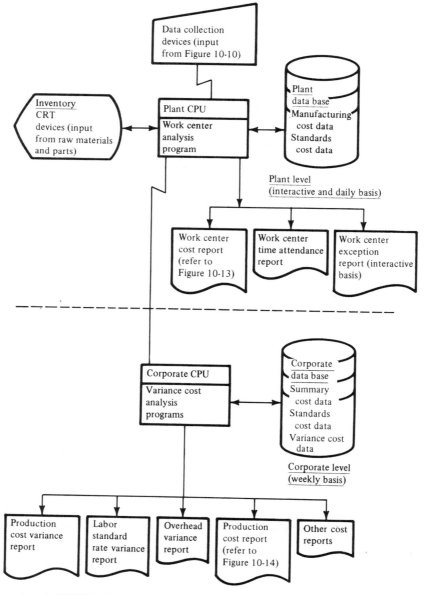

FIGURE 10–12. Cost accounting data flow for a distributed processing accounting subsystem.

system, capable of retrieval by cost accounting. In a similar manner, work center data collection devices within the manufacturing subsystem provide the input for costing analysis at the plant level. Basically, raw materials and labor data are compared to standards stored on the plant data base.

An important daily report being generated at the plant level is the work center cost report, illustrated in Figure 10-13. Several daily variances are calculated—namely, materials usage, labor, and operation. Other reports, such as work center time attendance and exception reports, are generated daily and on an interactive basis, respectively. In addition to the programs needed to produce these outputs, a program is triggered at the end of each week to transfer summary cost information from the plant to corporate headquarters. These cost figures are used for longer-range analysis—in particular, to improve the operations of a specific plant as well as to compare one plant against another. Also, these analyses verify cost standard accuracy or lack thereof.

As shown in Figure 10-12, weekly costs analyses are processed at the corporate level. They include production cost variance, labor standard rate variance, and overhead variance. Of special interest is the weekly production cost report (Figure 10-14) that brings together information generated on other reports. This report is reviewed by manufacturing, inventory, and accounting management. Generally, the information contained in this report is the basis for weekly meetings and evaluation at the corporate and plant levels.

Work Center No. 10   Date: 12/15/7-

Materials Usage Variance

$$\frac{\text{Total cost of actual materials used}}{(\text{Unit standard materials cost} \times \text{actual units})} \times 100$$

$$\frac{\$3,150}{(\$3.09 \times 1000)} \times 100 = 102\% \text{ or } \$60.00 \text{ unfavorable variance}$$

Labor Variance

$$\frac{\text{Total actual direct labor cost}}{(\text{Standard hours} \times \text{standard labor cost rate})} \times 100$$

$$\frac{\$1,410}{(220 \times \$6.00)} \times 100 = 107\% \text{ or } \$90.00 \text{ unfavorable variance}$$

Operation Variance

(Actual unit variable costs − standard unit variable costs) × actual production

Product 11: ($2.95 − $3.00) × 1000 = $50 favorable variance
Product 40: ($2.90 − $2.85) ×   800 = $40 unfavorable variance

FIGURE 10-13. Daily work center cost report—analysis for work center 10 in a distributed processing environment.

Weekly Production Cost Report (Unit Basis)

Analysis of Product 15   Week Ending 5/8/7-

Work Center	Materials		Labor		Overhead		Total Manufactured Costs		Quantity
	Actual	Standard	Actual	Standard	Actual	Standard	Actual	Standard	
12 (machine shop)	$1.60	$1.55	$1.41	$1.35	$ .64	$ .60	$3.65	$3.50	1500
35 (minor assembly)	1.04	1.05	.60	.60	.45	.45	2.09	2.10	1500
54 (major assembly)	1.26	1.25	1.26	1.25	.76	.75	3.28	3.25	1500
72 (inspection)	-	-	.17	.15	.12	.10	.29	.25	1500
	$3.90	$3.85	$3.44	$3.35	$1.97	$1.90	$9.31	$9.10	

FIGURE 10-14. Weekly production cost report (unit basis)—analysis for product 15.

In addition to the above cost reports, other period analyses are generated at the corporate level. A monthly listing of materials, labor, and overhead costs to be absorbed by the financial statements is prepared. Also, a listing of raw materials, work in process, and finished goods is processed. On a quarterly basis, a cost analysis, similar to Figure 10-14, is run. Standard costs are evaluated in view of rising costs and are changed to reflect current operations.

FINANCIAL STATEMENTS AND TAX RETURNS MODULES

Financial statements, in a distributed processing environment, are prepared at the corporate level based on general ledger data contained in the corporate data base which have been forwarded from the three manufacturing plants. The general ledger updating program, shown in Figure 10-15 at the corporate level, is used throughout the month to keep the data base updated. Data are fed from within and outside the accounting subsystem. At the end of the week, a listing of general ledger entries is produced by the computer to indicate the various debits and credits to specific accounts. In a similar manner, after all transactions have been processed for the last day of the month, general ledger balances and their detailed transactions are printed as well as written onto magnetic tape. The reason for this tape file is that general ledger items must be capable of being processed against the corporate data base the very next working day. Thus, the general ledger magnetic tape file can be changed at a later date to effect corrections and entry of special items. Of course, changes made to this file must also be made to the corporate data base for uniformity of accounting data.

For monthly financial statements, the magnetic tape file output per Figure 10-15 is computer-processed. Although the essential elements for these balance sheet items (on this tape) originate outside the accounting department as depicted in Figure 10-16, their physical flow is reflected in accounting entries, which are summarized for the month-end balance sheet. Similarly, income and expenses are the result of activities in other departments which flow into the corporate data base under program control, as general ledger entries. The resulting income and expenses

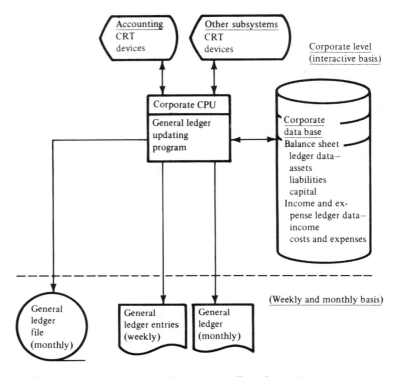

FIGURE 10-15. General ledger data flow for a distributed processing accounting subsystem.

are compared to budgeted values for meaningful analyses. (The responsibility for maintaining budgeted data base elements belongs to the corporate planning subsystem.) The profit after taxes, in the form of retained earnings and depreciation plus specific balance sheet items as shown in Figure 10-17, provides the source of funds for the firm, which, in turn, are applied to financing specific projects.

From the foregoing presentation, the preparation of financial statements in a distributed processing environment parallels that of an integrated MIS. However, financial reports have been forwarded to the user on a timely basis. But equally important to management is the provision for timely exception reports which highlight income and expenses that fall outside predetermined limits. Interactive processing can, for example, compare actual sales against typical patterns and control limits, leading to identification of *in-control* or *out-of-control* conditions as they occur. The same approach can be applied to the firm's costs and expenses. Comparisons, then, can be retrieved upon demand—enabling the capabilities of the new accounting information subsystem to exceed those of its predecessor.

The design approaches outlined above for financial statements is also applicable to the preparation of tax returns. By and large, data can be extracted from the data base as of a closing date and written onto magnetic tape. At a later date,

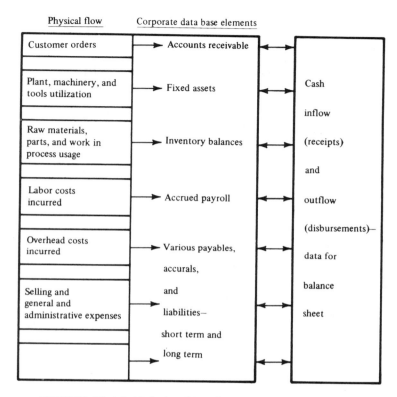

Physical flow   Corporate data base elements

Customer orders	→ Accounts receivable	↔
Plant, machinery, and tools utilization	→ Fixed assets	Cash
		inflow
Raw materials, parts, and work in process usage	→ Inventory balances	(receipts)
		and
Labor costs incurred	→ Accrued payroll	outflow
		(disbursements)—
Overhead costs incurred	→ Various payables, accurals,	data for
	and	balance
Selling and general and administrative expenses	→ liabilities—	sheet
	short term and	
	long term	

FIGURE 10–16. Relationship of the physical flow to the balance sheet in a distributed processing environment.

tax returns can be prepared in a batch processing mode. In this manner, governmental reports and returns on the federal, state, and local levels present no major obstacle for the firm.

CHAPTER SUMMARY

The accounting subsystem of the American Products Corporation is an integral part of the marketing, purchasing, manufacturing, inventory, and physical distribution subsystems in a distributed processing environment. Marketing is linked to accounts receivable, purchasing to accounts payable, manufacturing to payroll, and inventory and physical distribution to cost accounting. Despite this high degree of integration, there are numerous methods and procedures that operate within the accounting subsystem itself without reference to other subsystems. Thus, design considerations in this environment are extremely difficult.

A most important advantage of a distributing computing approach over prior ones centers on timely accounting information at the plant level. Accounting

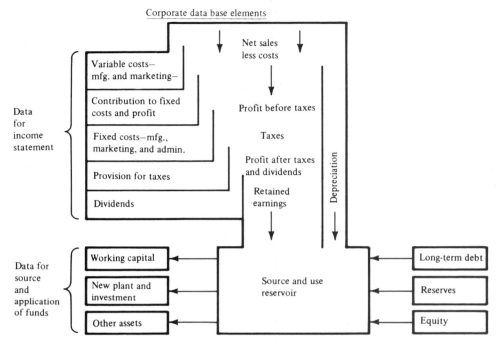

Corporate data base elements

FIGURE 10-17. Relationship of the income statement to the source and application of funds statement in a distributed processing environment.

personnel and their managers are capable of retrieving current accounts-receivable data for checking customer credit, checking on the status of overpayments to or credits due from vendors, determining the accuracy of plant personnel attendance, analyzing actual versus standard costs, and retrieving current general ledger balances, among other things. In essence, information can be isolated and evaluated now about other subsystems and the accounting function itself, enabling the firm to be forward-looking in its approaches to accounting decisions.

QUESTIONS

1. What advantages does a distributed processing accounting subsystem have over the integrated MIS accounting subsystem?

2. Referring to the cost accounting data base elements in Figure 10-7, define their detailed parts.

3. Suggest cost accounting formulas that would be found in a distributed processing environment.

4. Determine the major modules for the customer billing program.

5. Suggest changes to the payroll section in a distributed processing environment that include the utilization of the plant and corporate data bases.

6. Referring to the section on cost accounting, suggest changes that reflect an ideal distributed processing operating mode.

7. What is the relationship of flexible budgets to the accounting subsystem in a distributed processing system?

SELECTED REFERENCES

Blum, J. D., "Decision Tree Analysis for Accounting Decisions," *Management Accounting,* Dec. 1976.

Cook, W. F., and Bost, W. J., "Standard Cost System: A Module of a Management Information System," *Journal of Systems Management,* March 1969.

Davall, D. M., and Wilkinson, J. W., "Simulating an Accounting Information System Model," *Management Accounting,* Jan. 1971.

Enrick, N. L., "Be Mean About Management Reporting," *Computer Decisions,* Sept. 1970.

Hand, A. B., and Rives W. L., "Constructing a Data Processing Cost Accounting System," *The Magazine of Bank Administration,* April 1974.

Klein, C. E., "Computerizing Accounts Receivable," *Credit and Financial Management,* Aug. 1975.

Magee, R. P., "A Simulation Analysis of Alternative Cost Variance Investigation Models," *The Accounting Review,* July 1976.

Nichols, G. E., "Accounting and the Total Information System," *Management Accounting,* March 1971.

O'Brien, J. J., *Management Information Systems,* New York: Van Nostrand Reinhold Company, 1971, Chap. 10.

Roy, H. J. H., "Credit Scoring: An Update," *Credit and Financial Management,* Aug. 1974.

Rupli, R. G., "How To Improve Profits Through Simulation," *Management Accounting,* Nov. 1973.

Sauls, E., "An On-Line System for Accounts Payable," *Journal of Systems Management,* May 1973.

Theil, H., "On the Use of Information Theory Concept in the Analysis of Financial Statements," *Management Science,* May 1969.

Thierauf, R. J., *Systems Analysis and Design of Real-Time Management Informaton Systems,* Englewood Cliffs, N.J.: Prentice-Hall, Inc., 1975.

Thorne, J. F., "Real Time System in Accounting Applications," *Journal of Data Management,* Jan. 1970.

Wiener, H., "Putting Your Credit Line Online," *Computer Decisions,* Sept. 1973.

part four

FUTURE DEVELOPMENTS IN DISTRIBUTED PROCESSING SYSTEMS

DEVELOPMENTS FOR FUTURE DISTRIBUTED PROCESSING SYSTEMS 11

Present distributed computing, as discussed in the prior chapters, provides identifiable advantages for meeting business user needs. Currently, the many advantages of dispersed data processing include computer power located where it is needed, the ability of prolonging mainframe life and investment, utilization of easy-to-learn languages for local and regional processing, balanced loading of processing tasks on host computers as well as local and regional processors, network communications capabilities, use and selection of versatile applications at the appropriate processing level, reduction of data entry errors, and the employment of unskilled personnel at the local and regional processing levels. Overall, distributed processing systems that give the user the ability to install low-cost computers at remote points and connect them to a host computer via communication networks in a distributed processing environment is having a considerable impact on current information processing.

By no means do present systems represent the end state of distributed computing. Rather, dispersed data processing will mature in the future into what might be called the *electronic office*. Computer power and powerful software will be commonplace in virtually every business office. In light of these predictions, in this chapter we shall examine the emerging characteristics of future distributed processing systems. Accent will be placed not only on distributing computing power further at the lower levels but also on accelerating the use of computing capabilities at the higher levels. In effect, future distributed processing systems will touch on every organizational level so that there is a more effective approach to planning, organizing, directing, and controlling business activities.

DIRECTIONS IN DISTRIBUTED PROCESSING SYSTEMS

Historically, business information systems have been aimed at administrative and record-keeping types of applications which normally have been run on computerized batch systems that update a master file and produce managerial reports. For the most part, these applications and the systems to meet their processing requirements have been developed. However, the emphasis has been and is currently shifting. The attention of business has been and is turning to day-to-day problems—into the interactive world, i.e., real time, and toward systems where data entered for immediate processing requires immediate verification. In such systems, the operator is allowed to correct input errors as they are detected, before further processing, especially in terms of maintaining the correctness of the company's data base.

Although there is general agreement that there will be more transaction processing at the local and regional levels in an interactive mode as well as the preparation of operational and functional management reports at these same levels, there still is some disagreement about what will happen at the headquarters level. Since there are many computer programs that are executed in a large, mainframe environment, many feel that distributed computing will supplement centralized computing, not replace or displace it. Furthermore, because many corporations have invested heavily in hardware and applications software, they have no intention of parting with this investment in the near future. In such an environment, there is no question that various types of processors and minicomputers will supplement the centralized computer.

The foregoing represents one point of view—a need for both distributed and centralized computing facilities. From another viewpoint, there is a recognition that the entire computer industry is currently in the throes of a transition from producing small- to large-sized computers to much smaller computers and processors along with "intelligent" terminal equipment. As some computer futurists view distributed computing, a terminal rivaling the performance of sophisticated minicomputers will rent for less than its operator's salary in a few years. After that, the focus will be on distributing data files as well as processing power. The flow of communication between remote terminals and central processors will slow to a trickle. In about 10 years, there will not be a need for a central processor, except to maintain a central file. From the latter viewpoint, the focus will be more on distributed computing and very little on centralized processing.

Within the framework of these two opposing views, there are varying degrees, resulting in a wide range of opinions. No matter what viewpoint is held, there is one clear picture that is emerging. In the future, there will be more distributed processing systems than there are currently. Likewise, the installations will become more sophisticated and capable of performing more tasks at a lower cost. In light of the increased numbers of future distributed processing installations and their level of sophistication, in the remainder of the chapter we shall explore their new and emerging characteristics. By getting a "handle" on these characteristics, systems designers will be in a better position to design these future systems. But, before doing so, information as needed in future distributed processing is discussed.

INFORMATION IN FUTURE DISTRIBUTED COMPUTING

Based on the current distributed processing systems (first, second, and third levels) explored in the first part of the text, there is generally adequate information produced for the *operational* level. Not only are reports prepared on past operations, but they are also available on current and forthcoming activities. However, the question can be asked whether or not an organization's resources (men, money, materials, machines, and managers) at the lowest level are allocated in the most optimum manner. Depending on the level of complexity involved and the competence of lower management, they may or may not be. Generally, they are not, because optimization comes from the top. In current systems, mathematical models, if used, basically are directed at one specific area or its related parts, but overall optimization is not employed. Hence, operational information is generally deficient from an overview standpoint.

The question asked about operational information can also be asked about *tactical* information; that is, are an organization's resources at the middle organization level allocated in the most optimum way for distributed computing? The same answer can be given. Largely, they are not because current distributed processing systems do not employ comprehensive mathematical models whereby all of an organization's inputs and outputs are automatically coordinated. Of greater importance is *strategic* information, which is paramount if a system is to optimize overall results. Generally, current distributed computing does not have the capability to provide top-level information that is capable of predicting tomorrow's results.

Although present distributed processing systems are deficient in meeting many of management's needs as set forth above, in particular, at the higher levels, future distributed systems are directed toward improving the situation. As will be noted in the remaining sections of this chapter and in the next chapter, improvements are necessary in certain areas if future distributed computing is going to assist all management levels. Thus, the focus will be on new approaches, concepts, and models that provide the appropriate management level with meaningful and timely information.

EMERGING CHARACTERISTICS OF FUTURE DISTRIBUTED PROCESSING SYSTEMS

Prior to discussing these emerging characteristics of future distributed processing systems per Figure 11-1, it would be helpful to review the essential characteristics of current systems, as presented in Chapter 2. The rationale is that future systems will build upon those currently in operation. By way of review, the distinguishing characteristics found currently in a distributed processing environment are

- *three-level system approach*—the first-level system focuses primarily on the local processing of source data entry, the second-level system combines local processing of source data entry and transaction processing with the preparation of managerial reports, and the third-level system provides a network of distributed processing for meeting the user's needs at the local, regional, and headquarters levels. (Future systems will focus on improving operations at all levels.)

- *interactive processing mode and/or batch processing modes*—allows the user the option of interactive processing, batch processing, or a

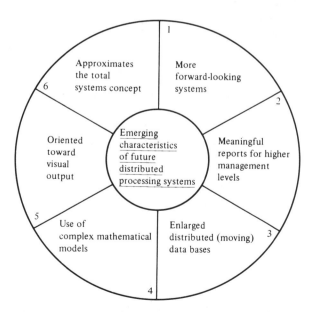

FIGURE 11-1. Emerging characteristics of future distributed processing systems.

combination of the two. (Future systems will stress the interactive processing mode.)

- *utilization of various I/O terminal devices*—consists of employing preprogrammed ("smart") and programmable ("intelligent") terminals, with accent on the latter. (Future systems will focus primarily on programmable terminals since these units are capable of performing many routine tasks that a computer can perform.)

- *timely reports that utilize management by exception*—provides timely managerial reports that set forth exception items. (Future systems will continue to employ this concept plus a new one called *management by perception*—to be discussed in this chapter.)

- *distribute data base at the appropriate level*—provides for locating the data bases where they are needed in dispersed computing. (Future systems will incorporate larger distributed data bases that employ the "moving" file concept—to be discussed in this chapter.)

- *simplified approach to programming and implementation*—incorporates an easy-to-program approach as well as a simplified method for installation. (Future systems will keep in mind the user's needs, in particular, those of operating personnel.)

- *local autonomy of data processing operations*—allows personnel at the local and regional levels to develop more of their data processing applications without extensive systems support from the centralized systems group. (Future systems will stress more local autonomy of distributed processing operations.)

MORE FORWARD-LOOKING SYSTEMS

A most distinguishing characteristic of this next phase is that it will be a more forward-looking system. In addition to receiving a response from the system in time to satisfy their requirements, company personnel will be able to project the life cycles of products in developing strategic plans for the firm. This approach is extremely desirable in the increasingly complex business world. The environmental factors that affect success and failure are so dynamic that top management must be able to understand and react to them quickly and decisively. High operational costs provide another strong incentive for creating more forward-looking control systems.

The life cycle of a typical product, shown in Figure 11-2, helps to illustrate the corporate integration that management must accommodate. For operating and middle management to plan and schedule effectively, there must first be an awareness of the original product plan set forth by top management; there must be a continuous appraisal of actual performance and changes in the plan across the organization. Distributed processing systems will be designed to process operational data so that organization-wide information requirements—in particular, those for strategic planning—can be satisfied.

Within such an environment, a new management principle, namely, *management by perception,* is required. This principle refers to the ability of management

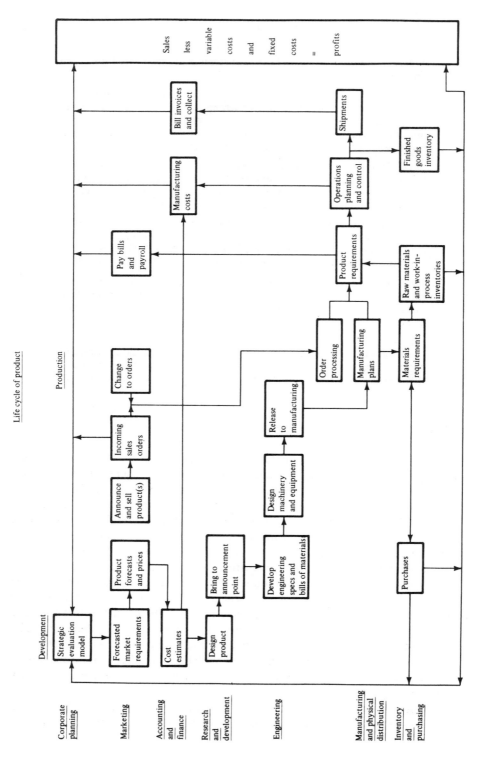

FIGURE 11-2. Future distributed processing systems—more forward-looking in their consideration of the life cycle of products for developing long-range plans.

to perceive future external and internal trends before they occur and to determine their impact on new products so as to improve overall organizational performance. It should be noted that this principle is forward-looking as opposed to the backward-looking approach of *management by exception,* which focuses on comparison after the fact. However, both have their place in the managerial process.

To elaborate further on management by perception, management must be able to perceive those political and social trends which are developing that have relevance to the organization. By perceiving these trends before they occur, management can adjust its strategic plans for new products and, in turn, its tactical and operational plans for these products. In this manner, top managers can optimize overall performance for the organization. In effect, top management needs to stand back and take a look at the total picture in which the company operates. It must "look at the forest instead of the trees." To state it another way, what may be appropriate yesterday may not be proper today and in the future. Thus, future systems, especially those which are distributed and focus on satisfying managerial needs at the highest level, will be even more forward-looking into the future than past systems.

MEANINGFUL REPORTS FOR HIGHER MANAGEMENT LEVELS

An essential difference between current and future distributed systems is their reporting function. Output and exception reports from current distributed computing are oriented mainly toward lower and middle management. Sample outputs focus on the following areas: accurate market forecasts, service to customers, marketing budgets, allocation of departmental manufacturing facilities, vendor performance, alternative investments of short-term assets, and negotiations with labor unions. On the other hand, reports from future distributed processing systems will be designed to satisfy more management requests. Representative applications that apply to present and future conditions include

- setting long-range plans and objectives for an entire organization that are fully integrated into the major subsystems and their related parts
- planning and evaluating new products over their life cycles (as discussed in the preceding section)
- determining manpower requirements and allocating organization personnel so that the best person is placed in the appropriate job
- allocating factory capacity in the most efficient manner for the entire organization
- determining materials requirements that reduce overall costs for the entire organization
- acquiring short-, intermediate-, and long-term capital funds as needed for the entire organization
- determining profit profiles or large alternative investment plans
- indicating improvements in operating revenues and costs

Future systems, then, are quite different from their predecessors. While current distributed computing is concerned with maximizing decisions for one major subsystem or one of its parts, future systems cut across the entire organization for optimal decisions. Thus, a new kind of business structure is needed to handle difficult and complex conditions. At the heart of the structure must be a system in which external and internal data interact with each other in countless variations. Such a system will allow management to be involved and will be dependent on a highly integrated, total corporate planning model that interacts with all of the organization's major subsystems and their related parts. A large computer will become central to this type of future system for assessing external and internal data that have meaning to top management.

ENLARGED DISTRIBUTED (MOVING) DATA BASES

The data base structure of future distributed processing systems will be both horizontal and vertical in nature (Figure 11–3). For this approach to become operational, the systems designer must determine how the data base elements form a data base for the important needs of all management levels. He or she must ask questions regarding, for instance, whether or not current data being employed for lower-management day-to-day decisions are valid when projected for the long run. Can the major business functions utilize the same inventory figures as those needed by top management for long-range planning? An even more important question concerns whether or not the requirements of top management are so different as to be incompatible with lower- and middle-management needs. This type of question presents a new challenge to the information system designer. Not only must the data base be integrated to serve all functions (subsystems and their related parts), but it must also be capable of servicing all management levels with their respective information needs. Thus, data sufficient to answer questions in the short or intermediate runs may not be adquate for the long run.

To accommodate the needs of management, distributed data bases could be structured as illustrated in Figure 11–4. Basically, data must be classified according to their usage. Operational information pertaining to individual products or customers is needed for maintenance of the company's records and is of little interest to top management. Management control data consist of information on exception conditions triggered by the operational-level systems. It involves summaries, recaps, and comparable information generally for use by middle management in controlling the company's operations on a short-term basis. Planning information is intended for usage by top management in exercising its broad responsibilities for directing the long-range activities of the organization. In essence, operational distributed data must be summarized for tactical or middle-management needs, which, in turn, must be summarized for strategic or top-management requirements.

Although the foregoing approach to a distributed hierarchical data base provides historical information about current operations, there is another type of information that is of more value and interest than, say, monthly operating state-

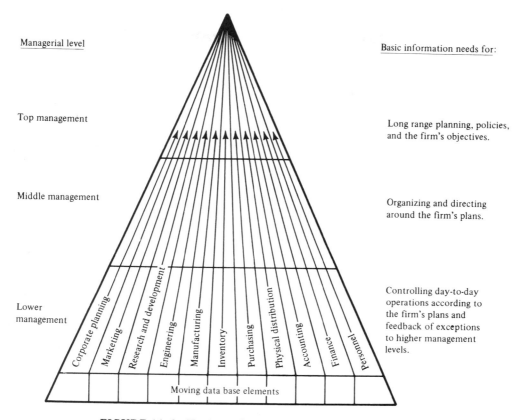

Managerial level

Basic information needs for:

Top management

Long range planning, policies, and the firm's objectives.

Middle management

Organizing and directing around the firm's plans.

Lower management

Controlling day-to-day operations according to the firm's plans and feedback of exceptions to higher management levels.

Corporate planning — Marketing — Research and development — Engineering — Manufacturing — Inventory — Purchasing — Physical distribution — Accounting — Finance — Personnel

Moving data base elements

FIGURE 11-3. Horizontal and vertical structure of the data base for the major subsystems in a future distributed processing system.

ments and budget performance analyses. This is information that pertains to future operations, being predictive in nature since it augments the manager's own judgment about what performance is going to be like in the future. Here there is need for a wide array of quantitative and qualitative techniques for exploiting the information in the data base, ranging from simple extrapolations to the employment of complex mathematical models with the capability of manipulating numerous variables. Information techniques pertaining to probable future performance are more difficult to design and develop and, consequently, have not progressed so far as those techniques using historical information.

To produce meaningful future information, there is need to procure a certain amount of environmental or external information that is compatible with internal information contained in the distributed data base. This includes information about the industry in which the firm is competing as well as the pricing structure, advertising campaigns, and locations of its competing firms. Other external information not having to do directly with competition but still of great potential importance to management includes economic indicators, information about securities markets, and demographic data of many kinds. Acquisition and usage of such information is limited by the nature of the business, the difficulty of procuring the data, and its cost versus its value in management decision making.

It should be noted that environmental data need not necessarily be captured and stored in the data base on a continually recurring basis. Data may be obtained when needed to perform a particular type of analysis. For example, census data and other descriptive information might be stored on magnetic tape to assist in making an occasional determination of the best location for new manufacturing plants or sales offices.

A distributed data base that is capable of handling the foregoing structural requirements could be built upon a *moving file* concept—that is, as operating data are received, appropriate adjustments will be made automatically through the system to the higher data levels. The "moving data bases" reflect not only actual day-by-day operating activities but also the planned performance of these same activities at all levels. The lower-level (local) distributed data bases feed the next (regional) level, where data are summarized to reflect longer time periods, which, in turn, are fed to the highest (centralized) level of the data base for producing strategic information. This orderly arrangement of the data base allows the user to ask "what if" questions in order to determine if the overall organization performance or some part of it can be improved or if plans should be modified. The dynamics of the moving file concept are very responsive to the changing environment in which all levels of management must plan, organize, direct, and control the business.

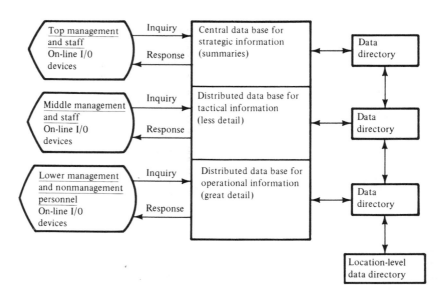

FIGURE 11-4. A dictionary/directory system used in a "moving data base" environment for a future distributed processing system.

To operate the distributed moving data bases in an efficient manner, it is necessary to develop an organization-wide data element dictionary/directory which includes standard definitions, an index system, mathematical routines for deriving higher levels of data from the stored data base elements, and security rules for file access. Also, the dictionary/directory system is so designed that only critical data are referenced in memory or auxiliary storage devices, while less critical and more voluminous files are retrievable from magnetic tape or some other low-cost storage medium. As illustrated in Figure 11-4, the lowest level of the data base elements for operational information can be referenced by the data directory as well as the highest level of data for strategic information. This approach permits large on-line files to be handled on an interactive basis from the lowest to the highest level where data items can be sorted, manipulated, and chosen according to many criteria.

In the final analysis, a logical method must be selected as the optimum approach to organizing the data bases after giving consideration to operational, tactical, and strategic information needed by the various subsystems. Likewise, thought must be given to growth that can be anticipated in volume of records (data sets). In general, the insertion of additional or new records in the data bases should not upset the file organization to the point that it will be necessary to reorganize them at frequent intervals. Thus, an approach to designing large, moving data bases in a distributed processing environment is a challenge for any group of systems analysts (and may take years to solve).

USE OF COMPLEX MATHEMATICAL MODELS

Even though present-level mathematical business models are adequate for solving specific operational business problems, operations researchers, working with systems designers, must be capable of developing more advanced mathematical models that encompass one or more of the organization's subsystems. Thus, to create an effective and efficient overall mathematical model that relates various managerial needs in a logical manner, there must be a marriage of systems with mathematics. This combined effort is imperative. Although most operations research projects presently are centered around solving well-structured problems, the future trend is heading in two directions. First, many of the standard OR (operations research) models are being combined into larger and more sophisticated models. Second, the large number of problems that are difficult to structure are getting increased attention from operations researchers.

In reference to the last item, typical problems which are poorly structured and unstructured problems which do not lend themselves to mathematical modeling are

- determining organization objectives
- selecting, developing, and motivating employees
- improving collective bargaining relations
- humanizing the work environment

- facilitating company relations with federal, state, and local governments

- learning to interact with the community that buys its wares and from which it draws both employees and public support

These aspects of the managerial job will rise in importance and will require broadly trained personnel who are sensitive to social, political, and technical changes. The assistance of operations research, then, will allow the manager to relegate certain problem types to the computing capabilities of the system while time is spent on problems that are not logical candidates for OR solution.

In the next chapter, operations research models that are applicable to future distributed processing are set forth. Likewise, possible applications are presented.

ORIENTED TOWARD VISUAL OUTPUT

In a future distributed processing environment, output will be away from printed output, to a more visual form of output. Visual display screen devices include CRT units, picturephones, computer graphic devices, large-screen display systems, and management control centers. Key managers will sit around a large display screen and will ask "what if"-type questions of the computer. The answers will be displayed on the screen, and after discussions and iterations, a decision will be reached.

An example of "what if" questions would be the proposed introduction of a new product. A staff specialist (capable of mathematical programming and operations research), working with a marketing manager and using a CRT unit, might employ a mathematical model, such as venture analysis, that incorporates estimates of sales, costs, competitor reactions, and comparable data from a centralized data base. To make a final decision on the proposed new product, the staff specialist would vary the inputs rather than entering only one estimate for each of the variables, constraints, and similar restrictions. For example, he might ask, "If I assumed sales to be X, *what* would happen *if* the sales value were set at some other value?" Or, "*What if* the various competitors did A rather than B or C?"

To answer "what if" questions, certain computer graphic devices that have been programmed to produce charts and graphs on the screen can be employed. By touching the screen with a light pen, the specialist can order the computer to calculate new values and redraw the graphs almost instantaneously. Thus, the manager and specialist team can test all or most possible feasible alternatives and can select the best one by analyzing quantitative data.

APPROXIMATES THE TOTAL SYSTEMS CONCEPT

Future distributed processing systems will be approximating the *total systems concept,* which, though it tends to be utopian when carried to its highest level of achievement, is still an ultimate goal by and large for systems analysts. Basically, this concept refers to the condition in which all of an organization's inputs, processing methods and procedures, and outputs are automatically coordinated to accomplish the organization's objectives.

To accomplish this Herculean feat, it is necessary, in most situations, to utilize mathematical models that cut across the entire organization. As discussed, these corporate models must coordinate their resources in an optimum manner in order to achieve the desired objectives. These models must not only be integrated and interacting on the highest level in an organization but must also be related directly to the many subparts of the major subsystems. Only in this manner will overall optimization of the entire organization result.

To approximate the total systems concept, the ability to extract desired information from the multiple-level, distributed data bases is essential. Because this type of data base will be structured on the moving file concept, it must be possible to retrieve the required information for most types of OR models. It should be pointed out that the present state of the art in data base designing and OR modeling has not reached this level of sophistication.

Additionally, there must be greater use of hardware and software before this next phase in distributed processing systems can approximate the total systems concept. For example, there must be greater utilization of microprocessors, microcomputers, and minicomputers at the production level. As illustrated in Figure 11–5, microprocessors control the individual machines. However, for newer machines, such as mechanical robots, either a microcomputer or a minicomputer is required. In most cases, nevertheless, data are fed from the microprocessors to the microcomputers to control the process flow of one work center. In turn, output of the process-flow control system for all work centers is input for the minicomputer whose main function is the scheduling and control of all manufacturing operations. As data are fed into the production scheduling and control system, the minicomputer analyzes the data. Where manufactured goods are running ahead or

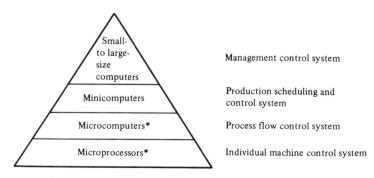

*Depending upon the application, a minicomputer might be utilized.

FIGURE 11–5. Hierarchy of computing devices in a future distributed processing manufacturing environment.

behind schedule, appropriate adjustments are made to the schedule so that production control is optimized for current manufacturing activities. Last, critical production data, as compiled by the minicomputer, become input for the main computer. Thus, this hierarchy of distributed computing devices (Figure 11–5) assists an organization in automatically coordinating its production activities that are the basis for input to other functional areas.

Although the foregoing discussion has centered on applying the total systems concept to an individual organization, system approaches that extend beyond the organization will be explored in the next chapter. This presentation brings into sharp focus the need for the total systems concept as a practical design goal for future distributed processing systems.

RECAP OF EMERGING CHARACTERISTICS OF DISTRIBUTED PROCESSING SYSTEMS

The new and emerging characteristics that set future distributed processing systems apart from current ones have been discussed in the preceding section. As stated in the opening section, these characteristics build upon the ones found in present systems; they are complementary as well as supplementary. For the reader's convenience, they are summarized in Figure 11-6. It should be noted that as future systems become operational, other characteristics from those set forth will probably emerge. The foregoing characteristics, then, should not be seen as an absolute guide. Rather, they should serve as a general guide to the evolution of future distributed processing systems.

COMPARISON OF PRESENT AND FUTURE DISTRIBUTED PROCESSING SYSTEMS

A comparison of important characteristics for current and future distributed processing systems is set forth in Figure 11-7. An examination of these characteristics reveals more management involvement, particularly at the highest level. The interaction of external factors with internal factors and their resulting impact on the organization will take on new importance within a future distributed processing environment. Likewise, there will be more nonmanagement, i.e., operating personnel, involvement, because these systems will be the very heart of the business structure. More company personnel will interact with the computer via I/O terminal devices in order to obtain desired responses; user/machine interaction will evolve in a way that will facilitate more advanced applications than are possible with current systems. This increased interactive mode will lead to solving far more complex and qualitatively different high-level problems. Overall, such future systems will be important links that allow organization personnel (management and nonmanagement) to interact with tomorrow's dynamic environment. This processing mode will allow an organization to approach the total systems concept that was espoused by sales and systems personnel in the early days of computers.

1. *More forward-looking systems.* Utilizes a longer time framework in the future when solving a problem, resulting in *management by perception*—the ability to perceive future trends before they occur and determine their ultimate impact on the organization.

2. *Meaningful reports for higher management levels.* Recognizes the need to produce more than operational and functional information for lower and middle management, respectively, but also to generate strategic information that is critical to optimizing the scarce resources of an organization.

3. *Enlarged distributed (moving) data bases.* Employs distributed data bases that allow for the moving of summary data to the centralized data base for meeting the needs of top management.

4. *Use of complex mathematical models.* Centers on the need to solve mathematical problems (using operations research techniques) that cut across part or all of an organization's subsystems versus just solving for one specific operational area.

5. *Oriented toward visual output.* Allows managers, assisted by their staff, to ask "what if" questions for an immediate visual response, thereby providing a means of evaluating feasible alternatives for selection of the best one.

6. *Approximates the total systems concept.* Comes close to the concept where an organization's inputs, methods, and procedures are automatically coordinated to produce the desired outputs.

FIGURE 11-6. New and emerging characteristics of future distributed processing systems.

FUTURE DISTRIBUTED PROCESSING SYSTEMS DEFINED

An integral part of any definition of future distributed processing systems should be reference to advanced mathematical models and distributed networks of data bases. While advanced mathematical models in such an environment will go beyond solving one specific problem area, distributed networks will involve the interconnection of several processors with their data bases that are within the same location, across town, across the country, or across company boundaries (refer to Chapter 12). The interconnections are established through common carrier communications channels, using data link control to establish paths and manage the message transactions.

In view of the importance of these items plus examining the foregoing emerging characteristics, future distributed computing can be defined as an approach to placing low-cost computing power at the various organizational levels (from the lowest to the highest) and linking these points with a centralized computer via a distributed communications network. At the lower organizational level, the accent is on capturing source data, performing transaction processing, and preparing operational management reports. At the higher levels, the focus is on the preparation of informational reports for middle and top management that assist in accom-

Important Characteristics of Distributed Processing Systems	Current Systems	Future Systems
Type of system	Forward- and backward-looking system	More forward-looking system
Reports prepared	Output reports directed mainly to lower and middle management for past, current, and future operations	Output reports directed to lower and higher levels of management for past, current, and future operations
Basis of reporting	Current plans and objectives used for management exception reports	Current plans and objectives used for more management exception reports and for management by perception
Information orientation	Input/output-oriented with I/O terminals	————————————→
Processing mode	Interactive processing and remote batch processing	————————————→
Data elements	Distributed data base	Enlarged distributed data base, including a moving data base concept
Type of files	Accent on random access on-line file storage	————————————→
Mathematical models	Use of standard operation research models for well-structured problems	Greater use of standard and complex operations research models for well-structured and poorly structured problems
Type of output	Accent on written and visual output	Oriented toward visual output
Total systems concept	Contains elements of the total systems concept	Approximates the total systems concept

————————→ *denotes continued use and development.*

FIGURE 11-7. Comparison of important characteristics for current and future distributed processing systems.

plishing overall and specific organization objectives. Thus, within a future distributed processing environment, data are recorded, manipulated, and retrieved from a large, moving data base via I/O terminals in order to plan, organize, direct, and control quantitative/qualitative managerial and operational activities in sufficient time to affect their operations on an immediate and a long-term basis. The use of the term *quantitative/qualitative* refers to the fact that operations research models will be employed to solve well-structured (quantitative) and poorly structured (qualitative) problems, respectively—necessary for providing meaningful managerial and operational information. In the final analysis, the value of information to an organization is that better decisions will be made.

CHAPTER SUMMARY

Currently, building and programming distributed processing systems are not too complex when only a few terminals and single-host computer are involved. It is many times greater where several hosts and hundreds of terminals, some of them small computers in their own right, are involved. To illustrate the degree of complexity, provision must be made for polling the demands of all the terminals, resolving their contention for common resources, queuing their requests, and prioritizing them. If a communications path is already in use, alternates must promptly be found, and when one terminal is connected to a host, the operating characteristics of both must be synchronized. Should the connection be interrupted, means must be provided to reestablish it—to recover quickly, without loss of data. Transmission errors must be detected, received messages must be checked and acknowledged, devices and the network itself must be managed, and the performance of the entire system—hosts, terminals, and communications lines—must be monitored. And all of that must be safeguarded with security measures. These functions and still others, in bewildering combinations, are, according to customer preferences and resources, assigned within the network structure.

As can be seen from the foregoing, building a network for present distributed processing requirements is no easy task. When consideration is given to superimposing the new and emerging characteristics of the future (as set forth in this chapter) on current systems, the job of systems designers is magnified several times. In short, the development and implementation of future distributed processing systems are quite complex. Considerable developmental work will be required before such systems can be operational. This is particularly true when consideration is given to satisfying the needs of top managers. For this reason, in the next (and final) chapter we shall center on mathematical models that assist the higher levels of management before presenting illustrative distributed processing systems of the future that, in some cases, extend beyond the organization.

QUESTIONS

1. What are the important differences between current and future distributed processing systems?

2. How are future distributed processing systems more forward-looking than current distributed processing systems?

3. Why is it that summarized operational data, as generated by current distributed processing systems, generally do not satisfy the needs of top management? Explain.

4. a. Explain what is meant by the moving data base concept.
   b. Is this concept the same as multiple data bases? Explain.

5. What type of mathematical models will be needed in a future distributed processing environment?

6. Explain why future distributed processing systems approximate the total systems concept while prior systems generally do not.

SELECTED REFERENCES

Alter, S. L., "How Effective Managers Use Information Systems," *Harvard Business Review,* Nov.–Dec. 1976.

Bielec, J. A., "Managing the Computer Non-Center of the Future," *Infosystems,* May 1977.

Buckelew, D. P., and Penniman, W. D., "The Outlook for Interactive Television, " *Datamation,* Aug. 1974.

Business Week Special Report, "Glowing Prospects for Brainy Computer Terminals," *Business Week,* Oct. 25, 1976.

Carlisle, J. H., "Evaluating the Impact of Office Automation on Top Management Communication," *AFIPS Conference Proceedings* (National Computer Conference), Vol. 45, 1976.

Chen, K. C., "A Framework for the Design of Advanced Manufacturing Information Systems," *AIDS Conference Proceedings,* 1976.

Chervany, N. L., and Perkins, W. C., "Organizational Relationships Between Management Science and Management Information Systems: Some Empirical Evidence," *AIDS Conference Proceedings,* 1975.

Gruenberger, F., *Computers and the Social Environment,* Los Angeles, Calif.: Melville Publishing Co., 1975.

Infosystems Staff, "Management Gets the Picture," *Infosystems,* April 1977.

Kindred, A. R., *Data Systems and Management,* Englewood Cliffs, N.J.: Prentice-Hall, Inc., 1973.

Murdick, R. G., and Ross, J. E., "Future Management Information Systems," *Journal of Systems Management,* April 1972.

Nanus, B., "The Future Oriented Corporation," *Business Horizons,* Feb. 1975.

Rue, J., "Power, Politics, and DP," *Datamation,* Dec. 1976.

Siegel, P., *Strategic Planning of Management Information Systems,* New York: Petrocelli Books, 1975.

Simonette, I., "Ring in Distributed Computing," *Computing Decisions,* Jan. 1976.

Sprague, R. H., and Watson, H. J., "Model Management in MIS," *AIDS Conference Proceedings,* 1975.

Sterling, T. D., and Laudon, K., "Guidelines for Humanizing Computerized Information Systems: A Report from Stanley House," *Communications of ACM,* Nov. 1974.

——, "Humanizing Information Systems," *Datamation,* Dec. 1976.

Surden, E., "Distributed Systems Seen Strengthening Central Site," *Computerworld,* March 28, 1977.

Thierauf, R. J., Klekamp, R. C., and Geeding, D. W., *Management Principles and Practices: A Contingency and Questionnaire Approach,* New York: Wiley/Hamilton, 1977.

Thorn, R. G., "Notes To Facilitate Workshop Discussion of Minicomputers in Production Operations," *AIDS Conference,* Nov. 1976.

Turn, R., *Computers in the 1980's,* New York: Columbia University Press, 1974.

Walker, P. D., and Catalino, S. D., "Next in MIS: 'Data Managed' System Design," *Computer Decisions,* Nov. 1969.

Withington, F. G., "Five Generations of Computers," *Harvard Business Review,* July–Aug. 1974.

FUTURE DISTRIBUTED PROCESSING SYSTEMS 12

The material of Chapter 11 stressed new, emerging characteristics of future distributed processing systems. Although the main thrust was on these items, the underlying theme was providing meaningful and timely information to operations and managerial personnel at the appropriate levels in an organization. Since information does not come into existence on its own, it must be acquired, evaluated, stored, transmitted, recalled, condensed, expanded, interpreted, and so forth to be of value to organizational personnel, in particular those involved in the decision-making process. Decision makers must possess the right kind of information at the right time in the right amount from the right source. Such is the conceptual foundation of future distributed processing systems where particular emphasis is placed on providing information for decision makers at all organization levels.

Within this chapter, the emerging characteristics of future distributed systems will be apparent throughout the discussion. After specifying the need for advanced mathematical models and presenting several of these to be found in future systems, the integration of paperless output and voice systems within the decision-making process is presented for a typical organization. Because true distributed processing systems will save time and money for their users by exchanging appropriate data among themselves, automatic funds transfer systems to financial institutions are explored along with vendor/customer-file interconnections. These interconnected systems will aid management action by exchanging data entailed by a management decision among all the organizational data bases concerned i.e., quickly and automatically.

THE NEED FOR NEWER MATHEMATICAL MODELS

Inasmuch as distributed processing is a method for implementing processing functions across a number of physical devices, so that each performs some part of the total processing required, it is most often accompanied by the formation of a distributed data base. A distributed data base exists when the data elements stored at multiple locations are interrelated or if a process (program execution) at one location requires access to data stored at another location. Although techniques are adequate to handle present distributed data bases, the same cannot be said for future, enlarged data bases that utilize the moving file concept (refer to Chapter 11). Various mathematical models must be developed to control the data as they move from the detail level to the summary level(s). Likewise, there is a great need for coordinating the distributed data bases as their data are periodically summarized for use at a higher level.

Additionally, mathematical models must be developed that allow the user to interact with the distributed data bases for solving a wide range of operational and managerial problems. Specifically, they must permit management to answer "what if" questions, such as

- What if product prices are changed; what will be the effect on cash flow and profits?
- What if a proposed new item of equipment is purchased or leased; what will be the effects on profits and cash flow of alternative financing methods?
- What if a wage increase is granted; what will be the effect on production rates, use of overtime, risk of seasonal inventory, and so forth for a production program?

At the highest level, for example, planning and evaluating new products over their life cycles, allocating available factory capacity in the most efficient manner, and setting organizational long-range plans and objectives are areas where answers are invaluable to top management. The need for advanced mathematical models is paramount not only for controlling and coordinating a distributed data base but also for interacting with detailed and summary data for answering a wide range of operational and managerial questions.

NEWER MATHEMATICAL MODELS

Based on the foregoing discussion, only advanced mathematical models that relate to answering specific questions for organizational personnel are presented. These models are treated within the framework of the three levels of management. Operational, tactical, and strategic mathematical models are designed to meet the needs of lower, middle, and top management, respectively.

Starting at the top, *strategic models* tend to be macro-oriented (overview of the organization) and subjective in nature. The time horizons for the models are often measured in years, as are top management's strategic planning responsibilities. The models are usually custom-built for the particular decision maker and the organization.

At the next level, *tactical models* are usually employed by middle management to assist in allocating and controlling the use of the organization's resources. The models are usually applicable to a subset of the organization (i.e., manufacturing, marketing, finance, etc.). The time horizon for the models usually varies from one month to less than two years. Some subjective and external data are needed, but the accent is on internal data. The models are much more likely to employ an analytic mode of analysis.

For the last level, *operational models* are usually employed to support short-time horizon decisions, that is, daily, weekly, and monthly. Since they are frequently found at the lower organizational levels, these models normally use internal, objective data in their operation. They employ an analytic mode of analysis and are often standard mathematical models.

Within each of these categories, newer types of mathematical models that have been developed by operations researchers can be found. Due to space limitations, emphasis is placed upon the mathematical tools of operations research that are oriented toward higher mangement levels, namely,

- corporate planning models
- goal programming
- venture analysis
- heuristic programming

Below, each of these are explained briefly.

CORPORATE PLANNING MODELS

Models which are capable of viewing the overall operations (macro) or a specific area (micro) of a firm are called *corporate planning models*. Generally, these models are concerned with the firm's finances and rely on simulation for their mathematical basis of analysis.[1] The most obvious use of a corporate planning

---

[1] Simulation can be defined simply as a systems model that has the desired characteristics of reality in order to reproduce the essence of the actual operation.

model is to assist in the development of short- to long-range corporate plans. An appropriately designed model is capable, in theory, of projecting the financial results of a company for an unlimited number of years. As a practical matter, the user will usually be restrained by his diminishing confidence in the correctness of assumed conditions in distant years. To develop a plan, a variety of alternative courses of action should be investigated under different sets of assumed conditions whereby the most appropriate corporate plans can be selected. Whenever new information causes changes to be made, the corporate model can be used to evaluate the effect of a revised plan quickly and inexpensively.

Macrosimulation

When the focus of a corporate planning model is on the entire firm, a global or overall management viewpoint is emphasized in the analysis of problems, thereby enhancing the likelihood of capturing the full impact of proposed financial courses of action. A macro corporate planning model demands company-wide effort to take advantage of the knowledge and expertise in all subsystems of the firm. For the macro approach to be highly successful in evaluating the financial results of alternative courses of action, the model must contain appropriate subsystem details.

Simulating complex relationships on the macro level should both depict those of interacting subsystems and consider the time factor within these subsystems. Relationships frequently change as time passes. For example, expenditures for research (R&D subsystem) are not expected to produce revenue (marketing subsystem) in the immediate period because they are investments in future revenue. Administrative expenses may follow changes in revenue and, in other cases, lag. It is essential, then, that the time relationship of the model be representative of the firm's own processes. Similarly, the simulation model must be consistent with the financial practice of the firm in order to reflect policies and procedures of management. An overview of a corporate planning simulation model that considers these factors is illustrated in Figure 12-1 with sample inputs and outputs as well as the required submodels.

Microsimulation

The overall or macro model illustrated in Figure 12-1 indicates that a series of submodels are required, resulting in a new simulation approach. Once the overview model has been validated, the next step is to diagram each submodel in more detail. Figure 12-2 illustrates how the marketing submodel, like the other submodels, would be structured. Basically, the marketing system is divided into six important parts:

1. The external environment model relates those forces in the environment that affect consumer demand.

2. The overall marketing decision model is tied in with its competitors' decision model. Also, it is related to other submodels (refer to Figure 12-1).

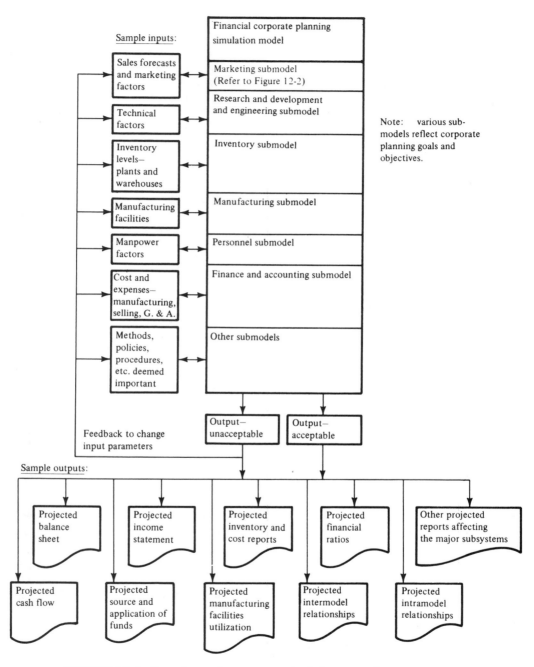

FIGURE 12-1. Overview of a macro-oriented corporate planning simulation model that depicts sample inputs and outputs.

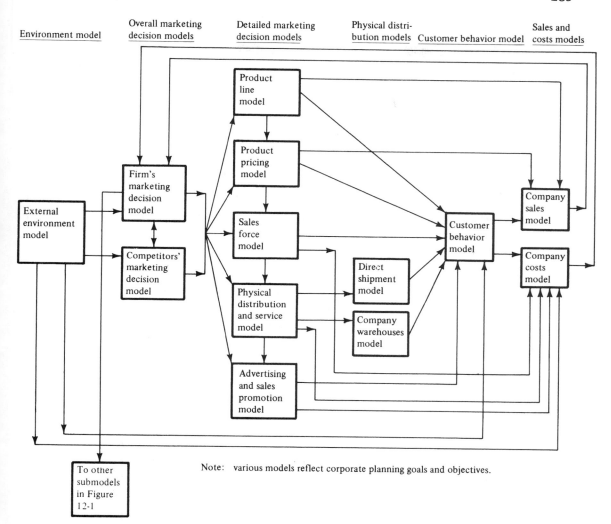

FIGURE 12-2. Complete marketing submodel, an essential part of a corporate planning simulation model.

3. The detailed marketing decision models are associated with product lines, product prices, sales force, physical distribution and service, and advertising and sales promotion.

4. The physical distribution models center on direct and nondirect shipments using company-owned warehouses.

5. The customer behavior model shows the response of customers to the detailed marketing decision models, physical distribution models, and the external environment model.

6. The sales and costs models reflect the output of the previous models in the illustration, which then provide input for the firm's marketing decision model (see 2 above).

The level of detail for the marketing submodel should not end here; further refinements in terms of inputs and outputs are necessary for each box in Figure 12-2. Thus, the attendant circumstances will dictate the level of detail necessary for each submodel of the corporate planning simulation model.

GOAL PROGRAMMING

Goal programming is a mathematical model that is capable of handling a single goal with multiple subgoals or multiple goals with multiple subgoals. Since goal programming is capable of handling multiple goals in multiple dimensions, conversion of various factors to costs or profits may not be necessary. In other words, two hours of idle time in work group A or two hours of overtime in work group B do not have to be expressed in terms of estimated costs. Since the multiple goals are often achieved only to the detriment of one another, a hierarchy of importance among these goals is required. This allows consideration of low-order goals only after higher-order goals are fulfilled. Therefore, various kinds of problems can be solved if management provides a ranking of goals in terms of their contribution or importance to the organization.

Management, for instance, might consider the costs of shortages to be higher than costs of changing the employment level and the latter costs to be higher than inventory costs, thus establishing three separate goals (the levels of production, employment, and inventories). The hierarchy among these incompatible multiple goals may be set in such a way that those with lower priorities are considered only after higher-priority goals are satisfied or have reached points beyond which they cannot be improved under the given conditions. This implies that there could be deviations from some or all goals, although the aim is to get as close to these goals as possible within the given constraints.

If shortages of one product are considered more critical than shortages of some other product, the largest weight should be assigned to the *deviational variables* for that product. In other words, we can assign differential weights to each variable within the same hierarchical order group, provided that they are in the same dimension. The same reasoning can be applied to all variables. If it is more important to avoid underemployment in some groups than in others, different weights can be assigned to variables in the various groups. Similarly, different weights can be assigned to deviations from goals in the lowest-order group representing excess inventories.

To illustrate goal programming, a manufacturing plant has a current operational capacity of 500 hours a day. With this capacity, the company produces two products: A and B. Production of either product requires 1 hour in the plant. Because of the limited sales demand, only 300 units of product A and 400 units of product B can be sold. The profit from the sale of product A is $10, whereas the profit from product B is $5.

The president of the company has listed the following goals in order of importance:

1. Avoid underutilization of production capacity.

2. Sell as many units as possible; however, since the profit from the sale of product A is twice that of product B, he is doubly anxious to achieve the sales goal for product A relative to product B.

3. Reduce overtime.

He must choose a strategy which will achieve all of his goals as nearly as possible. Hence, this mathematical model gives management a means of implementing a hierarchy of goals that further overall organizational objectives.

VENTURE ANALYSIS

One of the most extensive and sophisticated mathematical models that utilizes various operations research methods for assessing uncertainty and risk is called *venture analysis.* Its purpose is to analyze any investment opportunity that may be offered to an organization. For example, a company might consider introducing a new product (Figure 12-3), acquiring another company, building a new plant, or modernizing its distribution system. Whatever the objective, the computer evaluates the interactions of all the factors that might influence the project and the company's cash flow. With answers that the computer provides, a company is better able to maximize its profit at minimal risk.

When considering the introduction of a new product, several problem areas are troublesome to the manager—troublesome in the sense that they engender a desire to delay decisions until a reliable basis can be developed for choosing among

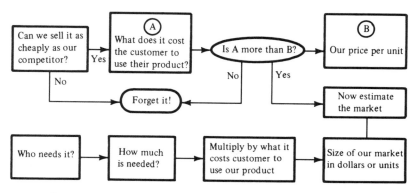

FIGURE 12-3. Venture analysis—basic steps in marketing a new product.

the many alternatives. The major ones are (1) the complexity of the market plus investment and cost factors influencing profitability of the venture, (2) the multitude of alternatives to be evaluated quantitatively before selecting a course of action, (3) the risks introduced by forecast uncertainties, and (4) the possible counteractions by customers and competitors.

Based on these problems, venture analysis evaluates alternative strategies, thereby permitting more explicit consideration of the risks introduced by the forecast uncertainties and the potential counteractions of customers and competitors (who must adjust their tactics in the face of a new factor in the market). Thus, for the commercialization of a new product, venture analysis is extremely helpful for developing decisions in the early stages of planning. As might be expected, this type of analysis relies heavily on computer programming and processing.

A typical venture analysis is a simulation model. All inputs are communicated to the model through a dialogue between management-user and the computer. The dialogue consists of answering a series of questions posed by the model. The answers form the data base for a particular analysis. A teletyped keyboard or video display terminal may be used for the dialogue.

The basis inputs to the model are of two types: probabilistic (i.e., uncertain) and deterministic (i.e., assumed known). Sales, cost of sales, capital purchases, engineering expenses, and general and administrative expenses are treated as probabilistic quantities; that is, uncertainty is considered. Interest rate, corporate assessment rate, number of years to be considered, depreciation life, depreciation type, and the like are considered to be deterministic, or known precisely. The probabilistic data convey to the model management's assessment of the uncertainty associated with each of the key variables. It consists of management's subjective estimates of the likelihood that the variables will attain specified values.

A set of standard financial computations is performed, thereby determining values of profit, cash flow, return on assets, and similar items. These computations are repeated a large number of times employing different combinations of values for the key variables, as described by management's uncertainty assessments. Each repetition of the computation produces new values (profit, cash flow, etc.). This information establishes the risk profiles of the performance measures. The risk profiles—the model outputs—are printed on the same Teletype keyboard or video display used to supply the input data. The outputs are available within several minutes after entering the data. Upon management review and evaluation, necessary input changes can be made and the computations repeated.

The values of key input variables and their uncertainty profiles are functions of many factors. For example, revenue is a function of selling price, total market, and market share. Thus, these factors may be interrelated; market share is a function of relative selling price, total market is a function of selling price, selling price may be related to manufacturing cost, and manufacturing cost may be a function of quantity manufactured, which is related to market size. No attempt has been made here to define these complex interrelationships within the model. Instead, it is assumed that meaningful estimates, based on a detailed analysis performed outside of the venture analysis model, can be made for all pertinent data.

The venture analysis model, in essence, is a management laboratory in which managers can experiment before the fact with a variety of investment alternatives. One experiment may consist of choosing a set of specific values for the key input variables and then utilizing these values to compute after-tax profit, cash flow, indebtedness, payback period, return on assets, and present worth (discounted cash flow). In each experiment, the choice of values for key variables is based on random sampling of the variables' probability distribution—the uncertainty profiles. The experiment is then repeated a large number of times, each time choosing, from the specified uncertainty profiles, a new set of values for the key variables and computing an after-tax profit. In this manner, frequency distributions—the number of times the computed results fall within specific intervals—are created for each of the computed quantities. The risk profiles are obtained directly from the frequency distributions and represent the chance that the committed quantity will exceed various specified values.

HEURISTIC PROGRAMMING

Heuristic programming, as it is known today, has its roots in the artificial intelligence research of Herbert Simon of Carnegie Institute of Technology, together with Allen Newell of Carnegie and J. C. Shaw of the Rand Corporation. Their goal in artificial intelligence research is to write programs instructing the computer on how to behave in a way that, in human beings, would be called "intelligent." Given enough observations, experiments, analysis, and modeling, they can instruct a digital computer to process information as humans do.

A simplified definition of heuristic programming that utilizes the computer as a major tool of analysis is given as follows:

> Heuristic programming utilizes rules of thumb or intuitive rules and guidelines and is generally under computer control to explore the most likely paths and to make educated guesses in arriving at a problem's solution rather than going through all of the possible alternatives to obtain an optimum one.

Because of the reliance on computers, most heuristic programming problems take the form of a set of instructions to solve a problem—the way the user might do it if he or she had enough time. To cover all contingencies likely to occur in a problem, generally a group of heuristics (intuitive rules) are needed. Since these heuristics are much too difficult to follow at the user's pace of problem solving, the computer identifies and evaluates the more feasible alternatives quickly and accurately.

Since a computer heuristic program, like a computer algorithm, terminates in a finite number of steps, a heuristic program produces a *good* answer, while an algorithm gives an *optimal* one. Although an algorithm appears better on the surface than a heuristic approach, many so-called algorithms end up in actual practice as heuristic programs because judgments have to be made by the user in their application which negate their optimality. Their principal difference is that a heuristic program can be constructed rather freely in a commonsense, intuitive manner. On the other hand, an algorithm must be constructed based on a mathematical model so that its optimiality proofs can be substantiated. Thus, a computerized heuristic program, in reality, appears preferable to an algorithm for many of the poorly structued and well-structured problems facing an organization.

PAPERLESS OUTPUT OF FUTURE DISTRIBUTED SYSTEMS

An integral part of future distributed processing systems will be paperless output. Within such an environment, the accent will be on meeting the user's needs by utilizing a management control station, i.e., a minicomputer-based unit that allows the creation, transmission, and receipt of information. Not only do the management control stations communicate with each other and higher-level computer systems, but also they permit the storage of file documents, i.e., on floppy disks or a comparable storage medium.

The applications of this control unit as a management tool are enormous. In banking, for example, there will be on-line risk asset management information at the fingertips of every senior corporate officer who needs it. For account and operations managers, the management control station will tie into transaction processing systems for up-to-the-minute monitoring of customer account status, lines of credit, investigations, quality, and timeliness of service delivery. Similar systems in manufacturing can give production planners instant access to inventory and plant capacity data, and product managers can have up-to-date reports on sales, distribution, special promotions, and competitive activity.

In any business organization, a department manager could, at the touch of a few *macro* keys, look up his or her current expenditures versus budget, current output versus goals, current project status versus schedule, plus all his or her business and personnel files. Although applications are virtually limitless, the point is that computerized information anywhere in an organization could be accessed from the management control station and displayed on the screen without loss of time or use of paper. And, according to each manager's needs, noncomputer documents can be fed into the system as well.

To get an idea of how the management control station terminal would operate, as part of a manager's daily routine via paperless output, consider the following scenario. A manager comes into the office in the morning and calls up an index of what is in his (or her) electronic "in-box." He can select any or all of the documents for display on the screen. To check on key commitments and due dates that may be approaching, the manager uses the "follow-up" file which lists all items in chronological order. In addition, he calls up the phone log to see what telephone messages are awaiting. So far, the manager has not touched a single piece of paper.

When generating memos, the secretary uses the system's word processing capability; that is, documents are created, edited on the screen, and kept on disk. Memos are transmitted electronically to all the management control stations on the distribution list over the distributed network, and other recipients get a hard copy produced by a printer on-line to their secretary's CRT. Such a distributed processing system provides planning, monitoring, and control support of day-by-day operations. To state it another way, the management control station provides access to visual information that the manager needs now.

Even though not included in the above scenario, accent in this distributed processing environment is on eliminating hard-copy management reports. Instead of a weekly, monthly, or some period basis, information can be retrieved on an up-to-the-minute basis at any time from the unit. Thus, this paperless mode places important information at management's fingertips when needed without wasted time and motion on the manager's part.

VOICE SYSTEMS OF FUTURE DISTRIBUTED SYSTEMS

Another important feature of future distributed processing systems is voice systems, i.e., audio response and voice recognition. *Audio response* allows computer users to add another output module to existing systems. This form of output opens up the ability to perform certain functions quickly, conveniently, and without often-compliated hardware and human processes. Currently, a mail-order firm allows its customers to enter orders over the telephone while an audio "voice" (an audio response unit is linked to a computer) verifies the order. Similarly, an air freight company is using audio response to allow its customers to check on the status of shipments. A computerized voice response might say, "Shipment number 2351 was delivered on July 25."

The equipment used in such systems is not that expensive. As illustrated in Figure 12–4, the touch-tone telephone is the most common terminal for an audio response unit. In areas where touch-tone is not available, a 10-key portable pad

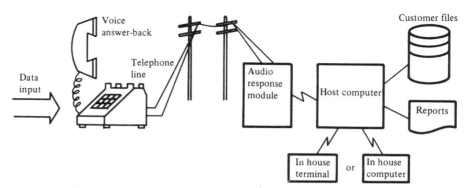

FIGURE 12–4. Audio response systems can be add-on modules to a computer system (per the above) or can function as stand-alone units.

which connects to the mouthpiece of any dial phone can be used to generate the same tones. (These generally sell for less than $100.) Hence, implementation of an audio response system does require the addition of new hardware to the host computer. However, the hardware required is, for most cases, a voice module, a tape drive, and a data set acting as an interface unit, translating phone input into proper form, and translating digitized computer output into speech.

Going a step further in future systems, distributed processing will employ *voice recognition systems.* In such an environment, the system converts the spoken word into data that a computer can understand. Before working with an individual, the machine needs a proper introduction. This means that the operator must tape his or her voice and utter the 30 to 50 words that generally make up the machine's vocabulary since such information is stored in the computer. Because a person's voice is as unique as one's fingerprints, each operator must make a separate recording. Thereafter, before talking to the computer, the operator must punch a code to remind the system of his or her voice.

Recently, a United Parcel Service distribution center installed a voice recognition system. A sorter on an arrival dock unloads a package onto a conveyor belt and utters a coded destination into the wireless headset. This spoken code becomes a command whereby the computer channels each parcel to the correct outgoing truck area. As another example, the Chicago Mercantile Exchange completed the installation of a system allowing an employee to call out prices on trades as they are being completed on the floor. The prices flash instantly on a screen. Such applications where an individual must use both hands to perform an ongoing task are natural applications for voice recognition systems.

DECISION MAKING WITH FUTURE DISTRIBUTED PROCESSING SYSTEMS

At a higher level in a future distributed processing environment, there will be the integration of paperless output and voice systems with decision systems. Currently, such systems are called *decision support systems* and they incorporate features found in management information systems and in computer simulation and mathematical optimization models. They emphasize direct support for managers in order to enhance the professional judgments required in making decisions. The use of interactive systems and video displays in decision support systems are examples of this point. Emphasis is placed on helping the manager make decisions rather than on actually making decisions for the manager. Also, presentation of information is in a form that is useful versus presenting all information that might be useful.

For example, Gould Inc. has combined a large visual display and video terminals with a computer information system. Designed to help managers make comparisons and analyze problems, it instantly prepared tables and charts in response to simple commands. IBM, working with the First National Bank of Chicago, has developed a similar system, which produces graphs and charts in color on a television screen.

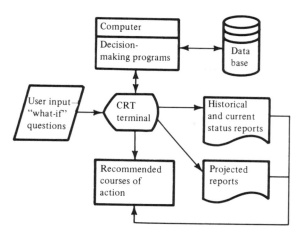

FIGURE 12-5. Interactive decision-making process of future distributed processing systems.

Because professional judgments and insights are critical in decision making, distributed decision systems of the future must be designed to support a manager's skills at all stages of decision making—from problem identification to choosing the relevant data with which to work, picking the approach to be used in making the decision, and evaluating the alternative courses of action. As shown in Figure 12-5, they must produce answers to "what if" questions that managers can understand, when such information is needed, and under their direct control. Hence, such future systems are intended to help managers dispersed throughout the organization at all levels in solving their myriad problems. The computer output as supplemented by the subjective feelings of the decision maker provides conclusive managerial decisions.

The rapidly decreasing costs of computer storage and improvements in data entry and data base management systems currently make it increasingly likely that much or all of the information a manager needs to reach a decision will be stored on-line, thereby making distributed decision systems a logical tool for analysis and solution to managers' problems. In addition, since personnel costs already exceed 50 percent of most data processing budgets, costs of providing information for managers can be reduced in the future. This reduction alone should be enough to justify distributed decision systems along with improved management productivity and improved decisions that result from increased use of sophisticated mathematical models.

Further developments in computer technology will not be enough to ensure the success of future distributed decision systems. Technology still must be assembled into systems that are compatible with managerial styles and provide support that managers feel is valuable. In essence, decision systems will have to fit into an environment where the decision-making processes may be difficult to specify. Also, they should be able to support decisions where compromise or time constraints may be more important factors in reaching a decision than optimal solutions or standard operating procedures. Achieving these goals will require new ways of using computer technology, uses that are different from how technology has been used previously in distributed systems or computer-based models. But because only managers know what representations, operations, and methods of control fit their styles of decision making, management involvement will be more important than computer technology in developing useful distributed decision systems for all management levels. Generally, the management operating mode at the local and regional levels is quite different from the home office level. Similarly, management's modus operandi can be quite different from those at the same level since each functional area dictates what management needs to know in order to plan, organize, direct, and control organizational activities effectively.

DISTRIBUTED SYSTEMS THAT EXTEND
BEYOND THE ORGANIZATION

Although the foregoing has concentrated on future systems that operate within their own organizational boundaries, a most important thrust is distributed computing that goes beyond the confines of the organization. Currently, such systems are just beginning to make their appearance in the area of cash management. Fundamentally, the foundation of cash management is efficient control of cash operations. Though businesses have used banks to consolidate a company's cash and have sent money across the country by such means as depository transfer checks that move over telegraph circuits, they are still confronted with the time-consuming daily task of phoning perhaps a dozen or more banks for an oral report on cash balances. Now, with the use of "intelligent" terminals, company treasurers can get cash-balance information in minutes from as many banks as are connected into the system. Balances can be determined as often as desired, permitting last-minute use of incoming cash.

The next step in such future distributed processing systems is connecting the corporate treasurer with the money market and currency departments. For example, the bank's system can tell a corporate treasurer at a specific time not only how much has already been collected but also how much will go into the company's accounts the following day from checks that require an additional day to clear. The computer also shows how much outflow there will be, allowing net cash amounts to be determined. Once the cash position is known, a decision can be made about investing the money. With some historical experience, a treasurer can take seasonal patterns into account and forecast cash receipts and payment needs. Direct from the company's computer terminal, transfers can be requested over the wire from the company's bank to any other bank on the line.

Typical of the transfers now electronically possible is a directive from the corporation's computer to transfer a specified amount from the headquarters account to the payroll accounts of distant subsidiaries. Within seconds, the headquarters balance is reduced by that amount and the subsidiaries balances increased by a like sum. Going a step further, a corporation's payroll will be completely computerized and directed from headquarters. Every week, the banks in cities where each branch or factory is located would be instructed by tape or wire how to pay bills—even how much should be put into each employee's account at that local bank. The worker could then draw immediately against his or her account. Since this is an essential part of electronic money, these aspects are a study unto themselves.

Distributed systems that extend beyond the organization, then, are currently focusing on cash management. Because a company's computer is connected directly to its bank's computer, a company has immediate access to considerable information that would have taken hours—or days—to generate by personal telephone calls or through the mail. The capability has developed because it connects any company through its own bank with the network of automatic clearinghouses and regional check processing centers.

DISTRIBUTED SYSTEMS THAT LINK MANUFACTURER WITH SUPPLIERS, DISTRIBUTORS, AND RETAILERS

Continuing with future distributed processing systems that go beyond the confines of the organization, a logical development to occur is one that links the suppliers, manufacturer, distributors, and retailers in a comprehensive total system. This linking approach is the total systems concept carried beyond the limits of the organization. In such a system, the demand response of customers at the retail level will be relayed instantaneously back to the raw material suppliers through a distributed communications network. As illustrated in Figure 12-6, the desired raw materials and/or purchased parts will be forwarded to the manufacturer for producing finished goods, which, in turn, will be shipped via the distribution channels to the retailers. Thus, sellers will have the right product available at the proper time and place for their customers in a minimum of time when an order is placed for immediate delivery.

Although data communication equipment is capable of handling computer-to-computer activities in a multiprocessing environment, the same cannot be said for operational intercompany programs. At this time, master mathematical models have not been developed that cross company boundaries for handling a supplier-manufacturer-distributor-retailer system whether it be order processing, production scheduling, or some other area. Considerable developmental work must be undertaken before this approach can become operational.

CONCLUSION

Once the present approaches, i.e., three-level systems to distributed processing, have reached their height, the next step in the evolving maturity of these systems will require a broader viewpoint of the organization structure, i.e., directed toward meeting more of the needs of all organization personnel. Not only will there be a

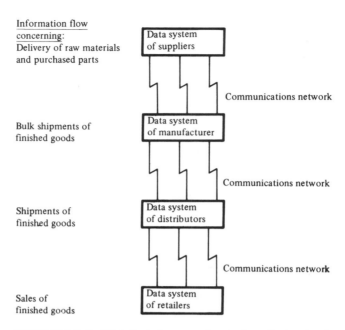

Information flow concerning:
Delivery of raw materials and purchased parts

Data system of suppliers

Communications network

Bulk shipments of finished goods

Data system of manufacturer

Communications network

Shipments of finished goods

Data system of distributors

Communications network

Sales of finished goods

Data system of retailers

FIGURE 12-6. Distributed processing system that extends beyond the firm—suppliers, manufacturer, distributors, and retailers are tied together by a distributed communications network (manufacturer is the focal point of the system).

concern for meeting the needs of functional areas or the management of business functions at the local and regional levels, but also there will be greater accent on the management of the entire corporation at the headquarters level. Thus, future distributed processing systems will evolve that allow an organization to adjust its operations to changing environmental factors that originate outside and within the organization.

Newer approaches to distributed computing are directed toward the total systems concept, the ultimate in automating data processing operations. Top management, with the aid of business systems analysts (well versed in programming and mathematical methods of operations research), will utilize the latest quantitative techniques to minimize the risk of doing business. Because the primary role of top management is to allocate scarce resources among the various factors of production, general managers, particularly in the future, must be able to recognize and assess alternative courses of action at the highest level. The dynamics of business, such as the complexity of an organization's product mixes and the shifting of markets, dictate that top management must have the capability of assessing the effects of both internal plans and external business conditions on organizational objectives and operating performance. Future distributed processing systems, which will utilize complex and sophisticated mathematical models, must be capable of producing timely and accurate information. The net result is that top management will be able to assess alternatives regarding the organization's future plans and select the optimum one. Needless to say, considerable research and developmental work are required before these systems can be operational.

Future system developments also include systems that extend beyond the organization as well as an electronic money system. Even though there are presently many barriers to such sophisticated distributed processing systems, acceptance or rejection of these innovations revolves around the human element. To ignore the "people factor" in planning and implementing advanced distributed processing systems is completely unrealistic. System advancements do not operate in a vacuum but are affected directly by the individuals who collectively form our society. In the final analysis, the key to successful newer and more complex distributed processing systems is *people.*

QUESTIONS

1. How important is the need for newer mathematical models in future distributed processing systems? Explain.

2. Why was the initial focus of the chapter on mathematical models for higher levels of mangement?

3. a. What part will paperless output play in future distributed processing systems?
   b. What part wlll voice systems play in future distributed processing systems?

4. What effect will current decision support systems have on future distributed processing systems?

5. Enumerate the essential characteristics of future distributed processing systems that cross company boundaries.

6. What effect will future distributed processing systems have on the individual within the organization and on the organization itself? Explain thoroughly.

SELECTED REFERENCES

Anderson, D. R., and Williams T. A., "Viewing MIS from the Top," *Journal of Systems Management,* July 1973.

Atler, S. L., "How Effective Managers Use Information Systems," *Harvard Business Review,* Nov.–Dec. 1976.

Bucatinsky, J., "Ask Your Computer 'What If . . .'," *Financial Executive,* July 1973.

Buckelew, D. P., and Penniman, W. D., "The Outlook for Interactive Television," *Datamation,* Aug. 1974.

Carlson, "Decision Support Systems: Personal Computing Services for Managers," *Management Review,* Jan. 1977.

Caswell, S. A., "Electronic Mail Delivers," *Computer Decisions,* April 1977.

Cerf, V. G., and Curran, A., "The Future of Computer Communications," *Datamation,* May 1977.

Davis, K. R., and Leitch, R. A., "Improving Marketing-Production Coordination Through On-Line Modeling," *Production & Inventory Management,* Second Quarter, 1976.

DeSafi, O. J., "EFT in 1988," *Datamation,* Jan. 1977.

Dilorio, A. M., "EFT Today," *Computer Decisions,* March 1976.

Edelman, F., and Greenberg, J. S., "Venture Analysis: The Assessment of Uncertainty and Risk." *Financial Executive,* Aug. 1969.

Ferreiro, J., and Niles, J. M., "Five-Year Planning for Data Communications," *Datamation,* Oct. 1976.

Flato, L., "Checking on EFTS," *Computer Decisions,* May 1975.

Fortune Special Advertising Section, "Information Processing/The Office of Tomorrow," *Fortune,* Oct. 1977.

Gibbs, T. E., "Goal Programming," *Journal of Systems Management,* May 1973.

Hammond, J. S., III, "Do's and Don't's of Computer Models for Planning," *Harvard Business Review,* March–April 1974.

Hansen, J. R., "The Computers Gets a Voice," *Infosystems,* Aug. 1977.

Hayes, R. H., and Nolan, R. L., "What Kind of Corporate Modeling Functions Best," *Harvard Business Review,* May–June 1974.

Hienan, D. A., and Addleman, R. B., "Quantitative Techniques for Today's Decision Makers," *Harvard Business Review,* May–June 1976.

Hirsch, P., "AT&T's Big Plans for a Value Added Service," *Datamation,* Jan. 1976.

Infosystems Staff, "Management Gets the Picture," *Infosystems,* April 1977.

Johnson, J. R., "The Changing DP Organization," *Datamation,* Jan. 1975.

Kaufman, F., "Data Systems that Cross Company Boundaries," *Harvard Business Review,* Jan.–Feb. 1966.

Kelley, N., "Bank of America Goes Distributive," *Infosystems,* March 1977.

Kramarsky, D., "Systems that Talk with You," *Administrative Management,* Aug. 1976.

Kutsch, J. A., "A Talking Computer Terminal," *AFIPS Conference Proceedings* (National Computer Conference), Vol. 46, 1977.

Laing, J. R., "Courts and the Public Slow up the Advance of Electronic Banking," *Wall Street Journal,* June 6, 1977.

Lampe, J. C., "Electronic Funds Transfer Systems," *Management Accounting,* March 1977.

Lee, S., and Jaaskelainen, "Goal Programming: Management's Math Model," *Industrial Engineering,* Feb. 1975.

Lope, W. A., "The Home Office of the Future," *Journal of Systems Management,* April 1972.

Lorange, P., and Vancil, R. F., *Strategic Planning Systems,* Englewood Cliffs, N.J.: Prentice-Hall, Inc., 1977.

Lucado, W. E., "Corporate Planning—A Current Status Report," *Managerial Planning,* Nov.–Dec. 1974.

Michael, G. C., "A Review of Heuristic Programming," *Decision Sciences,* Vol. 3, 1972.

Minor, W. H., "Talking to the Computer in a Natural Language," *Infosystems,* Sept. 1976.

Naylor, T. H., "The Future of Corporate Planning Models," *Managerial Planning,* March–April 1976.

Powell, J. R. P., and Vargin, R. C., "A Heuristic Model for Planning Corporate Planning," *Financial Management,* Summer 1975.

Rose, S., "More Bang for the Buck: The Magic of Electronic Banking," *Fortune,* May 1977.

Schill, R. L., "Interorganizational Management Information Systems: The Marketing Channel of Distribution," *AFIPS Conference Proceedings* (National Computer Conference), Vol. 44, 1975.

Smith, P., "Unique Tools for Marketers: PIMS," *Dun's Review,* Oct. 1976, and *Management Review,* Jan. 1977.

Tersine, R. J., "Organizational Objectives and Goal Programming: A Convergence," *Managerial Planning,* Sept.–Oct. 1976.

Thierauf, R. J., *Systems Analysis and Design of Real-Time Management Information Systems,* Englewood Cliffs, N.J.: Prentice-Hall, Inc., 1975.

Thierauf, R. J. and Klekamp, R. C., *Decision Making Through Operations Research,* New York: John Wiley & Sons, Inc., 1975.

Urban, G. L.," Building Models for Decision Makers, *Interfaces,* May 1974.

Wallenius, J., "Comparative Evaluation of Some Interactive Approaches to Multicriterion Optimization, *Management Science,* Aug. 1975.

Weberman, B., "Cash Like a Flash," *Forbes,* April 1, 1977.

White, R. B., "A Prototype for the Automated Office, " *Datamation,* April 1977.

Yasaki, E. K., "Toward the Automated Office," *Datamation,* Feb. 1975.

——, "Voice Recognition Comes of Age," *Datamation,* Aug. 1976.

Zani, W. M., "Beyond 1984: A Technology Forecast," *Datamation,* Jan. 1975.

INDEX